MW01033423

BISON
BOOKS

Oto and Ponca Indians. *Left*, Oto, painted by Carl Bodmer at Pilcher's Trading Post, May 12, 1834. *Right*, Ponca (Chief *Šúde-gáxe* or Smoke-maker), painted by Carl Bodmer at Pilcher's Trading Post, May 11, 1833.

THE PONCA TRIBE

SECOND EDITION

By JAMES H. HOWARD

In collaboration with
PETER LE CLAIRE, *tribal historian*
and other members of the tribe

Introduction to the Bison Books edition
by Donald N. Brown

Introduction to the new Bison Books edition
by Judi M. gaiashkibos

University of Nebraska Press
Lincoln and London

Manufactured in the United States of America

First Nebraska paperback printing: 1995

Reprinted from the original 1965 edition published by the Smithsonian Institution's Bureau of American Ethnology as bulletin 195.

Library of Congress Cataloging-in-Publication Data
Howard, James H. (James Henri), 1925–1982.
The Ponca tribe / James H. Howard; in collaboration with Peter Le Claire, tribal historian, and other members of the tribe; introduction to the new Bison Books edition by Judi M. gaiashkibos. — 2nd ed.
p. cm.
Includes bibliographical references and index.
ISBN 978-0-8032-2819-1 (paper: alk. paper)
1. Ponca Indians. I. Le Claire, Peter. II. Title.
E99.P7H6 2010
978'.0049752539—dc22 2009053350

INTRODUCTION TO THE NEW BISON BOOKS EDITION

Judi M. gaiashkibos

It was with great honor and humility that I accepted the invitation to write this new introduction for the most recent edition of James H. Howard's classic, *The Ponca Tribe*. This request was particularly meaningful to me because I have a personal connection with this book and the people that reside within it. I am a Ponca tribal member as well as the granddaughter of Otto B. Knudsen, who was the last chief of the Northern Ponca and informant for the young James Howard. Growing up in Norfolk, Nebraska, and as the first generation in my family off reservation, I was very fortunate to have spent my early childhood with my grandfather. During my childhood he was always close at hand, sharing his countless stories that came to shape many of my cultural values. My grandpa, as I called him, was my hero, and I followed him around like a little puppy. I fondly remember always trying to be near him, and in order to do so, I became his best little helper in whatever task he was engaged in. As a child, I did not understand the significance of and status afforded to my grandpa as an Indian chief. To me, my grandpa was a rock and man that I could count on; a full understanding of him did not come until much later in my life. Although I was only six years old when my grandfather left us for the spirit world, to this day, when I close my eyes, I can picture him just as vividly as if he were standing in front of me. He is there in his characteristic bib overalls, with his Stetson hat nearby, and I see his handsome face smiling and hear his clear, powerful voice sharing another great story with us.

So why, might you ask, did Otto Knudsen, the last chief of the Northern Ponca, spend his last ten years in Norfolk rather than on his family's ancestral lands? Well, it is a bit of a story. My mother, Eleanor Knudsen, was born in 1913 on the Ponca reservation along the Niobrara River in northeastern Nebraska. As a young girl she and two of her sisters attended the Genoa Indian School, where they learned the three Rs along with a western trade. Although my mother's training as a cook would come to serve her later in life, this school was not simply focused on bettering the lives of Indian people. This school was one of the many that Richard H. Pratt strategically placed throughout the United States, charged with assimilating the Indian into mainstream society. Their motto was, "Kill the Indian, and save the man." Although my mother faced much hardship during boarding school, once she returned home to the reservation she helped to raise her younger siblings and also served on the tribal council (a feat in itself as during this time not even non-Indian women were serving in elected positions). However in 1946 all of our lives were about to change as my mother and my Santee Sioux grandmother, along with three small children in tow, left the reservation in hopes of economic opportunities farther south in the small city of Norfolk, Nebraska.

The first challenge my mother and grandmother faced in Norfolk, which was ethnically predominantly German at the time, was finding a place to live. But as this was the 1940s, their prospects were limited. Few people were willing to rent property to a person of color, let alone two Indian women with three children and no husband. In the end it was an African American man, Henry Jones, the owner of a salvage junk yard, who offered them housing. The neighborhood quickly became referred to by the locals as Squaw Valley because of the influx of many other Indian families that followed my mother in search of a better life. Soon after arriving, my mother found a job cooking at the local hotel while my grandmother took care of the little ones. Not long after this, my grandfather too left his beloved homeland along the Niobrara River to be near his family. He chose to be by us; while once he was a respected chief and elder, he became a virtual stranger. And what a shock it must have been for him to see the signs that even I remember hanging in the local taverns and shop windows that stated, "No dogs and/or Indians allowed." And although we were poor and lived in poverty, I never really realized this until I went to school. This is because at home I was blessed with the love of my large family, which grew to ten brothers and sisters, grandma, aunties, uncles, cousins, and, of course, my dear grandpa.

I remember many times listening to my grandpa sing traditional Ponca songs as he sat with us in the evenings. Even as a child I could hear sadness in the songs and see that same sadness in my grandfather's handsome, all-knowing face. I enjoyed those nights, especially when he would also tell us old stories from home. During these times, he would act out the stories on the wall by making shadow puppets with his large hands and forming animals including eagles, buffalo, and horses. In each story Grandpa was able to find a "teachable moment," as we say today. He never preached to us, but through his stories we heard the message. At times, Grandpa would get so lonesome for home that I could tell he missed the life he had left behind. But just when he least expected, one of his many nephews or friends would magically appear from the reservation, and he would be so happy to sit in a circle with them in his little shack next door to ours and share food and stories from home. My mother would always cook something nice for the menfolk who came to visit, and many times she sent them on their way with her lovely homemade bread and some of her light and airy cinnamon rolls for the road back to Niobrara and the Ponca reservation. We never knew how long these visitors would stay or when they would finally leave; we never knew how long they would be gone. But they were our family and as such were always welcome. Looking back on this now, I can only imagine how lonely Grandpa must have been, living in these two worlds.

While Grandpa lived next door to us, he carried on many of his traditional ways. Toward the end of each summer, my grandpa would begin the task of drying corn for our family to save for the long, cold winter ahead, carrying on one of the many agricultural traditions of the Ponca people. My job as a small child was to shoo the flies, and that, I must say, I did quite well! Grandpa worked hard as he proudly turned the lathed screens that held the beautiful corn, and when he was finally finished he would end his work with a prayer and sing a song. Those were some of my favorite times with my grandpa. However, little did I know then that our time together was about to be cut short. In the fall of 1959 I found a small, dead sparrow in my grandpa's bed, and as a precocious six-year-old I proudly ran to tell my grandpa of this discovery. Only, he was not smiling as I had expected. He told me that this was a sign, a sign that he would soon be leaving us. Soon after, he asked my mother to bake him his last birthday cake—angel's food cake—for his final birthday celebration. I was with my grandpa that cold spring morning when he suddenly and quietly left us. Our dear grandpa, the last chief of the Northern Ponca, was buried in Norfolk and not in his homeland in Niobrara. I suppose this was for two reasons: one, we could not afford to take him home and two, my mother wanted him close by where we could go visit him. (That was March 1959, not 1954—the only correction I have to this great book.) My grandfather lived to be eighty-one.

Thirteen years later my dear mother was buried in the same cemetery next to my grandfather. The year was 1972, and she was now a citizen of the United States (at the time of her birth this was not true for Indians). However, due to the Ponca Tribe's termination in 1962, she was no longer officially a member of her own tribe. The Ponca people were now a landless people, with most of the members moving to nearby Sioux City, Norfolk, and Omaha. It was during this time that James Howard was preparing *The Ponca Tribe*. His book was published in 1965 as a bulletin of the Smithsonian Institution's Bureau of American Ethnology. Grandpa had been interviewed for this book when he was back on the Northern Ponca reservation, but because he was a very modest man, we were virtually unaware of this. My Santee Sioux grandmother knew of the publication, and through the stealthy research of my cousin, who was attending the

University of Nebraska, we were able to obtain a treasured copy. How amazing it was to read the stories of the great Ponca Tribe and learn more about my grandpa and our people.

In the late 1980s, more than twenty years after the first publication of *The Ponca Tribe*, the lasting devastation resulting from termination of the Northern Ponca became apparent, and federal restoration was sought. This was a hard-fought battle, one that was eventually won on Halloween 1990 by the efforts of the Northern Ponca Restoration Committee, led by Fred LeRoy, through Public Law 101-484. Much of the research necessary to support our restoration was gathered from James Howard's *The Ponca Tribe*. Without this history of our people as told through the voices of my grandfather Otto Knudsen and other informants, the Ponca Tribe of Nebraska might not have been restored. *The Ponca Tribe* was and continues to be the greatest resource for the Ponca Tribe of Nebraska as they struggle to reestablish their rightful place in Nebraska history.

In 1995 I became the executive director of the Nebraska Commission on Indian Affairs; as fate would have it, that same year James Howard's *The Ponca Tribe* was published and distributed in paperback for the first time for all to read. This book is a great source of personal pride as well as the greatest resource that I have utilized to learn about my people, who for almost twenty years legally did not exist. The Ponca Tribe of Nebraska will soon be celebrating their twentieth year of restoration, and we will also celebrate the forty-fifth anniversary of James Howard's *The Ponca Tribe*. I am thankful for James Howard's rigorous research methods as well as his descriptive style used to bring the Ponca tribal voices to life. This book is both his and our lasting legacy, and a treasure that will make sure the Ponca way of life will not be forgotten. We, the Southern and Northern Ponca, say, "Wi' Bluh Ho!" (Thank-you!)

INTRODUCTION

Donald N. Brown

In the thirty years since original publication, *The Ponca Tribe* has become a "classic" in the literature of the Plains Indians of North America. Its stature is due largely to the research interests and writing style of James H. Howard. He was dedicated to describing the traditional culture of Native Americans. As a cultural anthropologist, he knew the importance of field observation and participation in the local community for collecting information. He also was keenly aware of his dependence on interviews with tribal elders. He not only included their statements in his books and articles, but gave them full credit for their contributions.

Howard, born in eastern South Dakota in 1925, developed an early interest in the material culture and dance of the many Native American tribes that were located in the region. By his teenage years, he had begun constructing Plains Indian dance outfits and participating in the dances. This early interest became a professional passion.

After service in the U.S. Army in Europe during World War II, his interest in Native American traditions led him to the study of anthropology at the University of Nebraska, where he received both the bachelor (1949) and master (1950) degrees. In 1957 he was awarded the doctoral degree in anthropology from the University of Michigan. The research for his Ph.D. dissertation was the foundation for *The Ponca Tribe*.

Howard's professional career as an anthropologist included museum work, field archaeology, and teaching. He was on the staff of the North Dakota State Historical Museum (1950–53) and the Kansas City Museum (1955–57). After completion of the doctoral degree, he began his teaching career, first at the University of North Dakota (1957–63), then at the University of South Dakota (1963–68), and in 1968 at Oklahoma State University. He developed a variety of courses on Native American culture, including material culture and music. The locations of these professional positions were important to Howard, for they allowed easy access to the communities that he wanted to visit and study. In a sense, his fieldwork was in his backyard.

Howard was widely recognized as one of the most prolific authors in anthropology. He wrote over a hundred articles based on original research as well as many book reviews. He was equally comfortable publishing in professional journals for his colleagues and the journals and magazines for American Indian hobbyists. His 1955 article "Pan-Indian Culture of Oklahoma" (*The Scientific Monthly,* 81: 215–20) helped define the process by which "tribal" identity was being replaced by an "Indian" identity within the Native American world. In addition to *The Ponca Tribe,* he wrote books on the Plains-Ojibwas (1965, reprinted 1984), the Dakotas (1966, 1980), the Yanktonais (1976), and the Shawnees (1981). In 1968 he translated and edited *The Warrior Who Killed Custer: The Personal Narrative of Joseph White Bull.* Three manuscripts were published after his death: *The Canadian Sioux* (1984), *Oklahoma Seminoles* (1984), and *Choctaw Music and Dance* (1990).

Yet Howard was more than a researcher. He internalized what he discovered. To many colleagues, Howard was a "walking encyclopedia" on matters related to the Plains, Woodland, and Southeastern Tribes. Whether it was an item of material culture that a visitor wanted identified, or a question from a student about the scoring of the Kickapoo handgame, or an inquiry from an attorney about the traditional hunting lands of the Ponca, Howard was able to provide an answer and explanation. His breadth of knowledge made him a valued expert witness before the United States Indian Claims Commission in cases related to the Ponca Tribe, the Turtle Mountain band of Plains-Ojibwa, and the Yankton band of Dakota.

His passion to understand traditional Native American life led Howard to participate in many traditional activities. While living in Oklahoma, he would drive almost every weekend to one of the ceremonial grounds in eastern Oklahoma or to one of the pow-wows in western Oklahoma. He also regularly attended meetings of the Native American Church, where his knowledge of early peyote songs was highly respected. One of his special joys was to participate with the other members in the dances of the Ponca War Dance Society.

As mentioned above, *The Ponca Tribe* was based on research for Howard's doctoral dissertation. His purpose in conducting this study was twofold. First, he wanted to describe "aboriginal Ponca culture" (see page xii). Little anthropological research had been conducted among the Poncas, and much of the data about them was buried in studies of the Omahas. Usually considered a central Plains tribe, the Poncas included cultural elements from both the Plains and the Woodlands areas. Intrigued, Howard wanted to seek out the origins of these elements.

His second purpose emerged as he continued his research. The Poncas had been forcibly removed from their homeland centered on the Niobrara River in northeastern Nebraska and southeastern South Dakota in 1877. Two years later Chief Standing Bear and sixty-five other Poncas returned north to bury the chief's son. The result was a split between Northern and Southern Poncas. Howard noted the differences that had developed between these two groups and set out to document and explain them.

Drawing initially upon contacts made while he was a student at the University of Nebraska, Howard spent two periods of field research collecting information on the Poncas. In 1949 he worked two months among the Northern Poncas in Nebraska and South Dakota, assisted by four native informants. Five years later (1954), he spent two and one-half months with the Southern Poncas in Oklahoma. Here his primary informants included five elderly men and one woman who was fifteen years old at the time of the Ponca removal to Oklahoma in 1877. As recognized by Howard on the title page, the contributions of Northern Ponca historian Peter Le Claire to this study cannot be minimized. He provided a written "Ponca History" (pages 16–22) as well as many other insights into Ponca culture. He also acted as the interpreter for Howard among both groups.

In the thirty years since the original publication of *The Ponca Tribe* in 1965, both the Northern and the Southern Poncas have experienced many changes. Effective in 1966, the Northern tribe lost federal recognition through termination legislation. No longer were federal programs in health, education, economic development or tribal government available to the tribal members. According to Elizabeth S. Grobsmith and Beth R. Ritter, the result was that "their population dispersed, their economic status, health, and general welfare declined, and their ability to practice their culture diminished" ("The Ponca Tribe of Nebraska: The Process of Restoration of a Federally Terminated Tribe," *Human Organization,* 51(1992): 1–16). In 1990 the Northern Poncas were restored to federal recognition and there is an expectation of a rebirth of tribal activities. For the Southern Poncas, this thirty-year period saw a growth in participation in federally funded programs, a strengthened tribal government, and a renewed interest in the Ponca language and traditional activities, such as the women's Scalp Dance (Donald N. Brown and Lee Irwin, "Ponca," in *Handbook of North American Indians,* vol. 13 *Plains,* ed. Raymond J. DeMallie [Smithsonian Institution, in press]).

The sudden death of James Henri Howard on 1 October 1982 at the age of fifty-seven was a tragic loss to both his many friends in Native American communities in the United States and Canada and his many colleagues in anthropology throughout the world.

CONTENTS

ILLUSTRATIONS

PLATES

(All plates except frontispiece follow p. 172)

TEXT FIGURES

MAP

PREFACE

The Ponca tribe of American Indians has been in contact with White civilization for more than 150 years, yet no comprehensive ethnography of the tribe has ever been written. Although there is much material on the Ponca in the literature, it is scattered and uneven in quality. Many of the tribal institutions have been neglected entirely, and much of the material seems overgeneralized. It is even difficult to assess the cultural position of the Ponca. Thus, some ethnographers have stressed the Plains affiliations of the tribe, citing such features as the Sun dance, tribal bison hunt, and use of the skin tipi. Yet many complexes of Eastern Woodland derivation are present in Ponca culture as well; for example, the Medicine Lodge ceremony and organization, the stylized-floral decorative art tradition, and their well-developed horticulture. Like other tribes of the Missouri, the Ponca lie somewhere between High Plains and Woodlands in their cultural orientation, and some of the more typical Plains traits in their cultural inventory are known to be recent additions. A study of which Woodland Indian traits were retained by the Ponca in their movement out of the Southeast and into their historic location and which Plains traits were adopted in their new situation thus provides us with interesting data on human ecology.

It was with this problem in mind that my original Ponca research was initiated, and one of the primary purposes of this monograph is to present a more complete delineation of Ponca culture, under one cover, than has hitherto been done. To accomplish this, the existing literature has been closely examined. The results of this study were supplemented and checked by ethnographic fieldwork—2 months among the Northern Ponca of Nebraska and South Dakota in 1949 and 2½ months with the Southern band in Oklahoma in 1954, plus several shorter visits of a week or a few days to both groups on subsequent occasions. An attempt was made to trace the Ponca from their position as a village tribe on the Missouri to modern reservation and urban groups in Nebraska, South Dakota, and Oklahoma.

The reconstruction of Ponca culture of the precontact period, or even of the early historic era before the tribe had adopted much of the European pattern, is quite difficult. The Ponca were visited by White traders in the 18th century and acquired horses and a variety of trade goods well before we begin to get any extensive descriptions of their way of life. Furthermore, for the Ponca, we lack the precontact archeological sites which provide an "aboriginal baseline" for some other groups.

"Aboriginal Ponca culture," then, as used in this work, must of necessity be a construction. It consists of descriptions of Ponca culture of the 18th and 19th centuries from the published literature and documentary sources, plus 20th-century "memory culture" accounts of Ponca informants, with all recognizably European or White elements removed from consideration. Now, though this sort of treatment is admittedly risky, and traditional ethnographies constructed in this manner have received considerable criticism in recent years, there is, in my opinion, some justification for this approach. In the present instance it provides the only method of achieving a reasonably complete and well-rounded view of a culture which would otherwise remain a mere hodgepodge of disparate (though possibly well-dated) fragments. The criticism that this "free floating" Ponca culture does not accurately reflect *any* specific instant in time must be acknowledged, however, as valid. But until some sort of time machine is invented permitting us to revisit the past, we shall have to content ourself with such devices. It might also be noted that although all cultures are continually changing, the rate of change may vary from fast to slow. American Indian cultures of the precontact and even early historic periods were often not changing so rapidly that the concept "traditional culture" is entirely invalid.

Where it is possible to accurately trace change, of course, this has been done. The fieldwork among the two bands of the tribe, which were one until 1879, revealed that important differences had grown up in the relatively short period since their separation. On the whole, it was learned, the Southern Ponca have offered more resistance to the forces of White acculturation. Yet in certain respects, surprisingly, it was the Northern Ponca who were the more conservative. Out of this interesting discovery the second objective of this study developed: to show what differences exist between the two bands and to suggest factors that might be responsible for these differences.

In this connection the Southern Ponca participation in Oklahoma Pan-Indianism was examined. This interesting phenomenon, which seems to represent a sort of generalized intertribal "Indian" culture, takes many of its components from the older Prairie-Plains culture which was, to a great extent, shared by the Ponca. Other elements in Pan-Indianism derive from the cultures of the Eastern Woodlands and the Southwest, while yet others appear to be peculiar to Pan-Indianism and to have no roots in the Indian past. The third purpose of this study, then, is to trace the development of Pan-Indianism in Oklahoma, with particular reference to the Ponca. An attempt has been made to determine why some older traits were retained, why others were abandoned, and why certain new traits were adopted, and to show how these factors have contributed to the existing differences between Northern and Southern Ponca culture.

Since much of the information in this monograph is based on the testimony of Ponca informants, a brief sketch of some of the principal contributors may be valuable in evaluating their respective information.

NORTHERN PONCA INFORMANTS

Peter Le Claire (PLC) is of mixed French-Canadian and Ponca descent (pl. 21). He lives in a small apartment in Fairfax, S. Dak., at the present time (1962), though he was born near Niobrara, Nebr. He is 79 years of age but still quite active. PLC is recognized by both the Northern and Southern Ponca as the tribal historian, and often inquiries to other informants brought the response "You'd better ask Pete." PLC is one of the very few Northern Poncas who still own dancing costumes and participate in Indian dances. He is well liked by all who know him, Indian or White. A short autobiographical sketch of PLC, with an introduction by the present writer, appeared in 1961 (Le Claire, 1961).

Joseph Le Roy (JLR) is of mixed French-Canadian, Santee Dakota, and Ponca descent (pl. 20, *a*). He is 70 years of age (1962). His father was a Northern Ponca chief of the second rank. JLR now lives in Ponca City, Okla., but at the time of my fieldwork he resided in Niobrara, Nebr. Though his material is on the whole quite reliable, it sometimes shows what I believe to be Santee Dakota influence. For example, JLR gave me a rather lengthy account of *Windigo* cannibalism which he attributed to the Ponca, but which is more likely Santee.

Otto B. Knudsen (OK) was the last chief among the Northern Ponca, having been created a chief of the second rank at the last chief-making ceremony held in the north (pl. 20, *c*). His father was a Dane and his mother a Ponca. Because he learned most of his "Indian ways" from his mother, much of the material he supplied relates to women's activities, such as horticulture and the preservation of food. OK occasionally used feminine forms of speech when speaking *Đégiha.* He always laughed and corrected himself when such a slip occurred. He was 75 years old at the time of his death in 1954.

Edward Buffalo-chief or Buffalo-chip (EBC) was a fullblood Northern Ponca. He lived on a farm near Niobrara, Nebr. He came from a long line of Ponca chiefs and was himself a Peyote chief or "roadman." EBC was a cripple and inclined to be slightly misanthropic. He was much interested in the old Ponca religion and ceremonies, but frequently made gloomy comments to the effect "It is all gone now." He was not particularly talkative, and such information as was secured from him was usually the confirmation of data given by other informants. He did, however, contribute valuable original material on the Northern Ponca peyote religion. He died in 1950 at the age of 80.

SOUTHERN PONCA INFORMANTS

Mrs. Virginia Headman (VHM), nee Big-soldier, was the only Southern Ponca informant interviewed who was old enough at the time of the Ponca Removal to remember much of the old tribal life in Nebraska and South Dakota. She was 15 years old when the Ponca were brought to Baxter Springs, Kans., in 1877. Although hardly able to move about in 1954, her mind remained clear and her sense of humor keen. She was able to describe the tribal hunts along the Elkhorn and Keya Paha Rivers, and she vividly recalled a visit paid to a Pawnee earth-lodge village on the Platte when she was very small.

Leslie Red-leaf (LRL) was the last remaining chief (of the second rank) among the Southern Ponca. Blind and feeble, he still retained, in 1954, a clear memory of the old ways, and walked with the proud carriage of an oldtime Ponca chief. Dressed in his otterskin cap and red and blue broadcloth blanket he presented an imposing figure at various powwows in the Ponca City area. He was approximately 89 years old at the time of his death in 1955.

Louis MacDonald (LMD) was 2 years old when the Ponca tribe was moved south. As a boy he listened carefully to the words of the old men. A Carlisle graduate, he spent much of his life working for his tribe in Washington. He was, in 1954, one of the two remaining "soldiers" or Buffalo-police among the Southern Ponca. He was also prominent in Peyote affairs and was an informant on this subject for La Barre (1938, p. 3). He was 83 years of age at the time of his death in 1958.

Obie Yellow-bull, or Little-standing-buffalo (OYB), is particularly well versed in tribal mythology and custom. In 1954 he was still able to make and play the Indian flute, and was the last member of his tribe to do so (pl. 24, *c*). At present (1962) he is 79 years old, both blind and deaf. Though OYB was a willing informant, he often spoke so rapidly that it was not possible to secure a complete running translation of his remarks from PLC, who served as my interpreter.

Albert Makes-cry (AMC) was a particularly valuable informant because he was able to relate the tales he had heard from older Southern Ponca to landmarks in Nebraska and South Dakota, where he had visited for long periods as a boy. A deeply religious man, "Uncle Albert" is often called upon to lead the singing at church services and to pray for the group at tribal gatherings. He is 70 years old.

Walter Blue-back (WBB) or Black-eagle (his Sun dance name) was the *Xúbe* of the short biographical sketch of that title by Whitman (1939). WBB was the only Ponca youth of his generation to take part in the Sun dance and other old Ponca rituals. At one time he was a practicing Bear shaman. He later abandoned the practice in favor of the Peyote religion, in which he became a leader. Though still an active peyotist in 1954, he preferred to take a less active role. He died in 1955 at the age of 66.

The initials of the above-named informants following a sentence or paragraph in the text indicate that the information in the respective sentence or paragraph was supplied by one of them. Full names are used for informants who supplied lesser amounts of data. Quotations are not verbatim, but are paraphrases expanded from "shorthand" field notes.

PHONETIC KEY

There are almost as many different ways of transcribing *Đégiha*, the language spoken by the Ponca, Omaha, Osage, Kansa, and Quapaw, as there are authors who have worked with the tribes speaking the language. I believe that it is asking a great deal to require the reader of this monograph to learn a new alphabet in order to pronounce the native words herein. It is certainly asking too much to expect him, in addition, to work his way through each of the systems employed by others who have written on the Ponca and Omaha. Therefore, although it is a departure from the usual scholarly procedure, all *Đégiha* words in this study—even those in quotations—have been placed in a single uniform system. To insure complete accuracy, each word or phrase was read to Peter Le Claire and at least one other Ponca informant. The informants then pronounced it back and it was transcribed. The symbols employed and their values are as follows:

Vowels:

- i High, front, close, unrounded (as *ee* in American English *sheep*)
- ʃ High, front, open, unrounded (as *i* in American English *in*)
- e Mid, front, close, unrounded (as *A* in American English *April*)
- ϵ Mid, front, open, unrounded (as *e* in American English *extra*)
- a Low, front, open, unrounded (as *a* in American English *mama*)
- ɘ Mid, central, close, unrounded (as *e* in American English *the*)
- u High, back, close, rounded (as *oo* in American English *toot*)
- o Mid, back, close, rounded (as *o* in American English *open*)

i, ʃ, ϵ, a, ɘ, u, and o also have nasalized forms, as į, ʃ̨, ϵ̨, ą, ɘ̨, ų, and ǫ.

When *i* and *u* are phonemically consonants they are written *y* and *w*.

The symbol · adds length to the preceding vowel.

Consonants:

Stops:

- p Bilabial, unaspirated, voiceless
- b Bilabial, unaspirated, voiced
- t Alveolar, unaspirated, voiceless
- d Alveolar, unaspirated, voiced
- t^h Alveolar, aspirated, voiceless
- tš Alveo-palatal, affricated, voiceless (as *ch* in American English *church*)
- k Velar, unaspirated, voiceless
- g Velar, unaspirated, voiced
- ' Glottal, unaspirated, voiceless

Fricatives:

đ Interdental, flat, voiced (the sound of *th* in American English *the*)
s Alveolar, grooved, voiceless
z Alveolar, grooved, voiced
š Alveo-palatal, grooved, voiceless (as *sh* in American English *she*)
ž Alveo-palatal, grooved, voiced (as *z* in American English *azure*)
x Velar, flat, voiceless (as *ch* in the German *hoch*)
g Velar, flat voiced
h Glottal, flat, voiceless (as *h* in American English *hat*)

Frictionless:

m Bilabial, nasal, voiced
n Alveolar, nasal, voiced

The accents are indicated as follows:

ʹ Primary
ˋ Secondary

With the exception of the symbols ə, ', and g, all of the above-listed symbols are those of the "Michigan" system (Pike, 1947, pp. 5, 7).

THE PONCA TRIBE

By James H. Howard

INTRODUCTION

In the past four decades the data of archeology, ethnology, and ethnohistory have begun to provide us with at least the main outlines of what was undoubtedly one of the most highly developed North American Indian civilizations. This culture, which clearly shows its derivation from the high cultures of Middle America, has been termed "Middle Mississippi" by modern archeologists.[1] In technological advancement, social organization, and art it ranks just below the civilizations of the Aztec, Toltec, and Maya.

Middle Mississippi towns were usually built on the fertile floodplains of rivers. Each town was built around a great central plaza or "square ground" where important ceremonials were held. Nearby were huge pyramidal mounds with temples and chiefs' houses on their flattened summits. These mounds, the largest of which are as large or larger than the great pyramids of Egypt, were built up of earth and clay. In some instances the mound exteriors were faced with a smooth covering of clay analogous to the stone or plaster shells which covered Mexican pyramids. A wide ramp or stairway of earth or logs led to the summit of each mound. Also near the "square ground" was the "hothouse," a large, sometimes earth-covered lodge where councils were held.

Clustered around the square ground, mounds, and hothouse were the dwellings of the ordinary folk. These houses were generally rectangular in shape, with walls of wattle and daub construction and roofs of poles and thatch. The chiefs' houses and temples were similar but often boasted elaborately carved interior timbers and roof combs. Around the town there was frequently a palisade of upright posts supported by earthen embankments for protection against enemies.

No less impressive than their architectural works was the art of the Middle Mississippi people. Their pottery—buff, gray, or black in

[1] This description of Middle Mississippi culture was largely abstracted from "Indians before Columbus" (Martin, Quimby, and Collier, 1947, pp. 353–366).

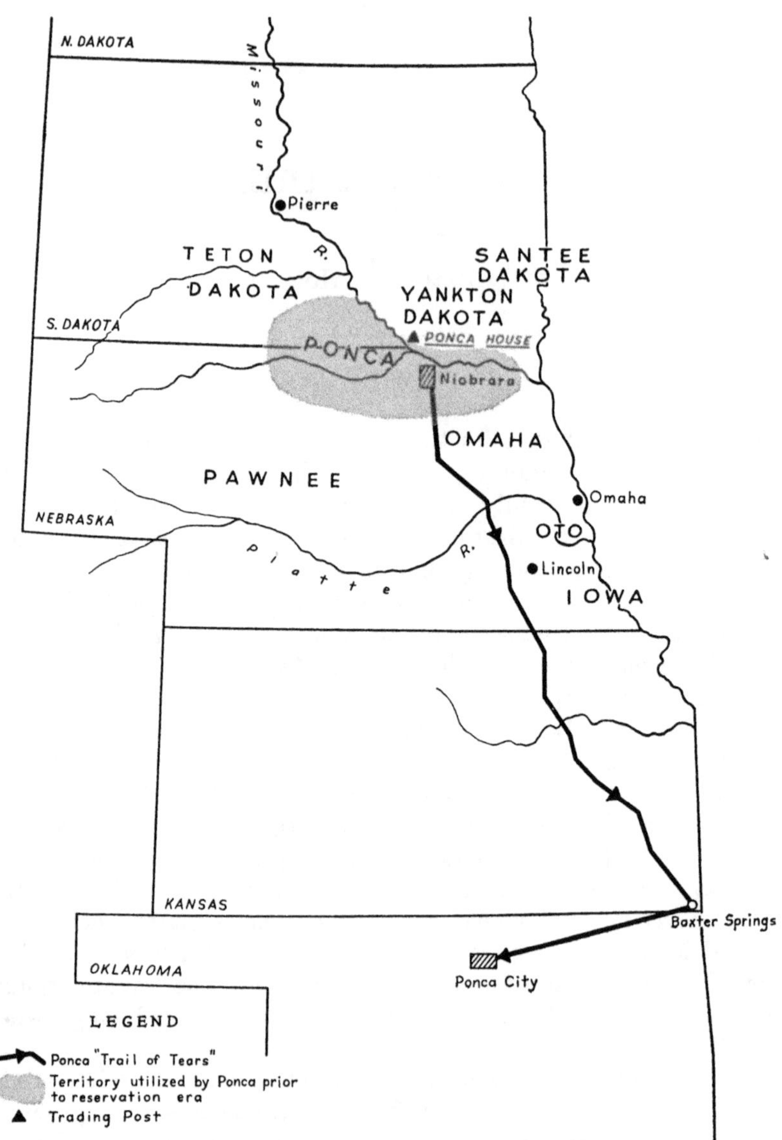

Map 1.—Author's conception of Ponca territory.

color—has been called the best in aboriginal North America. Some ceremonial vessels were made in the shape of animals, fish, and even human heads. Pots were decorated by polishing, incising, modeling, punctating, engraving, and painting.

Shellwork also was of a high order. Shell gorgets with engraved or cut and engraved figures remind one immediately of the elaborate ceremonial art of ancient Mexico. Gorgets with representations of feathered serpents, eagle warriors, and athletes playing the hoop and javelin game are characteristic. In some parts of the Middle Mississippi territory pear-shaped gorgets in the form of a human face with strange "weeping" eyes have been found.

The Middle Mississippi people were acquainted with copper and worked it into a variety of tools and ornaments. One excellent example of the coppersmith's art is an ornamental plate showing a dancing eagle warrior carrying a human trophy head in one hand and a mace in the other.

From stone the Middle Mississippi people made magnificent monolithic axes and maces that are masterpieces of primitive workmanship. Woodcarving, weaving, and featherwork also were of a high order, judging by the few examples that have survived.

Politically the Middle Mississippi Indians were advanced beyond the level of their neighbors to the north and west. The principal political unit seems to have been a city-state of the type found in ancient Mesopotamia and represented in the New World by the Maya. One large village culturally and politically dominated surrounding satellite villages. We know little of the political structure other than that there must have been some means of organizing cooperative labor on a large scale to effect the construction of the great temple mounds and fortifications. Perhaps a theocracy, with the principal chief and his priests acting as representatives of the gods, prevailed.

The construction of the great earthen pyramids and fortifications and to a lesser extent the elaborate works of art indicate a surplus economy which freed considerable time for these activities. Hence we are not surprised to learn that bottom-land agriculture was the principal economic base of Middle Mississippi civilization. Corn, squash, beans, gourds, and perhaps other crops were raised. This vegetal fare was supplemented by hunting, fishing, and the gathering of wild foods.

Middle Mississippi culture represents the most intensive Indian occupancy of Eastern North America and the highest cultural achievement north of Mexico. Nowhere was there a civilization which developed so rapidly and expanded so greatly in a few short centuries. From its center in the Southeast, Middle Mississippi influences radiated west and north into the Plains, and north into the Northeastern Woodlands.

Although a great deal has been learned about this civilization from the excavation of its sites, its genesis remains a mystery. Middle American influences are clearly discernible in the truncated pyramidal mounds, art motifs, weapons, and pottery styles. Yet, strangely enough, no Middle American trade pieces have ever been found in a Middle Mississippian site. Nor have archeologists found the neat string of connecting sites, either through the islands of the Caribbean or via the land route of the Southwest and northern Mexico, which would show how these exotic ideas reached the Southeast. It appears, rather, that certain basic Middle American ideas, once they were implanted among the Indians of the Southeast, developed there without additional stimulus.

Mysterious in its origins, the decline of this advanced culture is also imperfectly understood. Although De Soto and a few other very early explorers viewed Middle Mississippi culture before the great fortress towns and ceremonial centers had been abandoned, this culture seems to have passed its peak before the arrival of the White man. The coming of European explorers, traders, and colonists and the population displacement, tribal warfare, and disease which resulted merely hastened the fall of this once flourishing civilization.

No single tribe or linguistic group can be credited with Middle Mississippi culture. It was rather the product of many different tribes and linguistic groups. Among the historic tribes which were, at the time of their discovery, participants in this culture were the Cherokee, Chickasaw, Choctaw, and the numerous tribes of the Creek Confederacy. It was no mere accident that their descendants became known to the Whites as the "Five Civilized Tribes." They were carrying on, in their tribal life, many features derived from Middle Mississippi culture. Furthermore, their own relative advancement made it easier for them to adopt features of the newly introduced European civilization.

Other participants in the Middle Mississippi culture were the Caddoan tribes of the Central and Southern Plains and certain groups speaking languages of the Siouan linguistic stock. Apparently these Siouan-speaking groups, migrating out of the Southeast and receiving new cultural stimuli during their movements, carried Middle Mississippi ideas into the Prairie region.

Among these Siouan speakers were groups which became known in historic times as the Mandan tribe. Famous for their fortified earthlodge villages, intensive horticulture, and spectacular ceremonies directed by a priestly hierarchy, the members of this tribe became known as the "gentlemanly Mandan" to traders and explorers on the Missouri. They introduced their semisedentary way of life to many other groups in the Northern Plains, including the Hidatsa, and in late historic times, one division of the Dakota or Sioux.

Farther south, in the Central Plains, were tribes of the *Đégiha* and Chiwere divisions of the Siouan language family. The *Đégiha*-speaking tribes were the Ponca, Omaha, Osage, Kansa, and Quapaw, and the Chiwere groups were the Iowa, Oto, and Missouri. Like the Mandan, these "Southern Siouans" brought with them to the Plains certain advanced ideas derived from the Middle Mississippi centers in the Southeast, such as an agricultural way of life, a social and religious organization of a relatively complex nature, and, in the case of the Ponca, the custom of building fortified towns.

Neither the Mandan nor the Southern Siouans carried the highest form of the great southeastern culture into the Plains but rather a muted, simplified form. Nevertheless, throughout the cultures of all these tribes one can clearly see the impress of contact with the Middle Mississippi way of life.

It is with one of these Southern Siouan tribes, the Ponca, that this monograph is concerned. By the time they were contacted by White explorers, traders, and missionaries, the Ponca had become in most respects a typical Prairie tribe. Yet there remained many elements in their culture, the most notable being their custom of building bastioned earthen forts, which demonstrate their Middle Mississippi heritage. One who fails to take account of this Southeastern *leitmotif* in Ponca culture cannot, in my opinion, fully understand or appreciate it.

Without further ado, then, let us meet the Ponca.

The Ponca refer to themselves as *Pónka*, and they were known by this name to the Omaha, Osage, Kansa, Quapaw, Iowa, Oto, and Missouri tribes. Many American Indian tribal names have a meaning apart from their mere tribal designation. The name "Omaha" for example, means "Upstream people." If such a secondary meaning ever existed for the name "Ponca," it was lost long ago. Even the oldest members of the tribe do not know just why the tribe is called Ponca.

One fact, however, is certain; the name is not of foreign origin. It occurs as a clan or subclan name among three of the other four *Đégiha*-speaking tribes—the Osage, Kansa, and Quapaw. The fact that the Omaha tribe lacks a "Ponca" clan may have significance because of the tradition that the Ponca were a clan of the Omaha before the separation of the two tribes (Fletcher and La Flesche, 1911, p. 41).

As a result of the tragic Removal of 1877, the Ponca tribe is now divided into two bands, one in Nebraska and adjacent parts of South Dakota and the other in Oklahoma. These bands are generally known as the Northern and Southern Ponca. The native term for Northern Ponca is *Osní-Pònka*, which means "Cold Ponca" and refers to the relative coldness of their country as contrasted with Oklahoma where the Southern Ponca are settled. By the same token the Southern Ponca are called *Mašté-Pònka*, "Warm Ponca."

Concerning the term *Đégiha*, which is the name applied to the linguistic group consisting of the Omaha, Ponca, Osage, Kansa, and Quapaw, James O. Dorsey (1885 b, p. 919) states: "When an Omaha was challenged in the dark, if in his own territory, he usually replied, 'I am a *Đégiha*.' So might a Ponka reply under similar circumstances, when at home." I have heard this term used in speeches by Ponca and

718-071—65——2

Omaha on numerous occasions and its use was confirmed by my informants. The term means "The people of this group."

According to Dave Little-cook, a Southern Ponca, certain Southern Plains tribes refer to the Ponca as *Pá-masè*, or 'Head-cutters.' Little-cook knew no reason for the use of this term. The anthropologist Alanson Skinner (1915 c, p. 797) states, however: "When an enemy was killed, the Ponca scalped him, then cut off his head and threw it away. The sign for Ponca in the sign language indicates this custom." Apparently the Ponca, together with the Omaha and Osage, retained the old Middle Mississippian custom of removing the entire head from a slaughtered enemy. A common motif in Middle Mississippi art is a dancing warrior carrying such a trophy head.

The Pawnee names for the Ponca were *Ríhit* and *Díhit*, while the Caddo term was *Tšíaxosokuš* (Dorsey and Thomas, 1910, p. 279). James O. Dorsey lists the Winnebago name as *Kánka* in his vocabulary, compiled in 1896 (ibid., p. 279). In his "Omaha Sociology," he writes that from their custom of sometimes pitching their tipis in three concentric circles, the Ponca were sometimes called *Oyáte-yàmni* or the 'three nations' by the Dakota (1884 a, p. 219).

Before the 1877 Removal split the tribe into Northern and Southern Ponca, there were two important bands or village groups among the Ponca in Nebraska. The first of these was the *Waɫx̧ùde* or "Gray-blanket" band. This band maintained its winter village in the vicinity of the present Northern Ponca Community Building, 2 miles west and 3 miles south of Niobrara, Nebr. The name "Gray-blanket" derived from the fact that this group was once issued white blankets by the Government. Worn in the dust of the prairies these blankets soon, apparently, took on a grayish cast.

The second band was the *Hubđǫ́* or 'Fish-smell' village group, who camped about 2 miles east of the present town of Verdel, Nebr. Their name is said to refer to a year when dead fish, left behind by thawing ice in the nearby river, created a stench in the village that was remarkable even to the strong-stomached Ponca of that era.

The dialect spoken by the Ponca is one of four in the *Đégiha* language (Dorsey, 1885 b, pp. 919–920). The Ponca and Omaha dialects are the same except for a few words of modern origin, such as those for "cat" and "schoolhouse." The other three dialects in the language are Kansa, Osage, and Quapaw. The *Đégiha* language is a member of the widespread Siouan linguistic family. This language takes its name from the well-known Dakota or "Sioux" tribe. The fact that a tribe speaks a "Siouan" language, however, should not be taken to mean that they were politically allied with the Dakota. As a matter of fact most of the other members of the Siouan language family were bitter enemies of the Sioux tribe.

At the present time only older Ponca use their native tongue in ordinary conversation. The younger people of both bands customarily speak English. They may understand some *Đégiha*, but when addressed in this language by an older person they will reply in English. An informal census in 1961 revealed only 10 individuals under the age of 25 who could conduct a lengthy conversation in *Đégiha*. One cannot help regretting the extinction of this language, which will probably occur (in regard to the Ponca) in two or three generations. It is soft, resonant, yet capable of expressing dramatic action and deep emotion.

The Southern Ponca, as a result of their years in Oklahoma, now speak English with a slight Southern accent, and this has affected their pronunciation of *Đégiha* as well. This fact their Northern kinsmen find quite amusing. Yet the Northern Ponca, too, have changed. Members of this band, when speaking their native tongue, have the habit of interjecting an occasional Santee or Teton Dakota word, the result of their long contact with these groups in Nebraska and South Dakota. Even PLC, the tribal historian, does this occasionally. When asked the Ponca name for the women's menstrual hut, he first gave the Dakota *Išná-t*^{h}*i* instead of the *Đégiha* term *Oką-atì*.

According to older members of the tribe, the Ponca formerly hunted and ranged over most of the area now known as the Central Great Plains. The Black Hills of South Dakota they knew well, and sometimes even reached the Rockies in their search for game, scalps, and the adventure of seeing new territory. Their main seat, however, and the area where most of their permanent villages and forts were built, was what is now Knox County, in northeastern Nebraska. This was the heart of the Ponca domain in former times and is still the home of most of the Northern Ponca. Ponca folktales and accounts of great battles in the past almost invariably find their setting in this area.

Geographers and anthropologists agree that environment has an important conditioning effect upon the way of life of a region's inhabitants. What, then, was the Ponca country like? The climate of this Ponca "heartland" is of the general continental type. Summers are long and warm, and well suited to the raising of crops. The spring is usually cool, with considerable rainy weather, and the autumns are long and pleasant, with only occasionally rainy spells. Indeed, the Ponca preferred the fall of the year to both spring and summer.

The mean rainfall is 24.1 inches. About 77 percent of this occurs during the principal part of the growing season, from April to September, a very fortunate circumstance for the agricultural Ponca. In the summer most of the rainfall occurs as heavy thundershowers, but torrential rains are rare. Severe droughts are almost unknown during May and June, but in the latter part of July and through August the rainfall varies considerably and short dry spells may occur. The annual amount of snowfall varies from a few inches to several feet, with a mean of 30.6.

The Ponca country is part of a broad, nearly level plain which slopes gently downward toward the south and east (pl. 18). However, the Missouri River is so deeply entrenched along the northern edge of Knox County that much of the drainage locally is northward to that stream. About 90 percent of the land is upland and the remainder is alluvial. The land surfaces range from gently rolling to extremely rough and broken. Most of the upland area has been rather severely eroded, and this area includes a wide variety of wind- and water-formed physiographic features. When viewed from the crest of one of the Missouri bluffs, the landscape of the Ponca "heartland" is most inspiring. Tall, rounded, hills slope downward to rich green bottom lands. Away to the north stretches the mighty Missouri, outlined by its white chalk banks, the burial ground of unnumbered generations of Ponca.

Ponca villages, like the Middle Mississippi towns of the Southeast, were almost always located on river or creek terraces, preferably at a fork where a tributary entered a larger stream. The gardens were on nearby bottom lands which could be easily cultivated with a bison scapula hoe. The soils of the area, though not equally productive, are as a whole well suited to agriculture. The nearby hills and gullies provided both game and wild roots and berries.

Deposits of metal are significantly lacking in this area, but clay and sand suitable for ceramics are abundant at many places along the Missouri and its tributaries. Sandstone, used by the Ponca to polish wooden articles, is widely exposed along the Missouri bluffs.

The principal mammals in the area at the present time are the Virginia deer, coyote, beaver, raccoon, badger, muskrat, prairie dog, weasel, gopher, and field mouse. Formerly bison, antelope, and wapiti were found. The principal birds are the pinnated grouse, Canada goose, redhead, pintail, teal, and mallard duck, coot, rail, pelican, heron, golden eagle, bald eagle, and several varieties of hawks and owls, together with the other small birds of the general Nebraska area.

The fish which occur most commonly in rivers and streams of the Ponca country are the yellow and blue catfish, channel catfish, red horse, buffalo, carp, sunfish, and crappie. Of these, all are native except the carp. Both snapping turtles and painted turtles are found. Snakes most common in the area are the bull snake and garter snake, although an occasional rattlesnake is encountered.

The Ponca country is in the prairie region of the United States. In the virgin areas throughout the uplands and terraces, the predominant grasses are big bluestem, little bluestem, and slender wheatgrass. On the more sandy soils needlegrass predominates in most places. The bottoms support a great variety of moisture-loving grasses, except in the more poorly drained situations, where rushes and sedges grow. Native trees, including elm, oak, cottonwood, ash, hackberry, boxelder, and willow, occupy narrow strips adjacent to the stream channels in all the larger valleys, and walnut was formerly quite common as well. Trees are especially numerous on many of the lower slopes of bluffs bordering the Missouri River bottom lands.

The Ponca territory is a pleasant land, and the many tourists who annually visit Niobrara State Park, a small portion of the old Ponca domain which has been set aside as a recreation center, can readily appreciate the sorrow and bitterness of the Ponca when the Federal Government announced that the tribe must leave their homeland forever.

The Ponca were never, apparently, a very large tribe. Population figures vary greatly within a short span of time, probably because of poor estimates on the part of early observers. Nevertheless, a rough idea of Ponca population through the years can be gained from the various sources.

Will and Hyde write: "The traditions state that when they reached the Niobrara the Ponkas numbered three thousand people and encamped in three large concentric circles" (1917, p. 39). Mooney (1928, p. 7) gives 800 as the probable size of the tribe in 1788. The earliest historical estimate known to me is contained in a letter written by Esteban Rodriguez Miró, Governor General of Louisiana, to Antonio Renzel, Commandant of the Interior Provinces of Louisiana, in 1785. Miró states that the Ponca then had "not more than eighty warriors" (Nasatir, 1952, vol. 1, p. 126). Pierre Tabeau says that in 1804 they still had 80 men bearing arms, "but an invasion of the Bois Brules has since destroyed more than half of them" (Tabeau, 1939, p. 100). The "Bois Brules" mentioned by Tabeau were undoubtedly members of the Brulé subband of the Teton Dakota. Lewis and Clark estimated only 200 total population for the Ponca that same year, and this figure appears on Clark's map (Lewis, 1904–5).

Our next estimate comes from the explorer John Bradbury (1904, vol. 5, p. 96), writing in 1819 but probably referring to about a decade earlier. He states: "They now number about seven hundred." Edwin James (1905, p. 152), who accompanied S. H. Long's expedition of 1819–20, gives their number as 200. In 1832 Prince Maximilian of Wied, the famous Missouri explorer, visited the Ponca. He writes: "According to Dr. Morse's report, they numbered, in 1822, 1,750 in all, at present the total amount of their warriors is estimated at about 300" (Wied-Neuweid, 1906, vol. 22, p. 284). Gen. Henry Atkinson (1922, p. 10) in a letter written to Colonel Hamilton in 1825, lists the

Ponca as having 180 warriors. Dorsey and Thomas (1910, pt. 2, p. 278) give 600 as the number in 1829 and 800 in 1842.

In his diary the Rev. Moses Merrill (1892, p. 170) estimates their number as being from 800 to 1,000 in 1834. Seth K. Humphrey (1906, p. 47) notes: "In 1869 their number is given [as] 768." In 1874 the Government census, quoted by Fletcher and La Flesche (197, p. 51), lists their number as 733. In 1880 Dorsey and Thomas (1910, p. 279) give the number of Southern Ponca as 600 and Northern Ponca as 225, while in 1906 they list 570 for the Southern Ponca and 263 for the Northern band.

The census of 1910 gave 875 in all, including 619 in Oklahoma and 193 in Nebraska. The Report of the U.S. Indian Office for 1923 was 1,381. The census of 1930 returned 939. In 1937 the Indian Office gave 825 in Oklahoma and 397 in Nebraska. At the present time figures are approximately 1,000 for the Southern Ponca and 350 for the Northern Ponca, though the latter group is now so scattered as to make enumeration difficult.

ORIGINS

At the present time, archeology, "the handmaiden of history," can tell us little concerning the entrance of the Ponca into their historic territory. We can, however, spell out in a rough way the penetration of Middle Mississippi culture into the Prairie region, in which the ancestors of the Ponca and Omaha were undoubtedly involved. Perhaps the best scheme is that advanced by the archeologist James B. Griffin. He suggests that some of the later sites of the Mill Creek Aspect in South Dakota may represent the Ponca and Omaha, and that the Middle Mississippian influences which appear in the Plains ca. A.D. 1200–1300 are partly due to the movement of *égiha*-speaking tribes into the area:

> As a working hypothesis I have proposed elsewhere that the Mississippi Pattern influences in the Plains were the results of the movements of specific cultural units from the Mississippi Valley. The first of these is strongly associated, culturally, with sites in the Cahokia region. They moved from there into the Kansas City area . . . . Apparently this actual movement of people modified the eastern section of the Upper Republican giving rise to the Nebraska Aspect. Possibly a slightly earlier or concurrent movement from the Aztalan area to the west took place, producing first, the Cambria Focus in south-central Minnesota. Then it moved into western Iowa to become the Mill Creek Aspect. The later Mill Creek sites in South Dakota acquired Upper Republican and some Woodland traits. These sites were, one might postulate, occupied by the proto-historic Ponca and Omaha. [Griffin, 1946, p. 89.]

Many archeological sites of unknown affiliation in Nebraska and South Dakota, particularly in the Niobrara area, are claimed by the Ponca as former villages of their people. In 1936 and 1937 the University of Nebraska sponsored summer field parties in northeastern Nebraska in an effort to delineate the culture of the Ponca as it appears in archeological remains. By doing so, it was thought their claims could be disproved or verified.

One of the prime objectives of this work was the excavation of the famous Ponca Fort site, 25KX1, which is located near the mouth of Ponca Creek in Knox County, Nebr. This site, famous in Ponca tribal lore, was considered the most logical point from which to begin. It was definitely known to be Ponca by reason of its having been mentioned by a number of early explorers. Therefore, by excavating it and determining what Ponca pottery and other artifacts were like, it was believed that other sites in the area, by comparison, could be identified as Ponca or the remains of some other group or groups. Unfortunately, however, the work at 25KX1 has thus far raised more questions about Ponca archeology than it has answered.

The Ponca Fort site may be characterized as the remains of a fortified earth-lodge village. It is located in sec. 29, T. 33 N., R. 7 W., Knox County, Nebr. It is roughly 8 miles northwest of the town of Niobrara and 1 mile east of Verdel. The site is on the south side of the Missouri, and Ponca Creek, a tributary of the Missouri, is 2,000 feet north of the site, emptying into the Missouri a mile and a half to the east. The fort was well situated from a defensive point of view, being located on a prominence, one of the bluffs of the Missouri, some 50 or 60 feet above the floor of the valley of Ponca Creek.

The fort has an oval defensive ditch with an interior earthen embankment. This embankment supported, at the time the fort was occupied, a post palisade. The long axis of the ditch or moat is oriented east and west. The fort covers an area of 3 acres, and measures 380 feet east and west and 320 feet north and south. On at least one side of the fortification, protuberances or bastions were built from which the village inhabitants could rake attacking forces with a murderous crossfire. These bastions, still visible in an aerial photograph of the site (Wood, 1959, pl. 1), may have functioned primarily to protect the entrance to the fort which, according to J. O. Dorsey's map (1884 a, fig. 30, orientation corrected by Wood, 1959, map 1), was at the northwest end of the village.

Between 1953 and 1955 Raymond Wood, then a graduate student at the University of Nebraska, made an analysis of the material recovered from the Ponca Fort as well as from other purported Ponca sites in the area excavated by the Nebraska field parties in the thirties. Recently Wood has published on the Ponca Fort site (1959; 1960). He notes that the stockade surrounding the village was composed of posts that were quite widely spaced. Perhaps, in order to provide more adequate defense, logs or branches were interwoven between these uprights (Wood, 1960, p. 26).

Owing to repeated cultivation, no remains which could definitely be termed earth lodges were discovered inside the ditch, although numerous post molds were recovered in the 30 excavation units of the 1936 and 1937 fieldwork. Nevertheless, all traditional and historic accounts of the fort indicate the presence of earth lodges, and the Dorsey map (1884 a, fig. 30) indicates four lodges within the enclosure, the depressions of which may have been visible in the 1880's. Outside the fortification ditch, in natural hummocks or mounds, the inhabitants of the fort buried their dead. The crania from these mound burials show a roundheaded, broad-faced, narrow-nosed physical type in no way different from the present-day Ponca.

The Ponca Fort, or *N* as it is termed in *Đégiha*, seems to have been the last of its type built by the Ponca, though at least one other is mentioned in the traditional history of the tribe. In my opinion the construction of earthen forts of this sort is almost certainly a culture complex which the Ponca derived from their Middle Mississippi forebears in the Southeast or which diffused to them from this area.

Wood has identified three components at the site, one of which is prehistoric and two of which date from the early historic period. The prehistoric component is identified as belonging to the rather widespread Aksarben Aspect, which is thought by many Plains archeologists to represent the ancestors of the Pawnee, Arikara, and perhaps other groups and is dated A.D. 1000–1500. The second or "B" component yielded pottery of the type known as Stanley ware. Stanley ware has been found at several sites in South Dakota and is attributed to the Arikara Indians of the latter part of the 18th century. Component B has been identified, nevertheless, as representing the Ponca occupation of the site.

Aside from the pottery, Component B contained such native artifacts as grooved stone mauls, mealing slabs and mullers, shaft smoothers, grooved abraders, bowshaves, discoidal hammerstones, whetstones, cobble hammerstones, stone anvils, flint projectile points and scrapers, bone knife handles, a bone tube, fleshers, shaft wrenches, scapula hoes, an ulna pick, catlinite pipes and disks, fragments of twined matting, and a strip of bark in a roll. These artifacts, though valuable in indicating the general cultural orientation of the inhabitants of the site, are unfortunately not distinctive enough to specifically identify them, or to connect 25KX1 with other possible Ponca sites.

Numerous European trade objects were also recovered, including iron hoes, a hatchet, metal arrowpoints, coils of lead wire, button weights, pin brooches, and scraps of cloth. With one of the burials a conch shell gorget and a hair pipe were recovered. Finds of corn and beans indicate that the Ponca of this era were gardeners or farmers.

A very curious find from the site is a fragment of a catlinite bannerstone. These objects are usually regarded as weights or counterbalances used in connection with the atlatl or spear thrower, a very ancient American Indian weapon but one retained until the historic period by some Southeastern groups. Could this object from the Ponca Fort site represent a ceremonial retention of an old Middle Mississippi weapon by the Ponca? Certainly the bow and arrow was the principal weapon of war and the hunt at this period, and the find of a gun part indicates that the villagers were beginning to acquire a few firearms.

From the large amount of European trade goods present, Wood suggests that the occupation of the site by the Ponca occurred between 1790 and 1800, when the Ponca were acquiring huge quantities of goods through trade and the pillage of boats ascending the Missouri. In the last analysis, then, the Ponca Fort site not only tells us little about Ponca archeology but also presents us with the problem of accounting for the presence of Arikara pottery at a documented Ponca site. Wood suggests that this may indicate that some of the Ponca had taken Arikara women for wives. As unlikely as this explanation appears at first blush, it may have considerable merit, for the total amount of pottery recovered was small. Finds of kettle handles and brass kettle patches indicate that most of the women at the site, even at this date, were using metal vessels for cooking and carrying water. Furthermore, Peter Le Claire, the Ponca historian, states (letter of February 23, 1962) that the earliest Ponca traditions tell of friendly contacts and joint bison hunts with the "Sand Pawnee" or Arikara. Apparently these friendly contacts resulted in some intermarriage. Perhaps the Arikara wives, coming from a tribe farther upriver and hence a bit more removed from the influences of White civilization, continued to practice the ceramic arts at a time when they had been abandoned by their Ponca sisters-in-law.

Other sites which may represent the prehistoric and early historic Ponca are those of the Redbird Focus, recently described by Dr. Wood (MS., 1956). Here again, however, difficulties are encountered. All of the pottery occurring in sites of this focus is markedly different from that at the Ponca Fort site. These ceramics suggest that the Redbird Focus is related to both the Lower Loup Focus of the Central Plains, which is thought to represent the Pawnee of late prehistoric and early historic times, and the La Roche Focus of the Middle Missouri area, which seems to represent another Caddoan-speaking group, the Arikara.

We must say, then, that at the present time the prehistoric archeological remains of the Ponca tribe remain to be identified and that the archeology of north-central Nebraska is still too imperfectly understood to tell us much of the entry and occupation of the area by the Ponca. It is hoped that future research will clarify the relationships of the Ponca to other groups in the area and provide us with a more detailed account of their prehistory.

Since we lack archeological evidence in the form of a neat string of sites stretching back in time and space to the ancestral homeland of the Ponca, we must rely upon other sorts of data in reconstructing the tribe's past. One line of evidence is afforded by the tribal migration legends. Passed down from one generation to the next by word of mouth, such legends are of course subject to considerable distortion. Nevertheless they constitute one of our best sources for the reconstruction of Ponca history.

There are many Ponca and Omaha legends in the anthropological literature. Most of these agree in their main points, namely, that the Ponca, Omaha, Kansa, Osage, and Quapaw were once a single tribe in the Southeast, and that during the migration north and west the group split up, the Ponca and Omaha being the last to separate (Dorsey, 1884 a, pp. 211–213; Riggs, 1893, p. 190; McGee, 1897, p. 191; Anonymous, 1907, pp. 653–656; Dorsey and Thomas, 1910, pp. 278–279; Swanton, 1910, pp. 156–158; Fletcher and La Flesche, 1911, pp. 38–39; Miner, 1911, pp. xvii-xiii; Skinner, 1915 c, p. 779; La Flesche, 1917, pp. 460–462; Hyde, 1934 b, pp. 23–26; Strong, 1935, pp. 16–17; Wedel, 1936, p. 3). Many Southern Ponca, Omaha, and Osage interviewed in 1954 confirmed this tradition. Although the accounts agree in placing the ancestral home of the *égiha* tribes in the Southeast, they are vague as to the path followed when moving westward.

One traditional account from the Omaha tribe, cited by Fletcher and La Flesche (1911, pp. 72–81), states that after their separation from the Quapaw, the Omaha (and Ponca) followed the Des Moines River to its headwaters and then wandered to the northeast. The two tribes finally settled in a village on the Big Sioux River and lived there until a disastrous battle with the Dakota took place. They thereupon abandoned this village and turned southward, where they encountered the ancestors of the Arikara tribe, who then occupied the historic Omaha territory in northeastern Nebraska. At first they warred with the Arikara, but later a peace was concluded. During this peaceful interlude the Omaha and Ponca learned to build Plains-type earth lodges from the Arikara. The separation of the Omaha and Ponca supposedly took place shortly after this.

The Rev. James O. Dorsey, for many years a missionary among the Ponca and Omaha, gives a slightly more detailed account of the *Đégiha* migrations, combining native traditions with his own speculations. He says that the Omaha, Ponca, Osage, and other cognate tribes traveled down the Ohio River to its mouth from their original homeland in the Southeast. When they arrived at the Mississippi some went upriver, hence the name *Umą́hą* (Omaha), which means 'Upstream,' while the rest went downriver, and so earned the name *Ugáxpe* (Quapaw), meaning 'Downstream.' The former group contained the Omaha, Ponca, Osage, and Kansa. The latter group became the Quapaw.

The tribes which went upriver ranged for a time in the present Osage, Gasconade, and adjacent counties in Missouri. Here they were joined by a Chiwere Siouan-speaking group, the Iowa. At the mouth of the Osage River another separation took place, the Osage and Kansa leaving the main group. The Omaha, Ponca, and Iowa proceeded, by degrees, through Missouri, Iowa, and Minnesota to the pipestone quarries near the present city of Pipestone, Minn. From here they journeyed to the Big Sioux River, where they built a fort and a village. Game abounded in this locality.

The neighboring Dakota, however, made war on the three tribes and so they went west and southwest to a lake near the head of Chouteau Creek, now known as Lake Andes (?) in South Dakota. Here they cut the sacred pole, an important religious object, and assigned each clan and subclan its peculiar customs and duties. After leaving this lake they traveled up the Missouri River to the mouth of the White River, where they crossed over to the west bank. The Ponca then went on to the Black Hills while the Omaha and Iowa stayed in the vicinity.

Later the Ponca rejoined the others and the three tribes turned downstream. When they reached the vicinity of the present town of Niobrara, Nebr., the Ponca stopped. The Omaha removed to a place near Covington, Nebr. The Iowa passed the Omaha and later made a village near Florence, Nebr. (Dorsey, 1884 a, pp. 211–213.)

It is not possible to determine the assumed period of these different movements from either Dorsey's account or that of Fletcher and La Flesche. The former (1884 a, pp. 218–222) believed, however, that the Ponca separated from the Omaha around 1390, and that all migrations prior to the separation of the Iowa, Omaha, and Ponca occurred prior to 1673, and that the split between the Quapaw and the four other tribes took place before 1540. Fletcher and La Flesche (1911) imply that the Omaha-Ponca separation was late, but are not specific. W. J. McGee (1897, p. 191) believed that the separation took place ca. 1650.

Unpublished data accumulated by John L. Champe leads him to date the joint Omaha-Ponca occupancy of the village on the Big Sioux River, north of present-day Sioux City, Iowa, from 1700–1702, and the split of the two tribes at the mouth of the White River about 1715. Later the Ponca returned to the mouth of the White and, according to Champe (cited by Wood, 1959, p. 10), the Omaha moved to Bow Creek, near the present-day Wynot, Nebr., about 1735. This was the location of the Omaha "Bad Village," and it may have been here that the Ponca made their final break with the Omaha.

To the various traditional histories cited above we add another below, prepared by Peter Le Claire (PLC) several years ago. He gave it to me in 1949. This interesting document contains, in addition to the oral historical traditions of the tribe, a great deal of material on the customs, morals, and attitudes of the Ponca of his own and earlier generations. Although we will "get ahead of our story" with some of the later historical material included, it is thought best to present PLC's "Ponca History" as a unit at this point as an example of the traditional history of the tribe in its most recent form.

PLC secured much of his material from a man named *Mą́žą́hađè* (Mi-jin-ha-the in PLC's transcription from the *Đégiha*) or John Bull, a Southern Ponca chief (pl. 16). *Mą́žąhađè* died very shortly after imparting this information. PLC, in describing *Mą́žą́hađè*, said that he was a "good old man," an expert on tribal history and customs, and that he had participated in the Sun dance.

PLC has elaborated upon *Mą́žą́hađè's* material to some extent, injecting other stories and traditions with which he is familiar. The latter part of the history, for example, incorporates a great deal from published accounts of the Ponca Removal. The text in its present form was taken from a typewritten account prepared under PLC's direction in 1947. He had deposited this for safekeeping with a banker in Niobrara, Nebr., fearing that death might prevent his being able to pass it on. The text has been unaltered except for a few corrections made by PLC at a later date and the elimination of typographical errors. It was deemed best to leave native terms in PLC's own form of transcription.

PONCA HISTORY

By Peter Le Claire

(*a Ponca Indian*)

August 26, 1947

December 25th, 1928. A Xmas doings of the Poncas at the agency dance hall at Ponca City, Oklahoma when I visited Mi-jin-ha-the at his tent in the evening before the dance, this is what he said to me. "There is something that I want to tell you about the old Ponca history. At the present time there are some of them Poncas are older than I am that are living, but I was raised by two of my grandfathers and this is what they told me and I want you to know it, as we are living a different life now. No more long hair, no more old ways. You can write it on a tablet and try to get something out of it by having it published." [2] He told me this three times and I caught all of it; he died suddenly, shortly after.

[2] Apparently the older man thought that there would be a greater chance of the information being preserved if he promised PLC monetary gain.

The Poncas were in a big (Hu-tho-gah)[3] camp and where they were were people of light complexion and these people abused the Poncas and they wanted to get away from them. The chiefs gathered in their tent and prayed and they wanted someone to talk to God, and there was a stranger came in, a chief they didn't know, who sat in the door.[4] They wanted this man to go and talk to God. There was a mountain nearby and they told him to go up there and talk to God. He went up there and stayed four days and four nights and on the fourth night God talked to him in his sleep.[5] "You go back and tell them to cross this and do not look back when you are crossing. Don't take anything, only your dogs."

He woke up and started home, he was so weak that he just barely made the camp. They wet his lips with water and fed him little by little until he was able to talk. He told all he had heard and they moved. They crossed this water and they reached the end, there was all kinds of fruits and they were in a wonderful land.

They came on each side of the Ohio (Oh-hah-they) River and when they got to the Mississippi River they were on both sides of the river camping and one of the little chiefs[6] from the side sent a word that he wanted war, but the head chief refused and this was repeated four times and the head chief said, "Tomorrow morning we shall have war." Seven[7] of the chiefs in their tents heard a voice from heaven telling them, "Wake up, wake up. Put cold water on the children's eyes so they can open their eyes. There is a man coming. He is light complected and sweating and looking down.[8] He is going to eat from the ground.[9] As you go west (It-tah-xa-tah) there is plenty to eat and try everything, as you go, there are animals, in the water there is something to eat, there are birds, there are fruit trees with ripe berries."

They came and lived in Pipestone, Minnesota. While they were living there they found the pipe stone after a hard rain in a deep buffalo trail. They saw the red stone and the head chief was called and he told them to dig it and get it out as God has given us a pipe. The pipe was made there and the stem was made in Ponca, Nebraska. There is a creek they called Ash Creek across the river from Ponca. When they were in Pipestone they started marking their trail on the big boulders. This was done by the Medicine Men. It was a two-toned picture, part of the picture is already on the wall and it is finished and only a few Poncas can see it, make out what it is.[10] We will come to some more of these pictures later. Pa-dah-gah, he was the chief that kept the Sacred Pipe, he was the head chief and handed down to sons and grandsons for thousands of years until by some error, it fell into white mans hands.[11]

---

[3] The parentheses here, and throughout the History, are PLC's. He indicates, using his own syllabary, that "Hu-tho-gah" is the native term for a camp circle.

[4] It is a common custom among Plains Indians for a stranger to sit near the door, which is considered a place of little honor. In sitting here he indicates humbleness.

[5] "Four" is the most sacred number among the Ponca, and among Plains tribes in general.

[6] There were two classes of chiefs among the Ponca. The chiefs of the second rank, or "little" chiefs, were thought not to possess the judgment or wisdom of the "big" chiefs. This is probably the reason that a little chief is represented as the one trying to instigate a war.

[7] "Seven" is also a sacred number among the Ponca, and the Plains tribes in general. It seems to rank below "four" in importance, however.

[8] This description probably reflects White religious teachings. Pictures of the Crucifixion are favorite wall decorations in Ponca homes.

[9] Eating from the ground is a sign of extreme humbleness among the Ponca, according to PLC.

[10] This statement refers to the utilization of natural fissures in the boulders to save effort in carving the petroglyphs.

[11] This should read ". . . and (the sacred pipe was) handed down . . . ." The statement ". . . fell into White man's hands . . ." refers to the misappropriation of a Ponca clan pipe by an anthropologist in the 1930's. PLC thought that this was the tribal pipe when he wrote his history.

They moved to another place where the little town of St. Helena is and from St. Helena, Nebraska, to Santee, Nebraska where the old agency is now. On the Chalk rock walls near Springfield, S.D. is one more of the drawings of the Medicine Men.

From these villages, they would go on Wah-ni-sa (Buffalo hunt) up the Missouri River, way in the Rocky Mountains. They say where they step over the Nu-sho-day (Missouri River) they would follow the Rocky Mountains to Pikes Peak and they would come back to Nebraska and they would follow on the rivers back to Wah-ta where Fremont, Nebraska is. From Santee to Niobrara River,[12] here they saw a Pa-snu-tah [13] dead (an Elephant) and they also saw a prehistoric animal they called (Wah-kon-da-gee).

This animal was of long body, had forked feet, yellow hair, about 8 feet high, and about 40 feet long. They saw this animal go into its hole northwest of Verdel, Nebraska. This place they called (Way-kon-da-gi-mi-shon-da).[14] At the coldest days of the winter it would go into the hole. They found Niobrara River to be ideal place as they found everything they wanted to eat there, in the water, under the ground. They found wild beans and potatoes and fruits of all kinds.

There are old villages up the Niobrara River. There is one southwest of the Twin Buttes where the fork of the two rivers is (Ke-ah-pa-ha) and the Niobrara. The Twin Buttes were the places for the medicine men to perform. There is a cave in the east one there is where they saw a prehistoric animal, the Pah-snu-tah.[15]

Near Verdel, Nebraska, there is a dirt fort (Na-za)[16] where a battle took place 600 years or better.[17] The tribe they called Pa-du-kah.[18] They were from the south. They fought these Pa-du-kah four times and the last one they took a little boy as prisoner from the Poncas.

Very few of them went home. It is said that this boy prisoner came home, he was a good hundred years old. He said he came back to die and wished to be buried where his forefathers were buried at Ma-Ah-zee. This means "Chalk-rock-Bank" where the burying ground is, he told his family in the South, sons and grand-children, and five of them have come back to die and they were all hundred years old. The last one, Gish-ta-wah-gu died early part of 1900. He was so old that he was childish. He would cry for his mama and papa.

In the Big Horn mountains in Wyoming is the best trail marks there is made by the Poncas. It is a circle in the shape of a wagon wheel, rocks laid forming the shape. It represents a sun dance circle. All the colors that goes with the sun dance is found, the Black, red and white. Black represents weeping, and White is their prayers and the answer.

West of this circle is an arrow laid with rocks pointing directly toward it.

In the mountains the dwarfs is found and dreaded as it leads them away at nights and last until morning. "Mong-thu-jah-the-gah" is what they called them.

---

[12] This should read "(While traveling) from Santee to (the) Niobrara River . . ."

[13] PLC identified this animal as a "hairy elephant."

[14] "Way-kon-da-gi-mi-shon-da" may be translated "the lair of *Wakádagi.*"

[15] According to PLC this "hairy elephant" was alive.

[16] *Náza* is the Omaha and Ponca name for this fort. Whether or not the term is generic for all such fortifications was not learned.

[17] This should read ". . . took place 600 years (ago) or better."

[18] The Pa-du-kah were identified as Comanche by PLC, JLR, OYB, and VHM. LMD identified them as Shoshone. Recent ethnohistorical and archeological evidence indicates that previous to the 19th century the term "Padouca" was used in reference to the Lipan or Plains Apache. Later the term was transferred to the Comanche who had taken over much of the Lipan territory (Champe, 1949; Secoy, 1957).

The Ponca camp is called Hu-thu-gah, it is round the entrance in the east. There are seven bands in the Hu-thu-gah or camp. Each of these bands has duties in the camp. From the entrance left to right are the Wah-jah-ta. Their duty is to watch the entrance, they see who goes out, anyone going out and gets lost, they track them as they are expert trackers.

The next band are Ni-kah-pah-schna. Their duty is they know all about the human head and how it should be dressed.

The third band are Te-xa-da. This band when the camp is getting short of meats they would get their bows and arrows out and make believe they are shooting animals saying "I'll shoot this fat one."

The band in Center west are the Wah-sha-ba. The head is in this band. He gives out orders. He prays daily.[19]

The band next to them are the mi-ki-Medicine.[20] They know all about medicines.

The sixth band are Nu-xa-ice.[21] They know everything about water and ice.

The seventh band are called He-sah-da. The rain makers they know all about the heavens and the clouds.

In the center of the Hu-thu-gah or camp, all the chiefs have a tent in which they meet and pray. When the buffalo is found they meet with the Buffalo Police and plan the attack, sometimes they plan so perfect that not one of them gets away, some of the sharpshooters or fast shooters kill high as seven[22] buffaloes out of a herd that is surrounded. Most of these men that kill seven buffaloes give all their kill to the needy ones such as the old chiefs and orphans.

If the buffalo herd is far from the camp they would move the camp closer without disturbing the herd, when they are moving closer the Sacred Pipe is taken in the lead. When the herd is killed, they see that all of the camp is supplied equally, first the oldest are taken care of. They get the most tenderest meat.

The Buffalo Police are real strict if anyone disturbs the Buffalo herd before the attack, he is whipped good and hard. The police also keep the camp in order.

The commandments are few in the tribe.

1. Have one God.
2. Do not kill one another.
3. Do not steal from one another.
4. Be kind to one another.
5. Do not talk about each other.
6. Do not be stingy.
7. Have respect for the Sacred Pipe.

They have the Sun-dance in mid-summer when the corn is in silk. The dance lasts four days and four nights without drink, sleep, and without food, a real sacrifice. The dancers are in the shape of a wheel or representing the four winds they would swing every so often. The next branch of the sun dance is the Wah-Wan Pipe dance,[23] any one in the tribe that is needy makes a little bag of tobacco and hands it to anyone that has plenty and have things to spare and if this man accepts this bag of tobacco the dance is given, a pipe and gourd

---

[19] Note that the Ponca chief retained much of the character of a Southeastern (i.e., Middle Mississippi) priest-king in being both the political and religious head of the tribe.

[20] ". . . the mi-ki-Medicine," should read ". . . the Mi-ki (or) Medicine." *Maką́*, Medicine, is the Ponca name for this clan.

[21] As in the preceding instance, ". . . Nu-xa-ice" is the native term plus its English equivalent. This should read ". . . Nu-xa (or) Ice." *Núxe* is the Ponca and Omaha term for ice.

[22] Note the recurrence of the sacred number "seven."

[23] This should read ". . . the Wah-Wan [or] Pipe Dance . . ."

is used. The gourd has a rattle, little stones inside and it keeps time of the drum and the pipe on the left hand.[24] While the dance is on, it is passed on to anyone that wanted to dance with it and help give things to the needy ones.

When the Hu-thu-gah camp is moving the fire is kept alive in their travel. A dry oak with bark on is used, inside of the bark where the worms has eaten it leaves a powdered trail. This powder is lighted, the bark over it where the breeze keeps it alive until the next stop is reached. They use rotted grass and powdered ash wood that is rotted. The fire is made by blowing on it.

To start a new fire, the stem of a soap weed is used, fine sand, rotten powdered ash wood, and rotted dry blue stem grass, this is put on a flat rock, they rub with the big end on the rock where the powdered stuff is with a cupped hand over it until the flame is started and fire is made.

The arts of pottery and arrowhead making are lost. It is said they are very few of them that can make them. They say it was a gift of God to make them and they passed on with the secret. There is a butte east of Pikes Peak where they make supplies of it,[25] and left there for the next trip. The Ponca is very strict with the history. Anyone making a mistake is corrected by groups of old men.

There is a place between the Black Hills and the Rocky Mountains where the tribe split in two. They were passing sinew around the camp and some of them were left out as the sinew didn't go around the camp and this caused them[26] to get sore and they [27] sided in with them until they were equally divided and the sore bunch pulled for the North and this bunch are found in Canada.[28] Days and days passed. Finally they got four of the best trackers on their trail and the trail went straight north. It means no turning,[29] and they came back and told what it means. This place is so far back that the oldest men cannot remember the exact spot.[30]

In one of their trips to Pikes Peak one man stayed and farmed by the name of Tah-ha-wah-ti. He stayed there, raised corn, and stored it until they came again. This place is known as Tah-hah-wah-ti-hah-ah. It means "where the man farmed." This place is also too far back,[31] and the exact place is forgotten. It is said that this place is between the Black Hills and the Rockies.

The wind cave [32] in the Black Hills was found by the Poncas. It is called the hill that sucks in or the hill that swallows in. Pah-hah-wah-tha-hu-ni.[33]

How squaw corn was found. The camp was between two creeks. To the mouth of these creeks there came seven buffaloes and disappeared at the mouth. They were quickly surrounded and closed in on them, but there is no buffaloes to be found, but there were seven buffalo manures and they were tiny little plants on them.[34] The head chief was called to see them and he came and saw

---

[24] The feathered wand or "pipe" was swayed rhythmically back and forth.

[25] "It" refers to flint, which was used in the manufacture of projectile points, knives, and other artifacts.

[26] "Them" refers to the Ponca who did not receive any sinew.

[27] For "they" read "others."

[28] The alleged existence of a group of *Đégiha* speakers in Canada has never been verified. The belief that such a group exists, however, is still quite prevalent among both Omaha and Ponca.

[29] In other words the malcontents had not relented.

[30] This should read ". . . place is so far back [in time] that the . . ."

[31] Again, read ". . . too far back [in time], and the . . ."

[32] This is the present Wind Cave, a National Park in Custer County, S. Dak. The "sucking" phenomenon results from the difference in temperature of the air inside and outside of the cave mouth. The Teton Dakota have a similar name for the cave.

[33] *Pahé-wađáhoni* is the Ponca name for the cave.

[34] Note the recurrence of the sacred number "seven," also the association of bison with corn, important in Ponca and Omaha philosophy. The Yanktonai Dakota have a similar legend, in which corn sprouts from milk which drips from the udder of a supernatural buffalo cow.

them, he said let them grow and get ripe as God has given us some kind of fruit, we will move camp and when they are ripened we will come back. When they came back there stood the stalks and still they didn't know what they were. There was a man in the camp they called Mi-sah, this means "Smarty" or blowhard. He husked one of the ears and started a fire, he roasted it and ate some of it and said it is good. We call it Wah-tan-zee. The head chief said pick it all and pass it around camp, we will plant it in the Spring. There were four colors of it, red, white, blue, and yellow. After they started to plant it the Police were asked to watch it. No one is allowed to go near it, even the owners are kept away, until it is ripe and ready to be prepared for winter use.

The best dance is called Hay-thu-schka, known as the war dance; it is said that any one that is not well and feeling bad and anyone that is mourning, the sound of the drum will revive them and make them happy.

Long time ago before there were any kind of cut beads and bells there was another man they called Mi-sah (Smarty or blowhard) as he is known made remarks that he is going to have shiny beads, bells, and nice blankets on some day and all the girls will admire him while he is dancing. This dance ends up in prayers.

While the Ponca were living in their village near the town of Niobrara, there came wagons drawn by oxen they called them Monmona.[35] They were real friendly people. They camped near the little channel on the west side of it,[36] and stayed one year 1846 and one day chief Wah-gah-sah-pi told them of a good place out west part of his hunting ground, he told them that they might find a place that will suit them.

In the Spring of 1847 they moved on their way out west. All of the old people hold this meeting of the Mormons as a sacred thing, even of the present day. The younger ones feel the same.[37] When the Great Sioux Treaty of 1868 was made at Fort Laramie by some blunder that no one has ever been able to explain, the whole Ponca reservation which has been guaranteed to the tribe over and over again in repeated treaties with the National Government was given to their deadly enemies the Brule and Ogalala Sioux. Soon their enemies understood that the Ponca Territory had been given them by this treaty, their raids became more fierce and frequent. The seven years that followed this treaty were years when the Poncas were obliged to work their gardens and cornfields as did the Pilgrims in New England or the early settlers of Kentucky with hoe in one hand and rifles in the other. In 1876 Congress passed an act providing for the removal of the Poncas to Indian Territory in Oklahoma without their consent.

In the Spring of 1877 the Poncas were busy putting away their crops, many put in their corn and were engaged in gardening. A force of soldiers arrived and orders were sent out for all the Indians to prepare to move at once to Indian Territory but they were taken to Baxter Springs, Kansas where there was nothing but rocks and the Poncas didn't like the place at all. There were heartbreaking scenes in the little tribe. The Niobrara and Ponca had been their home for so long they knew no other. The graves of a dozen generations were there. The little fields were to be left. There were tears in the teepees and hot words in the councils. The cooler heads prevented an outbreak and so the long march to the South began. Arriving at their new home, the warm moist climate, so different from the dry bracing air of their Nebraska home, brought on sickness. Out of seven hundred and ten, one hundred and fifty-eight died the first year.

---

35 The term "Monmona" is the Ponca pronunciation of the English name "Mormon."

36 "It" refers to the Gray-blanket village, which was located approximately 2 miles west and 3 miles south of the present Niobrara, Nebr.

37 From this point on, PLC seems to have borrowed heavily from some historical account of the Ponca Removal.

718-071—65——3

Homesickness worst of all diseases in misery that it carries was in every lodge. In the midwinter of such a scene of wretchedness, Chief Standing Bear's oldest son died and the boy wanted to be buried in Nebraska and the chief with a little band slipped away from the reservation and turned their faces to the North. Seven of the party were very sick when they started. They were 10 weeks on the road and arrived, ragged and nearly starved at the Omaha Agency which was part of the Ponca territory in March. Their presence there was reported to Washington by the Agent and on request of the Secretary of Interior Carl Shiery, the commanding officer at Omaha, General Crook, was ordered to arrest them and return them under military guard to Indian Territory. When the party was brought to Omaha, March 26, 1879, the news of their misfortunes became known and in their behalf was brought one of the most important law suits to determine the status of Indians ever tried. Friends of the prisoners induced John L. Webster and A. J. Poppleton to volunteer their services in their behalf. This was the case of Standing Bear, versus George Crook, Brigadier General of the United States Army and asked that a writ of habeas corpus be issued to restore them to the liberty of which they had been unjustly deprived.

The case was ordered by Webster and Poppleton for the Poncas and the U.S. District Attorney Lamberton for the Government. The great issue raised was whether Indians were citizens and as such entitled to the protection of the constitution and laws of the U.S. Judge Dundy did not decide this question in his opinion, but held that an Indian was a person within the meaning of the law and had therefore the right to habeas corpus; that in addition an Indian had the right to serve his tribal relations and that Standing Bear and party having done this could not be imprisoned without trial and were entitled to their liberty. Standing Bear and his band remained in Nebraska.

All the chiefs that signed the treaties are as follows:

1817

Handsome Man
Rough Buffalohorn
Ho we na
Pa da gah xa
Gah he ga
Smoke Maker
Little Chief
Aquotha bee

Interpreters:

Solomon
Joe La Flesh

1825

Smoke
Ish ca da bee
The um ba bee
Wah the he
Na ji hah tanga
Wah sho shah
Nu gah they
Wa gee muza
Iude cow se
E pe Tha Gah
Way buc kee han
Ma han the gah no knife
Mi jin ha the
Ma cho shiga na pa bee
Black cros
Gah be gah
Na he tapee
Ne na pa shee
One that knows

1858 Treaty

Wah gah sah pi
Gish tah wah gu
Was Kon mi the
Ashna nika gah hi

PETER LE CLAIRE
Niobrara, Nebraska

In addition to archeology and traditional history, there are other lines of evidence which shed light on the Ponca past. Some interesting botanical evidence bearing upon the relationship of the Ponca to the Omaha is presented by Will and Hyde (1917, p. 296): "As might be supposed from their close relationship and intimacy in early times, the Ponkas and Omahas have the same varieties of corn today. Each tribe, however, preserves some varieties which the other appears to have lost."

The close connection between the Ponca and other Southern Siouan groups is evident to the trained observer even at the present time, and has been mentioned repeatedly in print. Fletcher and La Flesche, for example, write: "The five cognate tribes [Omaha, Ponca, Osage, Kansa, and Quapaw], of which the Omaha is one, bear a strong resemblance to one another, not only in language but in tribal organization and religious rites" (1911, p. 35). Some ceremonies and dances still performed today are claimed jointly by all of the *Đégiha* groups, the most notable being the well-known *Heđúška* or "War dance." Indeed, the separation of the Omaha and Ponca was recent enough that at least one artifact predating the separation is still in existence. This is the famous "sacred pole" of which J. O. Dorsey writes: "The *Waxđége, Žą-wáxube*, or sacred pole, is very old, having been cut more than two hundred years ago, before the separation of the Omahas, Ponkas, and Iowas" (1884 a, p. 234). Two of my own informants, LMD and OYB, knew of the sacred pole and mentioned that it had once been revered by both the Omaha and the Ponca. This intertribal relic now rests in the Peabody Museum, Harvard University. Its origin and functions are discussed at length by Fletcher and La Flesche in "The Omaha Tribe" (1911, pp. 217–269).

ENTER THE LONG-KNIVES

Some American Indian tribes, such as the Pawnee, Osage, and Dakota, owing to their great numbers or warlike reputation, became known to the Europeans long before explorers and traders had actually reached their territory. This was not true of the Ponca. From the fact that they are not noted on the earliest maps nor mentioned, by report, in the earliest explorers' chronicles relating to the Missouri country, we may reasonably assume that the Ponca tribe was neither especially large nor hostile. Even long after their "discovery," in fact, references to the group are scattered and infrequent.

The earliest European reference to a group that may be identified with the Ponca is on a map. This map, attributed to the famous French cartographer Guillaume De L'Isle, has a draft copy dated May 1718. It shows a tribe called the "Maha," very likely the Omaha, living near the "Aiaouez" (Iowa) north of the Missouri on the "R. du Rocher," probably the Big Sioux River. Far above, east of the Missouri, is another group, identified as "Les Mahas, Nation errante" [i.e., "Wandering Omahas"]. This last group is very likely the Ponca, which if true is the earliest mention of the tribe. The 1718 De L'Isle is considered a good "mother map" and has had many imitations.

The 1722 De L'Isle map shows "Les Maha" north of the Missouri in the vicinity of the present Sioux City, Iowa, but does not mention any group that might be identified with the Ponca. The 1744 Bellin map mentions neither the Omaha nor the Ponca. The 1755 Mitchell map, however, which seems to be largely a copy of the 1718 De L'Isle, shows the "Maha" and "Ajoues" on a river which seems to correspond to the Big Sioux or Vermillion. Again, as on the 1718 De L'Isle, we find another group of "Mahas" further identified as "Wandering Indians," upriver. It is possible that these earliest maps fail to mention the Ponca by name because they were then still a part of the Omaha tribe, or that because of the near identity of their dialect with that of the Omaha they were assumed to be a part of that tribe.

A widely reproduced map, the 1757 Du Pratz, shows neither the Ponca nor Omaha. An unsigned French map of 1786, however, entitled "Carte du Mississippi et ses embranchemens" (sic), shows the Ponca, identified by name, above the "Maha." Their village is placed on the Missouri, between Ponca Creek and the Niobrara. The map of Gen. George H. V. Collot (published in 1826 but referring to 1796) shows the Ponca just north of Ponca Creek on the Missouri. The Sellard-Perrin du Lac map of 1802 (which would appear to be a plagiarization of a Makay and Evans map) also shows the Ponca in this location.

The earliest mention of the Ponca tribe, other than on the 1718 De L'Isle map cited above, is in an unsigned letter, probably by Esteban Rodriguez Miro, the Governor General of Louisiana, to Antonio Renzel, who bore the title "Commandant of the Interior Provinces of Louisiana." In this letter, dated December 12, 1785, Miro writes (as recorded by Nasatir, 1952, vol. 1, p. 126):

> The Poncas have a village on the small river below the River-that-Runs [Niobrara]. Nevertheless they are nomadic, naturally ferocious and cruel, kill without mercy those whom they meet on the road, although if they find themselves inferior in strength, they make friends of them, and, in a word, although they are not more than eighty warriors, they only keep friendship with those whom necessity obliges to treat as friends.

The information contained in this letter was undoubtedly taken from the reports of Indians of other tribes, probably enemies of the Ponca, who lived closer to the settlements. The village mentioned was probably on Bazile Creek, as this is the first stream of any size below the mouth of the Niobrara.

The first European to actually visit the Ponca, or at any rate the first to leave a written record of his visit, was the trader Jean Baptiste Monier, known as "Juan Munie" in the Spanish accounts. Though of French descent, Monier, like most of the other traders on the Missouri, was a Spanish national. Monier visited and traded with the Ponca in 1789, and in 1793 we find him petitioning for the right to exclusive trade rights with the Ponca by reason of "having discovered and pacified the tribe" (ibid., pp. 194–195). However, in 1794 another trader, Jacques Clamorgan, complained of Monier's monopoly: "This new enterprise was . . . a violation of the usual trade which had formerly been made with the two nations [Omaha and Ponca] which are really one nation, since the Poncas are nothing but Mahas who have left the tribe." Clamorgan, who later purchased Monier's "monopoly" to the Ponca trade, locates the Ponca "on the bank of the Missouri, about thirty leagues above the village of the Maha nation" (ibid., p. 206).

Thus, as early as the last decade of the 18th century the Ponca were receiving European trade goods in very large amounts. The attraction of the rich Missouri Valley Indian trade soon drew others into the area, and in the years 1794–95 another French trader, Jean Baptiste Trudeau, established a post called "Ponca House." This post served not only the Ponca, as the name would indicate, but also the Omaha and Dakota. The site of Trudeau's "Ponca House" has never been located, but it is said to have been several miles up the Missouri from the mouth of Ponca Creek. Trudeau wrote (as recorded by Nasatir, 1952, vol. 2, 490): "The Ponca nation has its habitation placed at two leagues higher than the Niobrara's mouth. Their huts are built on a hill at the edge of a great plain about a league from the Missouri."

Trudeau was optimistic about prospects for the trade in the area, noting that, "The Buffalo, the deer, and beaver are common in this place." While Trudeau was trading out of Ponca House, another Frenchman, Solomon Petit, was also wintering in the vicinity, as well as employees of Jean Monier (ibid., vol. 1, pp. 88–89). In spite of the competition, Trudeau managed to obtain some furs from the Dakota, Omaha, and Ponca.

The Ponca were quick to apprehend the value of a middleman's position in the trade, and in 1795 they began the practice of stopping and raiding trading craft as they passed up the Missouri. Some of these stolen goods the Ponca then traded to the tribes farther upriver. This piracy was perhaps motivated not only by greed but also by a fear that the upriver tribes, such as the Arikara and Dakota, would acquire guns which would later be turned on the Ponca. The traders, of course, were anxious to deal directly with the upriver groups, since the farther one got from the settlements the less common trade items became, and the greater the number of furs that could be secured for them. This Indian piracy, which was practiced by both the Omaha and Ponca, as well as the various Dakota bands on the Missouri, delayed for a considerable period the development of trade on the Upper Missouri, not to mention the considerable financial loss to the companies involved. For example, Zenon Trudeau, Lieutenant Governor of Spanish Illinois and Commandant at St. Louis, reported that one trading expedition moving up the Missouri was pillaged by the Ponca, the loss involving a sum of 7,000 pesos (ibid., p. 374).

The Ponca were also, of course, securing many trade items through legitimate channels, sometimes from British posts to the northeast. Materials traded to the Ponca at this period, or stolen by them, probably included guns, powder and ball, gunflints, wormscrews, large and small knives, awls, hatchets, pickaxes, hammers, kettles, medals, flags, tobacco, combs, vermillion, cloth, and blankets, as all of these items are mentioned by J. B. Trudeau as items he carried with him as stock in trade (ibid., pp. 259–294). Wood (1959, p. 15) reports that of these items guns, hatchets, cooking kettles, and cloth were represented from burials and other features of the Ponca Fort, which was occupied by the Ponca at this time.

Less welcome "gifts" from the *Wá·ge* or White man were the various European diseases, to which the Ponca and other tribes of the area had little resistance. In the winter of 1800–1801, for example, a disastrous smallpox epidemic struck all of the tribes on the Missouri. Hardest hit were the Omaha and Dakota, the Ponca being affected to a lesser degree. So weakened by the disease were the Omaha that, although they set out on their customary fall and winter bison hunt, they were not able to hunt effectively, and starvation threatened the lives of the survivors. It was at this point that the Omaha accidentally encountered the Ponca, also engaged in their autumn hunt.

The Ponca "tribal memory" or traditional history clearly pictures this meeting—the initial shouts of friendly recognition which quickly fade as the Omaha draw nearer and the Ponca perceive the faces and bodies of the Omaha still covered with the hideous pustules and scurf left by the dread disease. Fearing another outbreak of the disease, the Ponca warned their Omaha kinsmen to come no closer. So desperate for food were the Omaha, however, that with their last strength they launched an attack on the Ponca, driving them from their camp and stores of dried meat. Fearing the disease more than their human antagonists, the Ponca offered little resistance.

Thus, by the time Meriwether Lewis and William Clark, on their epic journey of exploration, reached the Ponca, the tribe was quite familiar with Europeans—with their prized trade goods and their diseases. In their characteristic style and spelling, the explorers noted, on September 4, 1804, that there was a "Poncaries Village situated in a handsom Plain on the lower side of this Creek [Ponca Creek] about two miles from the Missouri" (Lewis, 1904–5, vol. 1, p. 140). On the Wm. Clark map of 1815 the "Poncarars, 200 souls" are shown a short distance above the mouth of Ponca Creek. Another explorer, H. M. Brackenridge (1904, p. 94), found their village there in 1811 and the Atkinson-O'Fallon party found them at the same place in 1825.

From this time on, the Ponca village was a regular stopping place for boats ascending and descending the Missouri, and the tribe was visited by most of the "greats" who traveled the river—military men, explorers, traders, and also artists and ethnographers such as George Catlin and Prince Maximilian of Wied. Relations between the Ponca tribe and the United States began in 1817, when the Government entered into a treaty of "perpetual peace and friendship" with them. This was followed in 1826 by another treaty, in which the Federal Government agreed to receive the Ponca "into their friendship and under their protection." Present-day Ponca are proud of the fact that they have never taken up arms against the United States of America.

The accounts of early 19th-century visitors to the Ponca, though customarily filled with the routine and trivia of everyday affairs, sometimes permit us an interesting glimpse of the life of the tribe. In 1824, for example, Peter Wilson, acting on behalf of Maj. Benjamin O'Fallon, visited a small group of Ponca at the mouth of the Niobrara. Wilson noted: "The cries and lamentations made by them while approaching convinced me that some sad disaster, or misfortune had happened." The cause of their distress was soon learned. A party of 30 Ponca, who were returning from a friendly visit to the Oglala subband of Teton Dakota, had been surprised and attacked by a large party of "Saones" (members of the Brulé subband of the Teton). Of the 30, only 12 escaped. Numbered among the dead were all of the Ponca chiefs, including the famous Smoke-maker (*Súde-gàxe*), the first Ponca chief of that name (frontis.; pls. 1 and 12, *a*). The son of Smoke-maker approached Wilson with tears in his eyes, bearing the chief's medal which had been given to his father by the Government. Wilson, after doing what he could to console the young man, appointed him chief of the tribe in his father's stead (pl. 1). (Report of Wilson to O'Fallon, 1824, National Archives, St. Louis Superintendency.)

Details of the fur trade with the Ponca are revealed in a letter from John Dougherty, agent to the Ponca, to Lewis Cass, Secretary of War. Dougherty states that goods were traded to the Ponca from a post of the American Fur Company located at the mouth of the Little Missouri. Specific items mentioned are powder, ball, blankets, strouds, calicoes, axes, hoes, tobacco, beads, and vermillion. It was the custom at this time (1830's) for a trader to establish "temporary" posts in the Indian villages, which might be some miles from the main post. When with the Ponca, the trader generally established himself in the earth lodge of a friendly chief, whose rank discouraged the pilfering of the trader's goods. It was not uncommon for the traders at these "temporary" posts to accompany the tribe on the tribal bison hunts.

The larger fur posts were staffed by 30 men each. These men loaded and unloaded the boats, some of them being delegated to take out goods to the temporary stations and bring back the furs. Regular cornfields and vegetable gardens surrounded the larger posts. The best months for fur trading were January, February, and March. After the spring trading season the furs were brought downriver in flatboats or barges, reaching St. Louis in the latter part of May or the first part of June. Even at this early date, Dougherty notes, the return of furs was diminishing as far north as the Ponca country, and he comments forebodingly that all of the tribes south of there must soon learn to "farm or perish" (letter of Dougherty to Cass, Nov. 19, 1831).

At this period the Ponca were allies of the Yankton and Teton Dakota, for in 1833 Dougherty reports that the Ponca were spending little time on the Missouri following the buffalo on the "Plains of the Eau-qui-cour [Niobrara] river. They are friendly with the Sioux and join them in war, against the Pawnees" (letter of Dougherty to Wm. Clark, Nov. 12, 1834). One suspects that for the Ponca this alliance was merely a means of self-preservation. Being a small group, they were afraid to stop warring on the Pawnee so long as the Dakota were still at war, since their country lay between the two tribes. The Pawnee, of course, often retaliated on the Ponca, and in 1835 Joshua Pilcher reported that "Two or three Ponca families farming at the mouth of the Niobrara had their horses stolen by the Pawnee" (Report of Pilcher, Oct. 5, 1835). Pilcher notes that the Ponca at that time inhabited the "country near L'eau-qui-court to its source in the Black Hills."

That same year Dougherty and Pilcher jointly recommended that the Ponca be attached to the Sioux Subagency. Their letter states that the tribe numbered between 75 and 100 men at that date, and goes on to note that the Ponca "formerly raised corn at the mouth of L'eau-qui-court but depredations of the Sioux forced them to join the

Sioux as bison hunters" (Report of Pilcher and Dougherty, Aug. 27, 1935).

At times the Ponca were even forced by their Dakota overlords to join the latter tribe in raids on the Omaha, close linguistic and cultural relatives of the Ponca. Thus Thos. H. Harvey, writing to Wm. Medill, Commissioner of Indian Affairs, notes:

> The Omahas are a poor dispirited people. They have for some years been living about eighty miles above Council Bluffs near the Missouri River. Owing to the frequent attacks of the Sioux and Poncas they have for several years made but little corn, and have consequently been exceedingly poor and destitute. [Letter of Harvey to Medill, Sept. 5, 1846.]

In this incessant raiding by the Dakota we see a pattern which was to become well-established in the latter half of the 19th century. The semisedentary village tribes, attached to their earth-lodge villages and cornfields, were no match for the well-mounted and well-armed Dakota, who always knew both the exact strength and the precise location of their victims. Young Dakota warriors, eager for war honors, would snipe at the settlements of the village tribes from a safe distance, or try to pick off isolated hunters or farmers. When pursuit was organized by their victims, they simply retreated to the Plains, where their pursuers feared to follow them because of the danger of ambush.

All of the village tribes were exposed to this harassment: Pawnee, Omaha, Ponca, Arikara, Mandan, and Hidatsa. These raids on the Ponca began shortly before midcentury and continued unabated until the time of the Ponca Removal in 1877. In his autobiography, Luther Standing Bear, a Teton Dakota chief, tells of his participation, as a small boy, in one of the last of such raids. Like most of the raids the Teton launched against the Ponca, this raid was motivated only by a "dislike" of the Ponca. However, all but two members of this particular raiding party were turned back before they reached the Ponca country by an aged Dakota chief bearing a peace pipe (Standing Bear, 1928, pp. 75–77).

In the autumn of 1846 a small group of Mormon settlers arrived in the Ponca country. This band of immigrants had been invited to the Niobrara villages by a group of Ponca who had found them camped near the Pawnee village at Genoa, Nebr. The Mormons had with them a small cannon, and it may have been the thought of how useful this item would be against the Dakota that prompted the Ponca invitation. The Mormons, called "Monmona" by the Ponca, were given some provisions to tide them over and assigned a camping spot near the "Gray blanket" village. In 1908 an impressive granite shaft was erected at this site.

The Mormons apparently got on famously with the Ponca, for their stay is recalled in the fondest manner in the tribal traditions. With the arrival of spring, however, the Mormons decided to move on to join their bretheren in the west. The Ponca chief *Wégasàpi* or 'Whip' (pl. 9), indicated the best route for the group to follow on the journey (Fry, 1922).

In 1855 a large-scale conflict took place between the Ponca and their old enemies, the Pawnee. Both tribes were on their tribal hunts, and the encounter was purely accidental. The Ponca were divided into two groups based on village affiliation, the "Gray blanket" group forming one and the *Húbdǫ* or 'Fish smellers' the other. The *Húbdǫ* band was the first to sight the Pawnee, and promptly gave chase. Arriving at the Pawnee hunting camp the Ponca surrounded it and, raising a great war whoop, charged. To their amazement, however, they found that the Pawnee had somehow managed to steal away without being seen. The "Fish smellers" therefore contented themselves with looting the deserted camp, appropriating for their own use the packs of dried meat, moccasins, leggings, and rawhide lariats left behind by the stealthy Caddoans. Then, careful to post guards over their horse herds, the *Húbdǫ* village group continued their bison hunting.

Meanwhile the "Gray blanket" village group encountered the fleeing Pawnee, and after a hot running fight, killed them to a man. Feeling against the Pawnee was high at this time because the year before a haughty Pawnee chief had forced his Ponca guest, a man who was seeking the return of some stolen horses, to eat two large pots of beans served in urine. This flouting of the customary laws of Indian hospitality infuriated the Ponca more than the fact that the Pawnee chief had demanded a gift of gunpowder in exchange for the stolen animals. Therefore, on the occasion of the slaughter of the Pawnee hunters, Chief Smoke-maker's newborn son was carried to the battlefield by an old woman and caused to put his feet on two of the Pawnee corpses, whereupon he was given the honorific title "Trod-on-two" (cf. J. O. Dorsey, 1890, pp. 377–383).

THE PONCA "TRAIL OF TEARS"

The tribal bison hunt of 1855 was to be the last successful one conducted by the Ponca. From this time forward, although the tribe attempted to go out semiannually in the traditional manner, their attempts to secure provender in this manner were invariably frustrated by prowling Teton war parties. Cut off from the buffalo plains and fearful of leaving their villages even to farm outlying fields, the Ponca were often on the point of starvation. To add to their woes, White settlers had for some time been percolating into the Ponca country, and the valuable bottom-land fields were fast being taken up by these squatters. In the winter of 1857–58 feeling was running so high in regard to their miserable situation that the Ponca destroyed the Niobrara sawmill and stole various items from the storehouse in protest against Government neglect.

Bowing to the inevitable, the chiefs of the Ponca tribe, on March 12, 1858, signed a treaty with the U.S. Government (Royce, 1899, p. 818). By the terms of this treaty the Ponca ceded to the Federal Government all lands which they owned or claimed except a tract bounded as follows: "Beginning at a point on the Niobrara river and running due N. so as to intersect the Ponca river 25 miles from its mouth; thence from said point of intersection up said river 20 miles; thence due S. to the Niobrara river; thence down said river to the place of beginning." In consideration of this cession, the Federal Government promised to protect the tribe in the possession of the remainder of their domain (the reservation as defined above) as their permanent home and to secure them in their persons and property. By a subsequent treaty in 1865, at the solicitation of the United States, the Ponca ceded an additional 30,000 acres of their reserved land (ibid., p. 836). In consideration for this cession and "by way of rewarding them for their constant fidelity to the government and citizens thereof, and with a view of returning to the said tribe of Ponca Indians their old burying-grounds, and cornfields," the Government in turn ceded certain lands back to the tribe. The lands thus held constituted a reservation of 96,000 acres (U.S. Congress, 1868, vol. 14, pp. 675–677).

In 1859 the Ponca attempted to make their customary spring and summer hunt, but encountered a combined party of Brulé, Oglala, and Cheyenne at the headwaters of the Elkhorn River. The Dakota-Cheyenne combination attacked the Ponca hunting camp, killing Heavy Cloud, the third chief of the tribe, another chief named "Podara," and 13 others. Three Ponca children were captured and carried off into slavery. The Dakota informed the Ponca that the reason for their attack was that the Ponca had sold their lands and made a treaty with the Whites (Letter of I. S. Gregory to Commissioner Greenwood, Aug. 27, 1859, National Archives, Ponca Agency).

Upon the return of the hunting party Chief *Wégasàpi* (pl. 9) angrily confronted Agent Gregory. Denouncing the Government for rewarding its enemies, the Sioux, while neglecting the Ponca, he displayed bloody arrows from the battle of the Elkhorn, and threatened to go to war. "I shall be a woman no longer, but go on the warpath with my tribe as I used to before my Great Father talked soft to me and tied my hands! It is better to die like warriors—like men—not wait until the Sioux come here to kill us" (ibid.).

The following spring Agent Gregory, in a rather weak move to placate the Ponca, requested that a part of the Ponca annuity be used to purchase a small fieldpiece for purposes of self-defense. He also asked for "large and small flags for the chiefs and soldiers" and a "chief's dress" for the head chief. Again that year the Ponca were driven from their hunt with great loss of horses and provisions. That fall Agent Gregory, in an endeavor to halt Dakota depredations on the Ponca, traveled to the Sioux country and counciled with the Brulé. Arrogantly, the Brulé promised to leave the Ponca alone the following season, as they expected "to be fully employed carrying on hostilities against the Omahas and Pawnees."

In 1861 Agent Gregory was replaced by J. B. Hoffman. As one of his first projects, Hoffman organized a constabulary recruited from among the warriors of the Ponca tribe. This group, which numbered 50, were outfitted in blue coats and gray trousers. In order to secure better protection the tribe's supplies were stored in a warehouse near the agency office. The following year a manual labor school was established on the Ponca Reserve, the first of its kind in that part of the country.

The agent's reports from this period reveal the progressive acculturation of the tribe since they had first been exposed to European trade items. In 1863, for example, the Ponca chiefs and headmen complained about the type of goods they were sent. No ammunition had been received for their rifles, no snaths with the scythes, and no thread with the dry goods. Agent Hoffman also reports that "half axes and squaw hatchets," once much desired by the Ponca, were by that date a comparatively worthless article. Fishhooks and lines also were of no value to them. Likewise the small round trade mirrors, once treasured as items of dance regalia, were no longer valued; after they had been distributed they could be found lying around the agency warehouse where they had been purposely dropped, and were picked up only by children to play with.

Poor as the situation of the Ponca was at this time, it was soon to get worse. In 1868 a United States commission sent to negotiate with the Dakota, through an inexplicable and almost criminal blunder, ceded to the Teton Dakota a tract of land which included all of the Ponca land, ceded and unceded. Now the Teton war parties had a perfect excuse for their raids on the Ponca—the Ponca were trespassers on Teton territory! The Federal Government made no effort whatever to correct this fantastic error or to protect the Ponca against their enemies as promised in the treaty of 1858, though they were frequently called upon to do so.

This lamentable condition of affairs was to continue for 8 years without correction or redress, the Government seeming to consent to the sacrifice of the rights and peace of a tribe that had never made war upon it and had never broken faith. During this period, in fact, the Government was supplying the Teton warriors with heavy-caliber rifles of the latest make, ostensibly for bison hunting.

Finally, in 1876, conditions had become so bad that Washington was forced to take cognizance of the situation. That year a provision was inserted in the Indian appropriation bill authorizing the Secretary of the Interior to use the sum of $25,000 for the removal of the Ponca to the Indian Territory if they consented to go. Though there had been some talk of removal in the Ponca councils, this action came as a surprise to the tribe. Eight chiefs were selected to accompany an agent of the Indian Bureau to the Indian Territory to select a new reservation there. However, the chiefs who went with the official, after examining various proposed areas, refused to select a site and begged to be allowed to go back. Being refused, they left the official and, in winter, with but a few dollars and one blanket each, started home, walking the 500-odd miles in 40 days.

Though the Ponca and their White friends, such as the Rev. J. O. Dorsey, repeatedly and forcefully appealed to the Secretary of the Interior and the Commissioner of Indian Affairs, representing that they did not consent to be removed, but, on the contrary, were bitterly opposed to leaving their homes, their appeals were disregarded. Since they refused to go of their own free will an order was issued on April 12, 1877, to force their removal, using Army troops if necessary. E. A. Howard, of Hillsdale, Mich., was appointed agent for the removal.

On April 28, 1877, Howard arrived at Columbus, Nebr., where he expected to meet Agent Lawrence with the assembled tribesmen. He found Lawrence with only 170 Ponca, the remainder having resisted removal, stating that they would rather die in defense of their homes than abandon their country and live in the "hot country" to the south. On April 30 E. C. Kemble, United States Indian Inspector, arrived and assumed control, arranging to conduct the first group of 170 Ponca to the Indian Territory. He ordered Agent Howard to visit the Niobrara Reservation and remove the remainder. Howard, after repeated councils, by his tact and kind treatment finally persuaded the recalcitrants that resistance would be useless and they prepared for the journey. Escorted by a detachment of 25 United States troops under Major Walker, the second group took their departure on May 16.

Their removal was a ghastly and miserable experience, recalled by present-day tribesmen as the Ponca "Trail of Tears." From start to finish the party was dogged by bad weather and calamity. At the beginning they had a terrible time crossing the flooded Niobrara River, the Ponca rescuing some of their soldier "guards" who were swept from their horses by the treacherous stream. Heavy rains fell nearly every day, and sickness added to the hardship of the march. After crossing the river it was not until May 21 that they were organized and got under way, one child having died during the delay in camp. On the 23d, in the midst of heavy rains, another child died, and they delayed the next day to give it burial. The roads were extremely bad, and much time was required to rebuild bridges which had been swept away and to repair the roads, deep in mud, through which they toiled.

The Ponca crossed Nebraska by way of Neligh, Columbus, Seward, and Beatrice. When they arrived at Columbus, Major Walker and the 25 troops under him, who had come along as guards to prevent escape, left the expedition and returned to Dakota. Every few days someone died of disease or exposure. On June 5, near the village of Milford, Prairie Flower, the daughter of Chief Standing Bear, died of consumption. She was given a Christian burial in the village cemetery by the townspeople. So overwhelmed was Chief Standing Bear by the kindness of the ladies of Milford in arranging the burial service that he stated to those around him at the grave that he wished to give up his Indian ways and become a Christian (pl. 10).

Later, on the day of the funeral, the camp was devastated by a tornado that carried away wagon boxes, camp gear, and even some of the people through the air as much as 300 yards. Several were seriously injured and one child was killed. After they broke camp the next day and proceeded on their way, another child died. Remembering the kindness of the citizens of Milford, the tiny coffin was sent back to be interred in the grave with Prairie Flower.

On June 16 the party reached Marysville, Kans. Their route through that State then led to Manhattan, Council Grove, Emporia, Iola, Columbus, and Baxter Springs. Deaths continued along the way, and two old women died in the camp near Council Grove. They, too, were given Christian burial, which was now becoming popular with the Ponca. Not far from Marysville four families, homesick and discouraged, dropped out of the line of march and turned back to Nebraska. As soon as they were missed, however, Agent Howard rode back to find them, and by the use of patience and diplomacy, succeeded in inducing them to return and rejoin the expedition.

It was not until July 9 that the party passed through Baxter Springs and crossed the line into the Indian Territory on the lands of the Quapaw tribe. After nearly 2 months the march ended in the same sort of weather in which it had begun. Agent Howard wrote: "Just after passing Baxter Springs and between that place and the reservation, a terrible thunder storm struck us. The wind blew a heavy gale and the rain fell in torrents, so that it was impossible to see more than four or five rods distant, thoroughly drenching every person and every article in the train" (National Archives, Ponca Agency).

The other band of Ponca that preceded those brought by Howard were all quartered in tents they had brought with them, no other provision having been made by the Government for their accommodation. Agent Howard was shocked at the lack of preparation for the comfort of his charges, by now broken down by sickness and the hardships of the journey. Discouraged, homesick, and hopeless, the Ponca found themselves on the lands of strangers, in the middle of a hot summer, with no crops nor prospects for any.

The Ponca thus placed in the Indian Territory numbered 681 persons, embracing 197 heads of families. Thirty-six had remained in the north with their Omaha kinsmen. The tribe had hardly established their tent city on the Quapaw Reservation when whisky smugglers from Baxter Springs, directly across the line in Kansas, began the surreptitious sale of liquor to them. Attempts by Agent Howard to prosecute these men were ineffectual.

The Ponca, unhappy and dissatisfied with their surroundings, asked for a more congenial home. Accordingly, some of the leading men of the tribe, with an Indian Inspector, made an examination of other locations. The one finally selected was on the west bank of the Arkansas River, covering both sides of the Salt Fork, in what is now north-central Oklahoma. This land, of which a reservation of 101,894 acres was afterward set apart for them, was a part of the country obtained from the Cherokee in the treaty of 1866. About May 1 a large party of dissatisfied Ponca left the Quapaw country for the location on the Salt Fork without consulting the agent and without assistance from him. They remained at their new home, without sufficient food and medical attention, and, as a result, a number of deaths occurred. Meanwhile, preparations were made by their agent for the removal of those remaining at the Quapaw Agency; finally the large amount of freight, consisting of personal effects, supplies, agricultural implements, and camp equipage, was loaded for the journey. There was also a large number of aged, decrepit, and sick Ponca, who were carried in the wagons.

The Ponca departed from the Quapaw Agency on July 21, 1878, and arrived at their new home, 185 miles distant, 8 days later. In spite of the great heat, which varied from 95 to 100 degrees every day, no further lives were lost on this last trip; but the people, oxen, horses, and mules, arrived exhausted from the hardships of the journey.

The new agency was located in the bend of the Salt Fork River about 2 miles above its confluence with the Arkansas. On the new reservation the Ponca first lived in tipis in one large village, but the agent at once began a movement to scatter them over the reservation, in order to prevent the spread of contagious diseases and to speed the beginning of agricultural work. He soon induced the so-called "half-breed band" to remove to the mouth of Chikaskia Creek, 8 miles from the agency. Having been on the move through the summers of 1877 and 1878, the Ponca had been unable to cultivate the soil for 2 years. Also in 1878 they suffered greatly from malaria, or "chills and fever" as it was then termed. As the Ponca had come from their northern home where such ills were little known, the disease was peculiarly fatal to them, and many died of it after they reached the Indian Territory. In fact, since the tribe left Nebraska one-third had died, and nearly all of the survivors were sick or disabled. Talk around the campfires was continually of the "old home" in the north.

Finally, the death of Chief Standing Bear's eldest son set in motion events which were to bring a measure of justice, and worldwide fame, to the chief and his tribe. Unwilling to bury his child in the strange country, Standing Bear gathered a few members of his tribe, and started for *Má-azì*, the Ponca burial ground in the north. Sixty-six, in all, the tribesmen set out on foot for Nebraska, following an old wagon drawn by two wornout horses. In the wagon was the body of Standing Bear's son.

When Secretary of the Interior Carl Schurz was notified of Standing Bear's "escape" he caused a telegram to be sent to Gen. George Crook, ordering him to arrest the runaways and return them to Indian Territory. In the meantime Iron Eyes, chief of the Omaha, met the Ponca and offered them food and asylum on his reservation. General Crook, however, pursuant to his orders, took the Indians into custody. On their way south the party camped near the city of Omaha. Their story was made known to the citizenry, and soon Omaha was seething with indignation at this latest evidence of the Government's cruelty. Sympathetic residents of the community, with the approval of General Crook, employed local legal talent to apply for a writ of habeas corpus in the Federal court in Omaha. The United States denied the prisoners' right to sue out a writ, on the grounds that "an Indian is not a person within the meaning of the law."

The trial aroused intense interest, and the courtroom was crowded with White sympathizers of the Ponca, who were spellbound by an eloquent speech by Standing Bear in his own defense. A newspaper reporter who was present wrote:

> There was silence in the court as the chief sat down. Tears ran down the judge's face. General Crook leaned forward and covered his face with his hands. Some of the ladies sobbed. All at once that audience by common impulse rose to its feet and such a shout went up as was never heard in a Nebraska court room. No one heard Judge Dundy say 'Court is adjourned.' There was a rush to Standing Bear. The first to reach him was General Crook.

I was second. The ladies flocked toward him and for an hour Standing Bear held a reception. [Foreman, 1946, p. 253.]

A few days later Judge Dundy filed his famous decision, a landmark in American jurisprudence, holding that an Indian is a person the same as a White man and similarly entitled to the protection of the Constitution.

Standing Bear and his followers were set free, and with his old wagon and the body of his dead child, he continued to the tribal burial grounds on the Missouri bluffs, where he buried his son with tribal honors.

By the summer of 1879, 26 more persons had died and 16 births had been recorded. The population of the Ponca in the Indian Territory now stood at only 530. However, those who had remained in the south were regaining some of their courage and fortitude. Under the direction of the agent, 70 houses were built for their homes; the logs were cut, hewn, and laid in place by the Ponca, who were paid for their labor. Cattle, horses, wagons, and harness were purchased for them, and 350 acres of sod were broken, which they planted in corn and vegetables. A day school was established and attended by 50 Ponca children. By 1880 the condition of the tribe had improved so that the birth rate slightly exceeded the death rate. From July 1, 1877, to December 31, 1880, there had been 129 births and 117 deaths, not including those who had prematurely moved to the Salt Fork. During the year 1880, 70 families had moved into log or frame houses, furnished with bedsteads and other furniture made by the agency carpenters (Foreman, 1946, pp. 253–254).

Meanwhile the complaints of the Ponca and their White friends in the East, of the abominable and unwarranted treatment of the tribe by the Government, had reached the proportions of a national scandal. The Ponca had a particularly vigorous champion in Thomas H. Tibbles, a former Indian agent and newspaperman. Touring the country with Chief Standing Bear and an Omaha Indian girl named Suzette ("Bright Eyes") La Flesche, he advertised the plight of the Ponca and also won the maiden's hand in marriage. The press of the country devoted much space to the Ponca, who had now become a cause celebre.

A committee of the U.S. Senate, after a full investigation of the subject, on May 31, 1880, reported their conclusions to that body. Both the majority and the minority of the committee agreed that: "a great wrong had been done the Ponca Indians." As a further result of the agitation, President Hayes, on December 18, 1880, appointed Generals George Crook and Nelson A. Miles, William Stickney of Washington, and Walter Allen of Boston as a commission to hold a conference with the Ponca and ascertain the facts relating to

718–071—65——4

their enforced removal from their home to the Indian Territory and inquire into their present condition.

The committee took testimony at the Ponca Agency in the Indian Territory and then proceeded to Niobrara, Nebr., where they heard the testimony of Standing Bear and his followers. The commission made its report to the President on January 25, 1881, showing the incredible ineptitude, indifference, and mismanagement that had made the experience of the Ponca needlessly disastrous and cruel.

As a result of the inquiry, an appropriation was made by Congress on March 3, 1881, of the sum of $165,000 to indemnify the tribe for losses sustained in consequence of the removal and for other purposes intended to ameliorate, make restitution, and promote their welfare. Under the adjustments provided by this act, the 537 Ponca then in the Indian Territory began to reconcile themselves to their new lot and settle down in the new reservation. A large brick industrial boarding school began operations on January 1, 1883, attended by 65 children. Others, equally desirious to enroll, were prevented by lack of room.

On the Niobrara Reservation, 170 Ponca under Standing Bear were living and cultivating the soil; raising corn, wheat, and potatoes. Formerly known as the "Poncas of Dakota," they became in 1882 the "Poncas of Nebraska" when the boundary line between the States was established on the 43d parallel. In September 1908, Chief Standing Bear died and was buried with his fathers. By his sufferings and courage he was instrumental in putting an end to enforced Indian removals in the United States.

It was only after the final arrangements had been made subsequent to the Removal that the Ponca tribe was permanently divided into "Northern" and "Southern" bands. The Southern Ponca, probably owing to their greater numbers and a lesser degree of White intermarriage, seem to have had through the years more resistance to the forces of White acculturation. In spite of the early "liquidation" policies of the Indian Bureau they have been able to preserve some of their tribal life up to the present day. Sun dances were performed by them for many years, and even today the *Hedúška* dance is a going concern.

The Northern Ponca, however, a small island of Indian culture in a sea of Whites, quickly began to assume their conquerors' ways. They were too few to stage the Sun dance, and even relatively minor ceremonies such as the *Hą́he-watši* tattooing required the services of Southern Ponca bundle owners. By the turn of the century most of the old Ponca religious ceremonies had disappeared in the north, and the last Northern Ponca *Hedúška* dance took place in the 1930's. On April 16, 1962, Senator Church, at the direction of the Northern

Ponca tribal council, introduced a bill calling for a division of the tribal assets and the termination of the Federal trust relationship to the Northern Ponca band. Complete assimilation into the major culture seems to be the goal of the majority of the tribal members in the north. Such is not yet true of the Southern Ponca, where "Indian ways" are still highly valued by many, and participation in the Peyote rite and Indian powwows continues to be important to a large proportion of the members of the band.

ECONOMY

As was true with most of the Missouri Valley tribes, the economic base of the Ponca rested upon a combination of hunting, fishing, gathering, and horticulture. Hunting, being the most exciting of these activities, was accorded the highest prestige in Ponca culture. The principal animal hunted by the Ponca was the bison, although elk, deer, and pronghorn antelope were also taken whenever the opportunity occurred. Smaller animals, such as rabbits and beaver, were hunted only when larger game was not available. Two kinds of hunting were recognized by the Ponca and their kinsmen, the Omaha. One termed *ábayè* referred to hunting by small groups of men without their families. The other, *t^{h}é-une* or *gax án*, referred to the tribal hunts when the entire group, with its belongings, moved in pursuit of the bison (Dorsey, 1884 a, p. 283).

There were two of these tribal hunts each year, one in the late spring or early summer, the other in the fall. The first of these began in late June or early July, the other in October or November. Their length depended upon the success of the hunt. Both were surrounded by ceremonial observations which were designed to obtain supernatural favor. PLC emphasized repeatedly in our interviews that: "The buffalo hunt was sacred to the Ponca because they depended upon the buffalo for their winter store of dried meat." Some idea of the tremendous importance of the bison to the people may be gained from Ponca ceremonies, nearly all of which have some bison symbolism.

Skinner (1915 c, p. 795) writes: "Every year when the squaw corn was about a foot high, the chiefs of the Ponca got together and counseled concerning the buffalo hunt. Two men were selected to be leaders, who took charge of everything. They picked the day that the village was to move, and they selected the camping ground." PLC, however, insisted that there was only one hunt leader, or *Nudá-hǫgà*, saying: "When the time came for the buffalo hunt the chiefs would appoint the leader. He was selected from among the bravest warriors. He had to have a good head and not to do things rashly or else the whole tribe would suffer." PLC's statement is probably the correct one, as it is consistent with the Omaha, Oto, and Iowa custom of naming only one leader for the hunt.

"Soldiers" or Buffalo-police also were appointed to assist the hunt leader in regulating the hunt. Skinner states that these men were appointed by the head chief of the tribe but PLC stated that they were chosen by the hunt leader himself. Among the Ponca the Buffalo-police were chosen from the bravest warriors of one of the military fraternities, but not the whole organization, as was true of the Teton Dakota.

The movement of the tribe on the communal hunt was a gala affair. At the head of the procession came the sacred tribal pipe in its bundle, carried on a beautiful but gentle horse, and tended by its priest or keeper, who rode alongside on another mount. Behind the pipe and pipe keeper rode the hunt leader, bearing his badge of office. This was a crooked staff wrapped with swanskin, ornamented with eagle feathers at the end and along the side and with a bunch of crow feathers at the tip (cf. Fletcher and La Flesche, 1911, p. 155).

A short distance behind came the hunters, riding their second best mounts and each leading his best "buffalo runner," which would be mounted when the herd was sighted and the time came to charge. Behind them, in turn, came the women and children with the camp equipage loaded on packhorses and dogs. Scouts preceded the entire party by several miles, searching out the best herds. These scouts reported each evening to the hunt leader.

Each night the *Húđuga* or camp circle was set up, the various clans camping in their traditional assigned areas. In the center of the circle was a special tent for the tribal pipe and its keeper and nearby the hunt leader's tent, which also served as the headquarters for the Buffalo-police and scouts. When the scouts located a suitable herd, the tribal chiefs of the first and second rank assembled with the hunt leader and Buffalo-police in this council lodge to pray for success. Each night, while in the buffalo country, a guard of Buffalo-police was posted at the edges of the camp to prevent any hunters from sneaking out to hunt ahead of the main body and thus endangering the public welfare by frightening away the herds. Such overzealous hunters, if caught, faced the possibility of being whipped by the Buffalo-police and having their tipi cover cut to shreds and their tipi poles broken.

The surround was the most common hunting procedure for the tribal hunt. Utilizing hummocks, ravines, and other natural features, the ranks of hunters would approach as near the herd as possible, endeavoring to encircle it. Then, on a signal from the hunt leader, all would charge and try to get the herd to milling. Occasionally a small herd would be driven over a bluff or, on the fall hunt, onto the ice of a river, where the slippery hooves of the bison would cause them to fall. Small parties of hunters could not employ these techniques for lack of sufficient personnel. They would instead "run" the bison, that is, charge in and shoot as many animals as possible before the herd escaped through flight.

Cows and young buffaloes were the ones most sought after, as their meat was tender and their hides were soft. Some bulls also were killed, however, as their thick neck hide was needed for the manufacture of shields and moccasin soles. PLC stated that although other tribes used animal disguises, such as wolf hides, in stalking the buffalo and other game, he had never heard of the Ponca doing so.

Like buffalo, elk and deer were sometimes hunted by driving them onto the ice in winter so that they would lose their footing and could be more easily killed. LMD and AMC told stories of winter bear hunts in the Black Hills region. AMC stated that Ponca hunters often painted the area around their eyes black when on a winter hunt to avoid snow blindness. When traveling in the Rockies, the Ponca hunted Rocky Mountain sheep.

PLC, OK, and AMC all mentioned hunting beaver and muskrat with dogs. A group of men and dogs would move along a stream, the men wading, looking for beaver and muskrat dens. When one was located the dogs would dig the animal out and the hunters would club it to death. Raccoons were hunted with dogs as well. PLC mentioned another type of hunting, in which dogs circled the game and caused it to keep doubling back by leaving their scent, which it would refuse to cross. Finally the circle would be small enough so that the animal would be within range of the hunter's arrow or bullet.[38]

Fowling does not seem to have been an important Ponca activity, though birds were hunted to some extent. According to PLC, birds were usually stalked by individual hunters. The area now forming the northern end of Niobrara State Park, near Niobrara, Nebr., was known as a good place to shoot ducks and geese (JLR). The late Northern Ponca Chief White-shirt once told JLR that he had brought down 100 birds with a single shot of his musket from a stand at the end of this island. JLR considered this somewhat of a sportsman's exaggeration, but admitted that the hunting was "awfully good" along the Missouri in the old days.

The main birds taken in the past were geese, ducks, and pinnated grouse. At the present time the Northern Ponca hunt ducks and geese as formerly, but the Chinese ringneck pheasant has now replaced the grouse as the principal upland game bird. Eagles, hawks, owls, crows,

[38] I find my credulity is strained a bit at this point. PLC insists that such a procedure was followed, however.

and pheasants are still hunted for their feathers, and hunting for feathers was probably important in the past as well.

Eagle feathers were particularly valued. Eagles were formerly secured by either of two methods. The first resembles the ceremonial eagle trapping of tribes farther up the Missouri, but apparently lacked the lengthy ritual observances of such groups as the Mandan, Hidatsa, and Yanktonai Dakota. Pits about 4 feet deep were dug on a high bluff, of a diameter sufficient to hold two men. These were carefully camouflaged with screens of woven branches covered with turf and leaves. A small hole was left in the center of the screen. A freshly killed rabbit was impaled on a stick and placed over this hole, so that the end of the stick would be moved by the men in the pit. They would move the rabbit about, making it appear that the rabbit was wounded. The eagle, flying overhead, would see what appeared to be a wounded rabbit and descend upon it. Once he had taken a grip on the decoy one of the men would reach up through the hole, grab the eagle's feet and pull it down into the pit, where the other man would club it to death (PLC).

The other method was to watch an eagle gorge itself on carrion, then quickly run over to where it sat and club it to death. According to PLC, the birds were often so heavy that they would topple over in their clumsy attempts to fly. When firearms became available to the Ponca both of these methods were abandoned. The Ponca continued to observe, however, the custom of leaving an eagle's carcass untouched for 4 days before plucking the feathers, lest they acquire "eagle sickness."

Trapping for furs does not seem to have been very important to the Ponca prior to the last quarter of the 18th century, as we find little mention of it in tribal traditions. However, when the European traders became established in the Ponca country, trapping became important, for then the Ponca could exchange furs for trade items. Beaver, muskrat, and raccoon were the important fur bearers in the Ponca region. The present term for 25 cents in *Đégiha*, *Mikáhiđawà*, means 'coonskin,' and is a survival from the days when a coonskin had this value in trade (JLR).

Trapping parties were of necessity small. One obscene Ponca story tells of two men and a woman making up such a party and another tells of a party of four men going on a trapping expedition during a time of famine (JLR). Traps were used in the manner taught by the Europeans, though some practices were elaborated by the Ponca themselves. Gilmore (1919, p. 89) mentions, for example, that traps were washed in a decoction of chokecherry bark boiled in water to remove the scent of previous catches. Trapping is still practiced to a small extent by some Northern Ponca. PLC (1961, p. 18) mentions learning to trap as a boy.

Concerning Ponca fishing practices, J. O. Dorsey writes:

> Both Ponkas and Omahas have been accustomed to fish as follows in the Missouri River: A man would fasten some bait to a hook at the end of a line, which he threw out into the stream, after securing the other end to a stake next the shore; but he took care to conceal the place by not allowing the top of the stick to appear above the surface of the water. Early the next morning he would go to examine his line, and if he went soon enough he was apt to find he had caught a fish . . . . [1884 a, p. 301.]

PLC described a somewhat similar method of fishing, but in this instance the fisherman remains on the bank. He throws out his baited line, but leaves a coil of loose line at his feet. When this begins to uncoil he knows he has a fish.

According to PLC, fish were once so abundant that they could be caught with the hands. Barbed spears were also extensively employed to take fish but: "Now there are too few fish to make this way of fishing any use" (PLC). According to PLC, bird claws were commonly used for hooks and lines were made of rawhide. Dorsey (1884 a, p. 301), however, says that the lines were of horsehair. After a successful fishing trip, the Ponca angler distributed a part of his catch among the old people in the camp, just as a hunter distributed meat after killing a deer, elk, or bison.

Turtles were, and still are, speared by the Ponca. Today a pitchfork is commonly used for this purpose. PLC was engaged in turtle spearing in Ponca Creek when I first visited him in 1949.

In addition to wild game and fish, an amazing number of wild plant foods were collected and used by the Ponca. As the tribe moved from place to place following the bison, the women, equipped with long digging sticks, kept a sharp watch for edible plants with which to supplement and vary the diet. M. R. Gilmore (1919) provides us the best listing and description of these. They included wildrice, wild onions, Indian-potatoes, wild sweetpeas, water chinquapin, and of course *tipsina* or 'prairie turnip,' the *pomme blanche* of the French. Milkweed sprouts, clusters, and the young fruit were valued as additions to the daily fare. The fruits of the blackhaw were eaten, but not gathered in quantity. Wild flaxseeds were used in soups. Morel was much esteemed and arrowleaf also was eaten on occasion. Even such unlikely items as corn smut and puffballs were used as foods when in a fresh state. James (1905, vol. 15, p. 171) mentions that the roots and nuts of *Nelumbium* were eaten by the Ponca. J. O. Dorsey (1884 a, p. 308) says that calamus roots were eaten as a food, but I am inclined to believe that they were restricted to medicinal use.

Although the Ponca raised beans in their gardens, they also utilized stores of wild beans that had been collected by rodents and stored by the animals in their burrows (OK). These beans were called "mouse-beans" by the Ponca, and are very likely the same as the "ground-beans" noted by Gilmore (1919, pp. 95–96).

Various fruits and berries native to the area were, of course, gathered as well. These included crabapples, wild strawberries, wild raspberries, juneberries, wild plums, sand cherries, chokecherries, wild grapes, buffaloberries, groundcherries, and elderberries.

Sugar was made from the sap of the maple, hickory, and boxelder trees. Wild honey also was used to sweeten things. A favorite dessert of the Ponca was wild honey mixed with nuts. Hickory nuts, black walnuts, hazelnuts, and hackberries were all used by the Ponca. Acorns were pounded into flour after they had been leached with a solution of basswood ashes to remove their bitter taste (Gilmore, 1919, p. 75).

Beverages, also, were made with various wild plants. PLC mentioned a beverage made from a plant "about 3 feet tall" called *xáde-maką́*, and Gilmore mentions several other wild-plant beverages used by the Ponca. Elderberry blossoms were dipped into hot water to make one type, and redroot or "Indian tea" was used in another. Other beverages were made of wild verbena, wild mint, and wild anise.

Salt was obtained from the salt flats 3 miles west of the present Lincoln, Nebr. The present Omaha and Ponca name for Lincoln, *Niskíđe-to̮wą́gđą* or 'Salt town,' refers to this. The salt was dug out in chunks with wooden spades, dried out on racks of wooden slabs, and then packed in parfleches for transport. Women did all of this work (PLC).

A few of the older people of both Ponca bands still make use of wild foods to some extent, though nowhere near the number of plants listed by Gilmore is utilized. A supply of *tipsina* bulbs, for use in soups, was noted in PLC's home in 1954. Bunches of other herbs, for use in soups and beverages, were seen drying on the porches of Southern Ponca homes. The Southern Ponca are probably more conservative in this respect than their northern kinsmen.

Like the other tribes of the Missouri, the Ponca raised extensive gardens, in some instances large enough to be termed "farms." Maize, beans, squash, pumpkins, gourds, and tobacco were the principal crops.

Corn was planted soon after the frost had left the ground. It was planted in a ritual manner that recalls the Ponca corn origin legend (see PLC's "History," pp. 20–21) and demonstrates the interrelation of corn and the bison in the Ponca scheme of things: "First a sod was removed from the ground to form a *mą́gđągè* or corn hill. Then the planter made a 'buffalo track' (i.e., a small depression) with his hand and dropped a few seeds into this. Then the hill was covered and smoothed" (PLC). PLC demonstrated the making of this "buffalo track" by making a fist with his right hand, but with the first and second fingers extended and bent at the first joint. Pressing his fist into the soft earth, he made a depression which very much resembled a bison's hoofprint.

Apparently, as was true throughout Eastern North America, most of the gardening was done by the women of the tribe. At least one story, however, tells of a man raising corn (cf. PLC's "History," p. 20). Will and Hyde (1917, p. 110) note that: "The women usually gave the patches two hoeings before the tribe started on the [summer] hunt, but sometimes, when the season was late, the corn was hoed only once." The corn was harvested in October, both the men and the women taking part in this activity. It was then dried on scaffolds and shelled as needed. PLC made an old-style Ponca corn sheller as an exhibit for an Indian Fair, and later gave it to me (pl. 22, *e*). It is a tapering wooden pin with a sharp point and a notch for the thumb. He stated that the point was run between the rows of kernels on the cob.

Beans, squashes, pumpkins, and, at least in the 19th century, a type of watermelon were important to the Ponca economy as well. Squash was planted in hills in the same manner as corn, and apparently interplanted with it. Detailed information on the planting of other vegetables could not be secured. The Ponca watermelons, according to JLR, were small, round, and full of shiny black seeds. He considered them to be aboriginal; but this seems unlikely, though the Ponca may have acquired them before Whites actually reached the Ponca country. These melons are described and pictured by Gilmore (1919, p. 120).

Fletcher and La Flesche (1911, p. 45) write that: "There were no ceremonies in the Ponca tribe relative to the planting and care of maize." Yet Skinner (1915 c, p. 789) states: "The object of the [Sun] dance . . . was to obtain rain for the crops." My informants PLC and WBB confirmed Skinner's statement. WBB mentioned that in later years the Ghost dance was performed for a similar reason.

At the present time the Ponca still raise their former crops, but the techniques and seeds used are those of the White man. Garden vegetables introduced by the Whites have been used by the Ponca for at least a century. Gourds for use in making Peyote rattles are raised by some Southern Ponca. Andrew Snake, a Southern Ponca gourd raiser, once told me that: "You've got to tend 'em like a baby—pour a little milk on 'em now and then." He also described how the growing gourds should be moved from time to time to keep them from being lopsided.

Corn was preserved for winter use by either boiling and drying it or parching it. Beans and squash also were dried, as were most wild roots, fruits, and berries. OK mentioned that turnips were preserved by first boiling them, then skinning them and splitting them in two. Meat was cut into thin strips, then smoked and dried over a cedar fire. This treatment not only preserved the meat but gave it a special flavor as well. Both meat and corn were pounded in a wooden mortar with a stone pestle. The corn thus prepared was made into corncakes which were apparently like the "corn balls" of the Mandan and Hidatsa. Pemmican or *dagádube* was the Ponca "emergency ration," carried by hunters and warriors. Bones were boiled until the "bone grease" or marrow fat rose to the surface. This was skimmed off, mixed with pounded meat and dried berries, and stored in sections of gut.

Ponca cookery was quite elementary if judged by European standards. Usually the meat was merely cut into pieces about the size of a man's hand and dropped into the kettle (PLC). *Wabásna*, or "roast," was made by cutting meat into pieces about 3 inches square and broiling it over an open fire on a green stick. Fish were also cooked in this manner. *Daní*, the special soup served at the *Heđúška* dance, was made of large pieces of meat boiled with squash, corn, and *tipsina*.

Fried bread or *umásnɛsnɛ̀*, still a popular dish at the present time, represents the first use to which the White man's flour was put by the Ponca. It is made of ordinary bread dough which is cut into pieces about 3 inches square, slit down the middle, and fried in hot grease. Occasionally the Ponca make "meat pie" by wrapping the fried bread dough around a piece of precooked meat before frying it. However, this is considered to be an Osage dish. In recent years the Ponca have learned many of the recipes of the Whites, and delicious cakes, pies, and other specialties are prepared for special occasions. The daily fare, however, remains quite simple in most families.

Formerly there were but two regular meals a day, one at noon and one in the evening about dusk (PLC, EBC). The entire family was present at these times. If a person became hungry at any other time he merely nibbled on a piece of dried meat. Nowadays there are usually three meals: breakfast, dinner (always the noon meal), and supper.

Usually there is little ceremony at meals, though many families begin each meal with a prayer in the native language. If a guest is present he is often asked to return thanks for the group. Formerly bison-horn spoons and hunting knives were the only eating utensils, but now plates, cups, table knives, forks, and spoons of White manufacture are in universal use. At a Teton Dakota dance near St.

Charles, S. Dak., PLC was observed eating a large piece of meat which he held on a wooden stick. He commented that this was the "old Indian way" employed before the Ponca had plates.

Usually the meal is served at the table, but at ceremonies, especially where many are present, people sit on the ground or floor picnic style. It is the usual form for the ceremonial dinner that follows a Peyote meeting or a funeral. The present-day Ponca, like other tribes of the Midwest, have the custom of deprecating the food they offer their guests. Thus, a visitor, invited in for "coffee," is usually offered a full meal with dessert. Then, after this sumptuous repast, his host may comment "We don't have much, we're just Indians."

The smoking of tobacco served as both a ceremonial act and as a form of indulgence to the Ponca. The tobacco originally cultivated by the Ponca was probably *Nicotiana quadrivalis* Pursh. (Gilmore, 1919, pp. 113–114.) It is no longer grown by either band of the tribe. Three types of additive or kinnikinnick which were mixed with the true tobacco were mentioned by PLC and OK. One of these was the inner bark of the red dogwood (*Cornus amomum*). Informants of Gilmore (1919, pp. 107–108) also mentioned three types, two of which were identified as red dogwood and redbrush (*C. stolonifera*). J. O. Dorsey (1884 a, pp. 309–310) mentions red willow as most common, with sumac leaves being used occasionally and arrowwood (probably *C. asperifolia* Michx.) only rarely. A small amount of kinnikinnick is still made by the Northern Ponca. Until recently the Teton Dakota paid regular visits to the Niobrara Reservation to trade for it. I bought a large sack of it from OK in 1949. He carefully instructed me to mix it with chopped "Horseshoe Plug" chewing tobacco before smoking it. Later, at the Omaha Indian powwow at Macy, Nebr., Mrs. James Poor-horse, a Southern Ponca woman, asked for some of this, and was elated when I gave her some "because it smokes so good, and is hard to get in our country."

Cigarettes are commonly smoked for pleasure by the Ponca of both sexes at the present time in place of the pipes formerly used. In the Peyote ceremony the cigarettes used in the ritual are equated with the calumet used in the older Ponca rites, and prayers are offered with them in the same way. The former method of praying with the pipe is described by J. O. Dorsey (1894, p. 375): "*Ábišude*, . . . is a word which refers to an old Omaha and Ponka custom, i.e., that of blowing the smoke downward to the ground while praying. The Omaha and Ponka used to hold the pipe in six directions while smoking: toward the four winds, the ground, and the upper world." Though accurate so far as it goes, Dorsey's statement fails to note that in addition to the four cardinal points, zenith, and nadir, the pipe is puffed a seventh time without moving it. This final smoking represents the locus of the individual who is praying, and completes the ritual number, seven.

Peyote (*Lophophora williamsi*), a spineless cactus plant containing narcotic alkaloids, is consumed by members of the "Native American Church" or Peyote religion at their ceremonies. It is usually eaten in the form of dried "buttons" cut from that portion of the cactus which grows above the ground. Occasionally several of the buttons are boiled in water to make "peyote tea." This is the form in which peyote is taken by people who are ill. From 1 to 50 buttons are consumed by a member in one night. Sometimes auditory and visual hallucinations are produced by the peyote. These "visions" are cherished experiences which older Ponca love to recount and interpret in terms of religious symbolism. Occasionally, however, the first experience with peyote is so frightening as to dissuade the user from further experimentation. PLC, for example, experienced such vivid visual hallucinations at the first meeting he attended that he has never returned. He stated, "The people's faces got long, then real short and wide—just like those mirrors they have at carnivals."

Before the introduction of the horse, the dog was the only domesticated animal known to the Ponca. At that time the dog was certainly the Ponca man's best friend. It guarded his camp; pulled his travois and carried his packs on the march; aided him in the hunt; and even provided hair which could be used, together with bison wool, to make finger-woven sashes, turbans, and garters. When other meat was not available or a special feast called for it, the faithful animal might be called upon to make the supreme sacrifice and to furnish the principal ingredient for dog soup.

JLR and AMC described a special breed of dog, now extinct, which was used to carry packs and pull the travois. This dog was large, with pointed ears. JLR said that of the "modern dogs" it most nearly resembled the Great Dane in appearance. It never barked, but whined when strangers approached. LMD and WBB both mentioned a time when the Ponca were traveling in the Rocky Mountains and found it necessary to make crude moccasins for the travois dogs' feet because of the rocky terrain.

A type of dog said to be of an aboriginal strain used as hunting dogs is now found on many Ponca farms. This dog resembles a small collie. It is black on its back and on the top of its head and neck, and tan below. Just above the eyes it has two tan spots, from which it gets its name, *Ištá-dùba* or "Four-eyes." A similar breed, also named "Four-eyes" is common to several other tribes, including the Omaha, Mandan, Hidatsa, and Yanktonai Dakota; hence the dog may well be an ancient and widespread aboriginal breed.

AMC mentioned a third type of dog which he said was raised chiefly for its hair and flesh. Of the "modern" breeds it most closely resembled the English Shepherd. It was fattened for the pot by being fed camp garbage.

Occasionally coyote pups were raised as pets. Crows were also tamed according to PLC. JLR told a story in which a *Heyóka* bird, identified as a "kind of hawk," the pet of a Ponca family, saved their lives when they were attacked by enemies. This type of bird was named after the Dakota-inspired clown cult of the Ponca, as the bird's appearance was similar to that of the clowns.

By the early 19th century the Ponca had acquired horses, mules, and donkeys from the Whites but not, apparently, cows, sheep, goats, or swine. James (1909, vol. 15, pp. 78–79) writes that "horses, mules, asses, and dogs" were the only domesticated animals possessed by the Missouri tribes at the time he was writing (1819–20). Fletcher and La Flesche (1911, pp. 77–80) cite Ponca traditions that horses were originally obtained from the Padouca, whom they identify as Comanche. Several of my informants confirmed this, though LMD stated that the *Pádǫka* or Padouca were Shoshone rather than Comanche. PLC insisted, however, that the Ponca had obtained their first horses from the Teton Dakota when the tribes met at a spot east of the Black Hills in what is now South Dakota.

Horses were highly valued by the Ponca. They were herded near the village by boys of the tribe. At night a man sometimes picketed his best stock, his war and hunting ponies, near his lodge. In summer they grazed daily on the rich prairie grass and in winter they were kept in the river-bottom timber where they could browse on willow and cottonwood boughs and rushes. The Ponca horseherds were maintained through natural increase, by stealing or buying stock from neighboring tribes, and, rarely, by introducing horses captured from wild herds. Usually wild horses were avoided, as they were generally "jugheads" or deformed or stunted in some fashion. Horses were broken to riding by having a small boy mount them in about 3 feet of water. The muddy footing and the water made bucking more difficult and even if the boy was bucked off he would not be hurt. Sometimes, if a horse was unusually wild, it was weakened beforehand by being starved (PLC).

Mules were valued equally with horses for use in the bison hunt and as "parade" animals. One Ponca story tells of a man whose horses were shot with arrows by jealous neighbors just before a bison hunt, but who managed to kill his quota of bison though he was mounted on a mule.

Ponca saddles were of the high "Spanish" type. The frame was of cut and steamed elk antler sewn in rawhide. Occasionally elmwood frames were used (Gilmore, 1919, p. 75). Stirrups were of bent wood sewn in rawhide, and saddles were padded with a piece of bison hide or a blanket. Rawhide or braided bison-hair halters were used which passed around the nose and jaw of the animal and had two reins attached. To allow the hunter more freedom of movement on the bison hunt, saddles were not used. The same type of saddle was used by both sexes. On ceremonial occasions horses were painted; feathers were fastened to manes, forelocks, and tails; and fancy hangings, martingales, and cruppers were displayed. In describing the decoration of a horse given away at a Northern Ponca puberty ceremony, PLC and OK mentioned that quillwork bands were fastened just above the fetlocks.

A man usually reserved his best stock for war and the chase, using the poorer animals to pull the travois and to carry the women and children. The travois or *ą́bawaį* was made of two tipi poles which were tied together so that they crossed at the horse's withers. Between the free ends a sort of sling was arranged, and on this the household goods were packed. The hooplike platform with laced-rawhide filling used by other Plains tribes was apparently not used by the Ponca.

At the present time the horse has lost most of its former importance to the Ponca, though its fame lives on in *Hedúška* dance songs and in the old stories of war and hunting. The few horses retained in the period of my fieldwork were draft stock used in farmwork.

The annual cycle of the Ponca at the time they were first contacted by Europeans reveals an alternating pattern of wandering in search of the bison interspersed with periods of sedentary, horticultural, village life. Crops were planted in the spring, hoed once or twice, and then the entire tribe departed for the summer hunt. They returned in time to harvest the crops in the fall, and then shortly afterward left on the fall or winter hunt. Returning to the permanent villages before winter closed in, they remained there until the following spring, hunting and trapping in the surrounding area. Most warfare took place during the summer months, although raids for horses were occasionally organized in the winter so that falling snow would obscure the tracks of the raiding party and their stolen horses.

The Sun dance, the major tribal ceremonial, was most commonly held in June. It took place at a spot near the permanent villages, shortly before the communal bison hunt. Late spring and summer was also the season for the various bundle rituals and warrior society initiations.

At the present time the Southern Ponca hold their ceremonial shinney games in the spring and their annual "Ponca powwow" in late August. Peyote ceremonies, hand games, and church services are held at any time throughout the year. Usually special Peyote meetings, hand games, and other festivities mark Easter, Memorial Day, Thanksgiving, Christmas, and New Year's Day.

MATERIAL CULTURE AND HOUSING

Ponca material culture shows both the Woodland heritage of the tribe and its later Prairie-Plains orientation. Thus the artifact inventory of the 19th-century Ponca includes not only most of the items common to the "classic" High Plains groups but also most of those common to the Central Algonquians as well. The material culture of the tribe was therefore rich and varied.

Ponca woodworking could not be termed highly developed, though many useful articles were made of wood. These included Woodland-type corn mortars, the smaller perfume and medicine mortars, bows, arrows, spears, war clubs, and quirt handles. The last mentioned, particularly, were often beautifully carved and ornamented. Articles were roughed out with an ax or knife, then finished by rubbing with sandstone, scoria, or the scouring-rush, all of which served the Ponca woodcarver in the same way as sandpaper does the contemporary craftsman.

Woodworking in the Indian style has all but disappeared among the Northern Ponca, though PLC still makes fine carved Indian canes, and in 1961 he made me an excellent carving of *Indáđingè*, the Ponca wood sprite. Among the Southern Ponca the Peyote religion has prompted a revival of woodcarving, and the wooden boxes in which the feathers, gourds, drumsticks, and other ritual objects are kept are sometimes decorated with fine geometric and realistic designs in bas-relief. The staffs and drumsticks also are beautifully worked. Often white Indian paint is rubbed over the finished carving on these objects to bring out the design. Well-carved cradleboards of the common Central Algonquian and Southern Siouan type were made until about 1915. Dance mirrors and batons also were beautifully done, sometimes with lead or pewter inlay work. One common type of dance mirror featured a horse's head as the mirror handle.

Until about 1900 collapsible "lazy-backs" or backrests, for use in the tipi, were made of willow rods threaded on sinew. These were kept rigid with chokecherry braces when in use. The bracing rods were unpeeled and were decorated with geometric designs cut into the bark. When not in use such backrests could be rolled up for storage or transport.

The inner bark of the *Tilia americana*, as well as nettle and elm bark fiber, was used for making cordage and ropes (Gilmore, 1919, pp. 102, 77, 76). Basketry was moderately developed, and Gilmore notes that "Sandbar willow stems were peeled and used in basketry by the Omaha and Ponca" (ibid., p. 73). Bulrush stems were used to weave mats, which were used as seats and floor coverings in the permanent dwellings. Smaller mats were used as wrappings for sacred bundles. A fragment of such matting was recovered at the Ponca Fort site.

Though definite information is lacking, it is almost certain that the Ponca manufactured finger-woven sashes, turbans, and knee bands in the finger-weaving technique. An old photograph in the Cross-Cultural Survey files at the Laboratory of Anthropology of the University of Nebraska shows two Ponca men wearing finger-woven turbans. Photographs labeled "Ponca" in the Morrow collection at the South Dakota Museum, University of South Dakota, also show such turbans worn by Ponca men. At the present time Ponca "straight dancers" generally purchase their finger-woven sashes and knee bands from the Osage, who still produce them.

Beautifully tanned skin garments, the skins colored in various ways, were formerly characteristic of the Ponca. PLC described the Ponca tanning process as follows:

> To tan hides the Ponca spread the green hide out on the ground and stake it down. Pieces of meat and fat still sticking to the hide are scraped off with an elk horn tool. After this the hide is dried and turned over, and the hair is scraped from it. You stop here for moccasin soles, parflêche, and other heavy pieces.
>
> If they want buckskin, bone grease (marrow) is rubbed into the hide. Then a sandstone or pumice stone is rubbed over the hide to make it soft and of an even thickness. A pit is then dug the same size as the hide and a fire is built in it. The hide is then smoked over the pit. This is said to make the skin waterproof. If they want a robe, the fur is left on the hide.

Various shades of yellow, tan, and brown buckskin were produced by using different sorts of twigs in the smoking process. Sometimes the buckskin was actually dyed. Maximilian (1906, vol. 22, p. 285), on his famous trip up the Missouri in 1832–34, noted a Ponca man "with a pair of shoes, made of elk leather, which were dyed black with the juice of a white walnut." The dyeing process noted by Maximilian may be akin to that described by Gilmore (1919, p. 101), who notes that soft maple twigs, grease, and a type of iron bearing clay were used in preparing a black dye used in coloring skins. Black moccasins are still made occasionally by the Southern Ponca, the only North American Indian tribe to make them. However, they now obtain black leather commercially.

The Ponca formerly made hoes of bison scapulae, and such hoes were recovered at the Ponca Fort site (Wood, 1960, pp. 57–58).

Adzlike tanning tools were made of elk antler, and fleshers were made of the cannon bone of the bison. Arrowshaft wrenches were made of bison ribs. Bone spreaders for the roach headdress were made of bison scapulae. The plume holders used in connection with these were usually made of dog leg bones. Large spoons, called *t*^{h}*é-he*, were made of bison horn which had been boiled, then cut and bent into shape. Some of these spoons hold almost a quart of liquid.

A type of neck disk favored by dancers was made from the smooth surface of marine shells, which were rounded and polished. PLC still makes these for use in dancing costumes, and he gave me one made of abalone shell in 1949. The usual material, however, is pink conch shell.

War club heads, mauls, and chokecherry pounders were made by pecking grooves in cobbles of the right size and shape. Arrowpoints, lance heads, and knives were made of flint quarried approximately 2 miles south of the present Butte, Nebr. Another Ponca quarry, located "east of Pike's Peak" is mentioned by PLC in his "History" (p. 20). Leonard Smith mentioned a type of blue stone that was called *Mǫhį-dù* (Blue-knife) by the Ponca because they so often used it for making knives and other flint implements, but he did not know the location of the quarry. PLC states in his "History" (p. 20) that the ability to make arrowheads was a "gift of God." This remark would indicate that the techniques involved in making chipped-stone tools had been in the hands of specialists before they disappeared completely.

According to my informants, the Ponca once made pottery of good quality. Native pottery, however, like stone tools, quickly disappeared in the face of the White man's iron kettle and porcelain dishes. James (1905, vol. 14, p. 75), writing in the early 19th century, states: "The original earthenware pots are now rarely used by the nations on the lower part of the Missouri . . . ." Yet this was only 31 years after Monier had "discovered" the Ponca! The accuracy of James' statement is borne out by the findings at the Ponca Fort site, where very little pottery was discovered; and what was found is apparently not Ponca in origin.

Leonard Smith contributed the following, rather fantastic account of pottery manufacture, which is presented to show how quickly a once common technological process may be forgotten:

> Ponca pottery was made from *Wasé-du* or blue clay, which was gathered along the Missouri. The pot was built up in a hole, which was the same shape as the pot. When it was shaped bluestem grass was put on top and a mat and water were put in the hole with the pot. The hole was then covered with a clay lid. It was then covered with dirt and a fire was built on top to harden the pot.

718-071—65——5

The actual process was probably somewhat as follows: The vessel was built up by either molding or coiling, then finished with a paddle in one hand, to slap the outside of the pot, while the other hand, inside, served as an "anvil." After the vessel was shaped it was decorated and allowed to dry until it was in a "leather" state. It was next covered with bison dung or wood, which was then fired to harden the pot.

The Ponca method of making fire by friction was described by PLC. First a piece of soft stone was found, selected usually with a small depression on one face. Some rotten ashwood was placed in this depression and just outside it. Then the fire maker took the stem of a yucca or soapweed plant and twirled it in the depression in the stone until enough heat had been generated to make the rotten wood smoulder. The fire maker then blew on this smouldering punk until he had a coal or spark large enough to ignite his dry-grass tinder.

A similar method, but one employing sand and dry bluestem grass, is mentioned by PLC in his "History" (p. 20). Gilmore (1919, p. 76), mentions the use of weathered slippery or red elm bark for catching the spark in fire making.

Since making a fire by friction in this manner was quite difficult, the fire was kept burning whenever possible. A method of keeping a fire while the tribe was moving was described by PLC, and is mentioned in his "History" (p. 20). A piece of rotten wood with "worm tracks" under the bark was obtained. The powder in these borings was ignited and the bark covering replaced. The smouldering powder acted as a slow match, and the fire could be kept for many hours.

The Ponca possessed little that could be termed machinery. The use of the lever was known, however, and levers were used to move heavy logs and stones. To carry large stones, such as those upon which petroglyphs were made, a large bison hide was used. The stone was rolled on the bison hide, then several young men would grab the edges of the hide and carry it (PLC).

The bow and arrow was the principal weapon of the Ponca in aboriginal times. According to PLC, Ponca bows were customarily made of seasoned ash and some of them measured 6 feet in length. This seems rather long to me, however, as I have never seen an American Indian bow longer than 4 feet. In addition to ash, Osage-orange or "bois d'arc" was also prized as a bow wood when it could be obtained from the tribes to the south (Gilmore, 1919, p. 76). Ponca bows were rounded on the outer surface and flat on the inner one. The top of the bow was pointed, perhaps so that it could be used as a crude spear in an emergency. The bottom was cut off straight. There was a slightly greater bend above the grip than below it. Bows were always unstrung when not in use (Dorsey, 1890, p. 47).

OK once watched Birdhead, the Northern Ponca chief, make a bowstring by lapping pieces of wet sinew and rolling them together on an old tabletop. When the sinew had dried "it would never come apart" (OK). A generation earlier, a Ponca would have probably used his thigh to roll the sinew.

Ponca arrows were slightly thicker at the butt so that they could be held more easily (PLC). Since the Ponca used the primary arrow release, pinching the arrow between the thumb and first finger, this was virtually essential. Gilmore (1919, pp. 108–109) states that arrows were made of rough dogwood or Juneberry shoots. PLC mentioned ash as the principal arrow wood.

Each man made his own arrowshafts, which carried his individual markings, but the arrowheads were made by specialists who traded them to the others (PLC). Ponca arrows were trifeathered. PLC stated that beveled stone points were used, but this information seems suspect, for PLC bases it on points which he has picked up at archeological sites. Points and feathers were bound to the arrowshaft with finely split sinew. Fletcher and La Flesche (1911, p. 42) mention clan markings on arrows in addition to the individual markings.

At the present time the bow and arrow is found only as a child's toy, and archery tackle has probably not been used in hunting for at least 50 years. It is interesting to note, however, that in the Peyote rite the staff of the leader is essentially an unstrung bow (in some cases complete with grip and nocks). It is referred to by peyotists as the "bow," while the drumstick is termed the "arrow." George Phillips, an Omaha peyotist, said that this was because of the great importance of the bow and arrow in obtaining food.

Spears were undoubtedly used as weapons by the Ponca at some time in the past, but after the introduction of firearms they functioned mainly as standards or symbols of warrior societies (Skinner, 1915 c, p. 786). Likewise rawhide shields were formerly used for defense (PLC). These were made of the thick neck hide of a bison bull. Both the shield and its soft buckskin cover were usually decorated with painted designs connected with the user's "medicine." One of these shields was still preserved by a Southern Ponca family in 1954, a family heirloom used as a wall decoration.

Wooden war clubs of the "rifle-stock" or "rabbit-leg" type were popular among the Ponca. Prince Maximilian was given such a club by a Ponca on his visit to the tribe (1906 a, p. 285). Clubs of this sort are a part of the Southeastern Woodland heritage of the Ponca. Stone-headed war clubs are said to have been borrowed from the Dakota in the 19th century (PLC, JLR).

Like other aspects of their material culture, the housing of the Ponca clearly reflects their mixed Woodland-Prairie-Plains orientation. Four different types of dwelling were in use among the Ponca at the time of White contact. The first was the *Mąítʰi*, or round earth lodge; the second was the *diuđipu*, which resembled the hemispherical bark wigwam of the Central Algonquians but was more often covered with hides instead of bark; the third was the *diúđipu-snèdɛ*, an elongated lodge of the *diúđipu* type; and the fourth was the *tʰiúkeđį*, or tipi.

PLC described the construction of the Ponca earth lodge as follows:

> There were four main posts in the center. They were as much as a foot thick. They had crotches in the top, and other poles were laid in these crotches. Then poles were leaned on these center poles all the way around. There was also a series of outer posts but there was no set number for these. The poles that were laid on the center poles also rested on these outside posts. When the framework had been built brush and a kind of red prairie grass were piled on. No wicker work was used in these houses. When this stuff had been piled on the whole thing was covered with dirt.

The description is a rather good account of the building of a standard Prairie Indian earth lodge, although PLC has neglected to mention the stringers connecting the outer ring of posts and the covered entryway, both of which were almost certainly present. Gilmore (1919, p. 75) notes that the posts used in the building of earth lodges were generally of elmwood. He also mentions that sloughgrass and "red hay" or *Andropogon furcatus* were used as thatching to support the earth covering that completed the lodge (ibid., pp. 66, 68). The latter is undoubtedly the "redgrass" mentioned by PLC. According to Skinner, the Southern Ponca were building earth lodges as late as 1880 (1915 c, p. 779).

Earth lodges were not built in the tribal circle arrangement, but rather according to individual fancy and convenience (Bushnell, 1922, p. 84; confirmed by PLC). The Ponca lacked any sacred rites in connection with the construction of the earth lodge. According to Bushnell (ibid.), earth lodges were built by the women, but PLC stated that the men aided in the heavy work of bringing in and setting up the heavy posts. PLC stated that earth lodges were always built facing the east in order to catch the morning sun.

The earth lodge persisted among the Southern Ponca as a ceremonial structure for several years after it had ceased to be used as a dwelling. The octagonal wooden dancehall, which was used for ceremonies by the Ponca and other Midwestern tribes until only a few years ago—and which still persists among the Omaha, Osage, and Plains-Ojibwa—seems to be a derivative of the earth lodge ceremonial structure. One of these dance houses stood on the Southern Ponca powwow grounds, near White Eagle, Okla., until about 1920.

PLC described the construction of the *diúđipu* and the *diúđipu-snêdɛ* as follows:

> The *diúđipu* was made by taking long green poles, sticking them into the ground, and bending them over and tying them at the top. Other poles or vines were tied around (horizontally) to make the framework. The whole thing was then covered with hides. The *diúđipu-snêdɛ* was made in the same way but was as much as forty feet long one way.

In 1949 I observed a Northern Ponca family, as well as several Omaha and Winnebago families, camping in lodges of these types, covered with canvas, at the Omaha Indian powwow at Macy, Nebr. PLC had a miniature *diúđipu* lodge, covered with old burlap sacking, at his home near Wewela, S. Dak., in 1951. It was used as a doghouse. PLC mentioned that these lodges, like tipis, were sometimes arranged in the tribal camping circle according to clan.

The fourth type of Ponca dwelling was the tipi. This was of the 3-pole foundation type, with from 12 to 20 poles used in all. The cover, usually of tanned bison hide, formed a rough half circle when spread on the ground. It had two projecting flaps, at the upper ends of which were sewn sockets to receive the two setting poles. This allowed the flaps to be moved in relation to the wind in order to regulate the draft of the center fire. (Skinner, 1915 c, p. 779; also PLC, JLR, OK, WBB, and OYB.)

The tipi was staked down with wooden stakes and the front laced together with slender wooden pins. In stormy weather a rope might be wound around the tipi to hold the cover in place (OK). The covers were often painted with clan and personal insignia. Tipis were pitched in the tribal circle arrangement on certain occasions, such as the bison hunt and the Sun dance encampments.

At the present time, the tipi is still used as a "powwow" dwelling by a dozen or so Southern Ponca families. It is also the "temple" in which the Peyote ceremony is held. Because of this the tipi has become, in the eyes of many of its members, a symbol of the Peyote religion. As a symbol it is frequently carved or painted on the boxes in which peyote regalia is kept, and it is represented in silver peyote jewelry. The adoption of the tipi as a special symbol by the peyotists is resented by some nonadherents. In 1954 I noticed a fine white tipi pitched on the grounds where a small Protestant church was holding a camp meeting. It was not used as a dwelling and did not figure in the church service in any way, but served as a symbol that this church, like the Peyote religion, was for Indians and not merely a "White man's church."

Some Southern Ponca families use wall tents as summer and emergency dwellings. Their method of setting up a wall tent, however, differs from that employed by most White campers and clearly identifies the occupants as Indians. Instead of the small stakes provided with the tent they stabilize it with four heavy wooden posts and two 2-by-4 crosspieces, two posts and a crosspiece on either "long" side of the tent. The tent ropes at the sides are tied to this crosspiece, which is lashed or nailed to the posts at either end.

There was generally little furniture in a Ponca dwelling. A fire for both cooking and warmth was built in the center. Pole beds, of the type used by the Mandan and other earth-lodge building tribes may have been used by the Ponca in the earth lodge and the *diúđipu-snèdɛ*, but were not mentioned by my informants. Corn mortars, of elmwood, were sometimes set in the earthen floor of the lodge.

The bed in a tipi or a *diúđipu* was merely one or more bison robes or blankets (PLC). Clothing and other gear were sometimes hung from a rope strung around inside of the tipi framework (OK). Willow rod "lazybacks" or backrests, in pairs, were generally reserved for the man of the house and his guests, and stood opposite the door of the lodge.

The Ponca homes which I visited were much like those of neighboring Whites, but were generally furnished much more simply, presenting a rather "bare" appearance in many instances. A few chairs, a table, a stove, and a woodbox were often the only furnishings. Pictures, when present, were usually of relatives or of religious subjects. Several snapshots placed together in a large frame was a common arrangement. Older persons sometimes hang their valuables from pegs in the wall to keep them out of the reach of children. The staff and "toolkit" of a Northern Ponca Peyote leader (EBC) were observed hanging from the wall in this manner. Extra clothing is customarily kept in large trunks.

Details concerning the cleaning and repair of the earth lodge, *diúđipu*, *diúđipu-snèdɛ*, and tipi could not be secured at this late date. Present-day Ponca dwellings are scrubbed and mopped quite regularly, but the frequency, of course, depends upon the particular family. Likewise, the yards of some homes visited were littered with garbage and trash while others were neat and orderly. Autumn is generally the season for repairing roofs and chinking cracks in the walls (PLC).

Cache pits were sometimes dug in or near the earth lodges. When dug inside they were usually south of the fireplace. If more than one was dug the second was placed to the west of the central fireplace, and if a third was dug it was to the north. In other words, as one entered the door, the cache pits followed a clockwise progression around the inside. Ponca cache pits were dug straight down for about 2 feet, then widened into a sphere, about 5 feet in total depth (PLC).

Menstrual huts are mentioned by J. O. Dorsey and Lowie (Dorsey, 1884 a, p. 247; Lowie, 1917, pp. 92–93), and were also noted by OK, JLR, PLC, and WBB. These were apart from the rest of the camp. Sweat lodges, built like the *diúđipu* but smaller, were used in the purification rites connected with certain ceremonies and with curing (PLC). A few Southern Ponca still take sweat baths, but the practice has completely disappeared in the north.

The earth lodge was the preferred structure for large gatherings among the Ponca. Bushnell (1922, p. 84), quoting Dorsey, writes: "Earth lodges were generally used for large gatherings such as feasts, councils, or dances." Among the Omaha the outdoor dancing ring where their annual powwow is held is still regarded as a symbolic earth lodge. If the Ponca ever had such a custom, they have long since abandoned it. At the present time the Southern Ponca hold their council meetings in the "Old Agency" building in White Eagle, Okla. In summer their dances are held outside, but in winter they use a large frame building near the "Old Agency" building.

The Northern Ponca hold council meetings, and until recent years had Rabbit dances, in the Ponca Self-help Community Building which was built with Government funds and Indian Work Projects Administration labor in the 1930's. This is located approximately 2 miles west and 3 miles south of Niobrara, Nebr. When PLC showed me the building in 1949 he commented that it had been intended for both "White" and Indian dances, and indicated where the *Heđúška* drum should stand, in the center of the ballroom floor. At that time the drum was still kept in a small room in the rear of the building. Southern Ponca visiting their Northern kinsmen would often ask to see the drum, which was in the keeping of Nancy Birdhead Knudsen. In 1954 the drum was removed to the Knudsen home at the insistence of the caretaker of the Self-help Building, who believed all Indian customs were "nonprogressive" and therefore undesirable.

Skinner (1920, p. 308) states that the ceremonies of the Ponca Medicine lodge (the equivalent of the Ojibwa *Midèwiwin* and the Omaha Pebble society) were held in a "long lodge roofed with tent-covers and brush" in the summer. This lodge was merely an extra long *diúđipu-snèđɛ*. JLR, however, stated that when his brother was "doctored" by the members of the Northern Ponca Medicine lodge group, the rites were held in a frame dwelling. This was confirmed by PLC, who further commented that this house had later become "haunted" by mysterious lights.

The Ponca Sun dance arbor was merely a semicircular screen of boughs the main purpose of which was to somewhat protect the dancers from the sun and wind. G. A. Dorsey (1905, p. 76), in his classic description of this famous Ponca ceremony, writes that on the third day of the dance:

> The Dog Soldiers went to the timber for additional boughs to complete the arbor forming the lodge. When these were in place women fastened four canvas tipis to the sides of the arbor and attached the free ends to the lodge poles, thus forming a better protection for the dancers from the burning rays of the sun.

Dorsey contrasts the simplicity of the Ponca Sun dance lodge with the more substantial Cheyenne or Arapaho structure.

The Ponca earth-lodge village was usually a mere aggregate of dwellings in no fixed order. The size of a village varied with the time and the place. James (1905, vol. 17, p. 152), writing in the early part of the 19th century, states: "The Puncahs have their residence in a small village of dirt lodges, about one hundred and eighty miles above Omawhaw creek . . . . Their number is about 200 souls." Half a century later the tribe was living in three villages: "The village at the United States agency contained [in 1874] 89 families and 377 persons. The village called *Ƕubđǫ́* . . . had 46 families and 144 persons. 'Point' village had 82 families and 248 persons" (Fletcher and La Flesche, 1911, p. 51). The "Point" village mentioned by these authors is very likely the "Gray-blanket" settlement of my informants.

At the present time the *Ƕubđǫ́* and Gray-blanket village areas are still recognized localities to the Northern Ponca, but neither could be termed a settlement. Most Northern Ponca live on farms in the Niobrara area or in the towns of Niobrara, Verdel, and Norfolk, Nebr. Most Southern Ponca live in and around Ponca City or the community of White Eagle, in Oklahoma. The latter, the site of the old Southern Ponca Agency, has a population of about 100, and is the only completely Ponca settlement in existence today.

DRESS AND ADORNMENT

In the early 19th century the Ponca man's clothing consisted of moccasins, leggings, breechcloth, and belt in the summer season. In winter a buckskin shirt, a fur cap, a robe or blanket, and perhaps a pair of mittens were added. A woman wore high-topped moccasins, knee-length leggings, a deer or elkskin dress, and a wide belt. Both sexes wore a buffalo robe or blanket as a kind of "overcoat" in winter and as an item of fancy dress at other times of the year. Children's clothing was cut on the same pattern as that of the adults.

For special occasions, such as feasts and ceremonies, special clothing was worn. Men wore otterskin bandoliers and porcupine and deer-hair roach headdresses, as well as other headdresses of fur. In the latter half of the 19th century breastplates of bone "hair pipes" were worn by both sexes, the pipes arranged horizontally in the man's ornament and vertically in the woman's. Women sometimes wore long beaded or quilled pendants hanging from their hair in back.

An early type of Ponca woman's dress, reflecting the Woodland affiliations of the tribe, is mentioned by Skinner (1915 c, p. 784), who writes:

> . . . At one time the two-piece, open skirt, woman's garment of Central Algonkin type was used, together with soft-soled moccasins. For many years these have been worn only by women who have been tattooed [i.e., women whose fathers or husbands had been admitted to the aristocratic Night-dance society, and who had been tattooed with its markings]. The ordinary females use the typical one-piece Plains garment.

The early "Woodland" type Ponca woman's costume was probably identical with that still worn as dance costume by conservative Meskwaki, Potawatomi, and Winnebago women. So far as I know, we have no good patterns or illustrations of the later "one-piece Plains garment" mentioned by Skinner, though it presumably resembled the Teton Dakota woman's dress.

An early account of Ponca male attire is given by Maximilian (1906, vol. 17, p. 98), who records his impressions of a chief's costume. "Schudegacheh's dress was remarkably handsome. His shirt was of beautiful otterskin, with a red cloth collar. He wore a cap of otter-skin, and a tobacco pouch of the same material. This dress was extremely becoming to this fine man." A very different impression of Ponca dress and appearance is given by the explorer Brackenridge (1904, pp. 93–94): "The greater part of the men were naked; the women were filthy and disgusting."

PLC recalled, from when he was a small boy, an old man who "dressed up" in the ancient style. This patriarch wore a wreath of sage about his head. His hair hung loose and fell to his shoulders. He wore a bandolier of twisted sage stems, a breechcloth, and moccasins. His body was painted in various designs and he carried a bow and a few arrows in his hands.

Although soft-soled moccasins were worn by the Ponca in the early 19th century, they were abandoned in favor of hard-soled footgear sometime before 1850. The typical Ponca moccasin for the past century is of the two-piece High Plains type with hard parfleche soles and soft buckskin uppers. PLC's dance moccasins are of this type, completely free of any decoration.

Beaded or quilled tobacco bags and eagle-wing fans were carried by men as items of dress on important occasions. In the 1830's Ponca men carried their weapons with them at all times (Maximilian, 1906, vol. 22, p. 293). Members of the Medicine Lodge society, when arrayed for the ceremonies of this organization, carried ornamented bags which were made of the skin of some small animal, such as mink or otter (Skinner, 1920, p. 307).

The ornament known as the "crow belt," the roach headdress, and war honor feathers were worn only by warriors who had earned the right to them according to both Skinner (1915 c, p. 794) and Fletcher and La Flesche (1911, p. 440). PLC stated, however, that during his lifetime dancers in the *Hed́úška* dance used any sort of feather ornament that suited their fancy.

A generation ago a type of costume called the "straight dance outfit" was favored by most Ponca men for use in Indian dances (fig. 1). This particular assemblage of costume pieces has remained *de rigueur* among the more conservative Osage, but is now worn by only a small minority of Ponca male dancers. Typically, a "straight" outfit consists of the following pieces. On the head the dancer wears a porcupine and deer-hair roach headdress, with bone spreader and plume holder. A single eagle tail feather stands erect in this headdress at the front. In addition to the roach most dancers wear two plumes falling over the eyes in front, or slightly to the side of the head, and two buckskin thongs with small pieces of silver crimped around the thong at regular intervals, suspended from a beaded or German-silver disk. The straight dancer also wears a brightly colored silk head scarf, rolled to form a narrow band and knotted over the forehead.

On the upper body the straight dancer wears a "choker" necklace, with a large shell disk in front, about the neck. His shirt is a loose-fitting, wide-sleeved style derived from those worn by Whites in the early 19th century. These are usually of a solid color, with a contrasting ribbon trim. This shirt is belted with a wide, loom-beaded

FIGURE 1.—Ponca "straight" dancer, front and back views.

belt with a stiff-leather backing. The dancer also wears German-silver armbands, a silk neckerchief with a German-silver slide, and two ornamental bandoliers. The bandoliers are usually made up of alternating silver beads and bone "hair pipes," though an occasional mescal-bean bandolier is seen. Attached to these bandoliers in back, so as to fall over either shoulder, are perfume bundles tied in silk handkerchiefs. Usually these handkerchiefs, the neckerchief, and the headband, are all of the same material and of a color that contrasts with the shirt, though sometimes the headband is an ordinary white handkerchief.

Tied at the dancer's neck, so as to fall down his back and stream out behind him when he dances, is a long otterskin dance tail, ornamented with beaded disks and eagle feathers. The thongs used to tie this ornament about the neck are concealed by the dancer's neckerchief. The Ponca claim to have introduced this otterskin tail into the Oklahoma area, and OYB said that formerly the otterskin was twisted and sewn round, like a rope. Those tails used at present, however, are flat.

On the lower part of his body the straight dancer wears leggings, a breechcloth, and a narrow "breechcloth tail." All of these are of dark-blue broadcloth, ornamented with matching ribbonwork designs at the outer edges. A straight dancer customarily wears his leggings backward because he wears knee bands and sleighbells at the knee, and if his leggings were worn in the usual manner the ribbonwork edging would be folded at the back of his leg and thus not show to the best advantage. At his waist the straight dancer wears a finger-woven yarn sash, the long ends hanging down on the left side. This is usually worn under the shirt and belt. Matching yarn knee bands are worn under the sleighbells at the knee, their long fringes hanging loose on the outside of the leg. Moccasins complete this part of the costume. Ponca straight dancers traditionally wear their shirt tucked inside the breechcloth, while the dancers of other tribes usually wear theirs hanging loose outside. Occasionally a few Ponca straight dancers omit the shirt and wear instead a blue broadcloth vest decorated with stylized floral beaded designs. As "props" straight dancers usually carry an eagle tail fan in the left hand and an ornamented baton in the right. Sometimes, however, a dance mirror in a wooden frame is substituted for this baton.

Another style of costume, the "feathers" outfit, is now preferred by all but a very few male Ponca dancers. This costume features a spectacular roach headdress, sometimes made of downy feathers, a "U-shaped" shoulder bustle, and a back bustle to match (fig. 2). This last ornament is derived from the "crow belt" of an earlier era. The breechcloth worn with the feathers costume is usually ornamented with beadwork in stylized floral and zoomorphic (generally horse) designs. The remainder of the beadwork worn with this costume, however, is generally in loom-beaded geometric designs. This consists of a beaded headband, choker necklace, armbands, gauntlets, "suspenders," and belt. Large knee bells, angora ankle bands, and moccasins complete this costume. As "props" the "feathers" dancer usually carries a set of peyote feathers and a straight wooden whistle.

FIGURE 2.—Southern Ponca "fancy" dancer, front and back views.

This whistle is sounded at the beginning of each *Hedúška* dance episode to encourage the other dancers. The "feathers" outfit is usually worn by the young, active, "fancy" dancers, while the man wearing the "straight" costume, though he may dance vigorously, always moves in a more restrained manner.

From about 1860 to 1930, eagle feather war bonnets were worn by Ponca men on state occasions, but these are no longer in vogue. They were apparently made and worn by any adult male who chose to do so, although both JLR and OK associated them with the chiefly class. PLC is the only Ponca dancer at the present time who customarily wears a war bonnet. The otterskin hat, rather than the war bonnet, was the Ponca "chief's" headdress, while a similar headdress of fox fur marked the experienced warrior.

The more traditional woman's dancing costume of the present day (fig. 3, *right*) is probably derived from the Central Algonquian woman's dress noted by Skinner (1915 c, p. 784). It consists of a long skirt, preferably of blue broadcloth, with bands of ribbonwork just above the hem. On her upper body the woman wears a loose silk blouse. Sometimes this has a large rectangular "middy" collar in the back. Both skirt and blouse were formerly decorated with many small German-silver brooches. This woman's costume style seems to be the feminine equivalent of the male "straight" outfit. It was formerly traditional among the Omaha as well.

In place of this traditional dress many Southern Ponca women, particularly younger women and teenage girls, prefer a white buckskin dress of Kiowa, Comanche, or Cheyenne cut (pl. 24, *a*, *b*). This item of apparel corresponds to the male "feathers" outfit. With it the contemporary Ponca girl wears a beaded coronet or "Princess crown" of Pan-Indian origin.

According to PLC, a chief's daughter could wear an eagle feather erect at the back of the head, though others denied this and said it was a recent addition to the woman's costume introduced by the wives and daughters of Poncas who served in the First World War. A chief wore a downy eagle plume erect in a socket at the back of his otterskin hat (LRL, Ed Primeaux). This custom has been continued up into the present era by the Peyote leader, who is called the "Road chief."

Although for most dances, ceremonies, and public events both men and women turned out in their finest attire, some rites called for special costuming. Writing of the dress of Ponca Sun dancers, George A. Dorsey (1905, pp. 82–83) comments:

> All dancers at all times wore their hair loose, and were naked, except for a loose, white skirt, over which hung in front the loose end of a red or blue loin-cloth. None of them at any time wore moccasins. Besides the paint which the dancers of each group wore in common, the members of each group wore or carried distinctive objects of a special nature . . . . Each dancer carried in one hand a bunch of sage, and all wore wrist and ankle bands of cotton, which are symbolic of clouds.

A special item of Sun dance attire which appears in one old photograph of the Ponca ceremony is a necklace of fur with a rawhide representation of a sunflower laced to the front. This showed that the Sun dancer, like the floral depiction he wore, followed the Sun with his gaze during the day. This costume piece is also known to

FIGURE 3.—*Left,* Southern Ponca peyote "roadman"; *right,* Ponca girl wearing cloth costume, showing the "middy" collar.

the Teton Dakota. Also characteristic of the Ponca Sun dancer were bandoliers made of fringes of red horsehair. Another type of Sun dance bandolier, according to Parrish Williams, was made of the hair from the tail of the bison in a "square braid" technique.

Each of the men's warrior societies also seems to have had its characteristic costume and style of painting. These are described later in this work.

Individual members of the Peyote cult in the Southern band usually wear dark shirts, neckties of red and blue broadcloth with symbolic tiepins of silver, and red and blue broadcloth or white sheeting blankets. Women members wear silk dresses and fringed shawls, and sometimes symbolic beaded or silver combs, brooches, and earrings.

Many rings, brooches, and bracelets were worn by members of the *Iskáiyuha* warrior society, according to Skinner (1915 c, p. 786). These ornaments were generally popular among the Ponca in the 19th century. Rings and bracelets continue to be popular with Ponca women and girls, and most Ponca men wear at least one finger ring.

Hair style apparently varied with the individual as well as the period, for Maximilian (1906, vol. 24, p. 97) writes that the Ponca he encountered " . . . had their hair cut short in the nape of the neck and across the forehead." The "young Ponca Indian" which Bodmer painted at Fort Pierre, however, has his hair dressed in two braids (Johnson, 1955, Leaf. No. 10). Perhaps the braids style was an imitation of the contemporary Dakota men's hair style. Old photographs in the files of the Laboratory of Anthropology, University of Nebraska, and in the Morrow Collection, South Dakota Museum, University of South Dakota, show Ponca men with their hair bobbed. PLC and Ed Primeaux remember both braids and short hair during their lifetimes. When the hair was worn in braids these were sometimes wrapped in otterskin (PLC, Ed Primeaux). The few old men who still wear their hair in braids at the present time usually wrap the braids in red or green yarn.

The Ponca man usually wore a small lock of hair called the *ásku* on the crown of the head. This was not intended as a "scalplock" or challenge to the enemy as some have contended, but was merely kept as a convenient device for attaching the roach headdress, silver chains, brooches, and other hair ornaments. According to Ed Primeaux (pl. 24, *d*), it was the custom of Ponca peyotists, in the period 1902–30, to wear a downy eagle plume, dyed red, attached to the *ásku*, as well as a silver button with two pendant buckskin strings, ornamented with silver and ending in two beaded tassels. This same headdress was sometimes worn, in connection with the roach headdress, by "straight" dancers.

Fletcher and La Flesche describe symbolic haircuts for boys representing the various Ponca clans (1911, pp. 42–46). PLC, OK, and JLR stated that this had not been the custom during their lifetimes.

According to PLC and Dave Little-cook, all hairdressing was done by members of the *Níkapàšna* clan. Hairbrushes were made of needlegrass awns tied in bundles (Gilmore, 1919, pp. 42–46). PLC still knows how to make these hairbrushes. *Monarda fistulosa* var. was used in a compound for dressing the hair (Gilmore, 1919, p. 111).

At the present time all of the Northern Ponca men cut their hair short in the style of the major "White" culture and dress in the same style as their White neighbors. Most of the Southern Ponca men do so as well, though in 1954 there were still three or four old men who wore moccasins and dressed their hair in braids. Younger women and girls in both bands follow current White styles in hairdress and clothing. Some of the older women in the Southern band, however, wear their hair parted in the middle and fastened in a bun at the back of the head, and they wear an "Indian style" dress. This consists of a loose blouse, worn outside the skirt, and a skirt of some dark material worn with many heavy petticoats.

Face and body painting were practiced by Ponca men in the 19th century, and male dancers still paint their faces. The common face-paint design for a straight dancer is a red line extending back from the corner of each eye for about 2 inches. Certain kinds of clay and plant juices supplied the coloring for this paint in aboriginal times, and buffalo fat formed the base. In 1954, PLC and I attempted to locate an old Ponca paint mine said to be in the bluffs just west of Niobrara State Park. Although some rather good yellow clay was found, the principal vein, which PLC remembered visiting as a boy, could not be located.

Yucca root was used as soap by the Ponca, particularly for washing the hair (Gilmore, 1919, p. 71; also PLC). Pieces of the root were chopped fine, a small amount of water was added, and the mixture was rubbed into suds between the palms.

PLC mentioned four plants used as perfumes by the Ponca, preferably in combination: *Péžį-bđàska* or "flat leaves," *Cogswellia daucifolia; Péžį-inùbđą-wažìde*, rose petals; *Inúbđą-kìđe* or "blue perfume," perhaps *Thalictrum purpurascens;* and *Maką́-inùbđą-kìđe-sàbe* or "black medicine perfume," *Aquilegia canadensis* L. or wild columbine. Gilmore (1919, p. 115) mentions that *Galium triflorum* Michx. was used as a perfume by the Ponca. Sweetgrass was used as a perfume and fumigant as well. Braids of it were sometimes worn around the neck, under the clothing.

Perfumes were pounded and mixed in small mortars made of elmwood (ibid., 1919, p. 75). Usually they were dampened to

718-071—65——6

increase their effect. PLC stated that formerly dancers in the *Heđúška* chewed dried perfumes while dancing and spit quantities of it onto their bodies and costumes from to time, disguising the act of spitting by the motions of the dance. Even at the present time the use of Indian perfume has not completely disappeared. We have noted that small perfume packets are tied to the bandoliers that are a part of the straight dance type of *Heđúška* costume, and some older men wear perfume bundles with their everyday dress. Because of its connection with "love medicine," the use of perfume of the Indian type makes the user the butt of much joking. At present, Ponca women and girls use commercial perfumes and cosmetics exclusively.

Ponca men formerly plucked their very light facial hair with clam shell or metal tweezers. In 1954 I observed an old man shaving in this manner while he was listening to a speech at a Peyote conference. He used a 2-inch section of door spring for tweezers. Most Ponca men now use razors, but they do not often use shaving soap.

Occasionally in the past, a Ponca man might sport a short beard of the "Uncle Sam" type. Photographs of Standing Bear, the Ponca chief, and Antoine, a Ponca mixblood chief, in the Morrow collection, South Dakota Museum, University of South Dakota, show this style (pl. 8, *c*).

LEARNING AND ART

A Ponca camp or village was kept informed of the orders of the chiefs and the reports of scouting parties by an old man called the *Eyą́pahà*, or crier. This man rode about the camp announcing the news in a loud voice. According to PLC some of these camp criers could be heard at a distance of more than a mile. Such criers are mentioned by both J. O. Dorsey (1884 a, p. 270; 1884 b, p. 156) and Alanson Skinner (1915 c, p. 798). Today the "announcer," or master of ceremonies, is still an important person at the annual Southern Ponca powwow, held each year in the latter part of August. Now, however, a public address system replaces the stentorian voice of tradition.

In communicating with tribes of alien speech, the 19th-century Ponca employed the Plains Indian sign language, but it is now almost completely forgotten. English has taken its place as an intertribal lingua franca. The sign for "Ponca" in the sign language was demonstrated by Dave Little-cook, who drew his first finger across his throat with a cutting motion. This means "Headcutters," which, Little-cook stated, was the name certain Plains tribes applied to the Ponca.

Both Little-cook and PLC denied that the "Language of the blanket," illustrated and described by Fletcher and La Flesche (1911, pls. 52 and 53, fig. 82), was used by the Ponca in aboriginal times. Dorsey (1884 a, pp. 262–263), however, describes one of the signs—that used for anger or embarrassment: "When he saw that his mother-in-law was seated there, he turned around very quickly, threw his blanket over his head, and went into another part of the house."

A gesture of affection which may have been introduced by the Dakota is also described by the Rev. J. O. Dorsey (ibid., pp. 269–270), who writes:

When the chief, Standing Grizzly Bear, met Peter Primeau, . . . and *Šahieda* at Niobrara in January, 1881, he embraced them, and seemed to be very deeply affected. La Flèche and Two Crows did not know about this custom, which may have been borrowed by the Ponkas from the Dakotas.

The Ponca claim to have made certain petroglyphs which are found in Nebraska and South Dakota. According to PLC and JLR, these served as trail markers, historical monuments, and places of prayer. PLC mentions these petroglyphs in his "History" (p. 17). JLR mentioned that certain men had "art visions," and as a result of these dreams made the rock pictures. Natural fissures in the rocks were utilized by the artists to complete their designs. Generally the main part of the design was made by pecking away at the boulders, which are often glacial erratics, with a hard river pebble, so that a shallow groove is produced.

WBB had an "art vision" in this tradition when camping near a sacred Pawnee spring, and made a drawing there:

I wanted to draw something, but I didn't know what to draw. All night I dreamt, all night long. I dreamt I went there and drew something. I went over next morning and drew what I had dreamt. I put my right foot next to the spring and drew. I drew the air. [Footnote in text: Black Eagle's symbol for air was a cross with lines radiating out bisecting each angle.] I saw it and I drew it. That spring was *xúbe* [sacred]. [Whitman, 1939, p. 190.]

The discovery of this well-defined Ponca tradition regarding their production of some of the petroglyphs in the Central Plains is rather interesting, as archeologists have long suspected a connection between these rock carvings and the expansion of Siouan-speaking groups into the Prairie region.

JLR stated that one of the chiefs of the second rank was designated as the tribal historian, and kept a "winter count" or calendrical record of the tribal history on a tanned bison hide. Each year a single important or unusual event was chosen and a pictograph of this event was painted upon the hide. This was apparently similar to the winter counts of the Dakota, Kiowa, Mandan, and Blackfoot. PLC confirmed this fact, and remembered hearing that one of the years recorded on the Ponca count was that of the great meteoric shower (1833–34). This year, known as the "winter the stars fell," appears on all Plains Indian winter counts known to me. PLC also mentioned that the tribal history was kept fresh in the people's minds by being retold at gatherings, which were held at regular intervals. Mistakes were corrected by older men.

Messages were conveyed by several different means. Lewis and Clark speak of setting the prairie afire to attract the attention of Indians on the Missouri, "this being the useal [sic] Signal" (Lewis 1904, vol. 1, p. 11). The use of this method of communication by the Ponca was confirmed by PLC and OK.

A heliograph signaling device consisted of a trade mirror set in a carved wooden frame. According to PLC the Ponca used sheets of mica for these heliograph mirrors before the days of the trade mirror. Later these mirrors became a favorite article of *Heđúška* dance paraphernalia. They also appear in old photographs as a part of the paraphernalia of Ponca Sun dancers (see pl. 17, *a*).

Messages to other tribes were carried by ambassadors who were safe from molestation. They transmitted the message verbally if they knew enough of the alien tribe's language. Otherwise the sign language was used (JLR).

Ponca numeration is based on the decimal system. The Ponca numerical terms are as follows:

Numeral	*Ponca term*	*Meaning of Ponca term*
1	*wíaktši*	one
2	*nampa*	two
3	*đa·bđi*	three
4	*dúba*	four
5	*sátą*	five
6	*šápe*	six
7	*péđąba*	seven
8	*peđábđi*	eight
9	*šǫ̀ka*	nine
10	*gđébą*	ten
11	*agđíwi*	add one (to ten)
12	*šápe-nampa*	two sixes
13	*agđí-đàbđi*	add three
14	*agđí-dúba*	add four
15	*agđí-sàtą*	add five
16	*agđí-šàpe*	add six
17	*agđí-pèđąba*	add seven
18	*agđí-peđabđi*	add eight
19	*agđí-šǫ̀ka*	add nine
20	*gđébą-nampa*	two tens
21	*gđébą-nampa gídi wíaktši*	two tens plus one
22	*gđébą-nàmpa gídi nàmpa*	two tens plus two

(The numerals proceed in this fashion to 30.)

30	*gđébą-dà·bđi*	three tens

(31, 32, etc. are formed by adding terms, as with 21, 22, above.)

40	*gđébą-dúba*	four tens
50	*gđébą-sàtą*	five tens
60	*gđébą-šàpe*	six tens
70	*gđébą-peđąba*	seven tens

Numeral	*Ponca term*	*Meaning of Ponca term*
80	*gđébą-pedàbđi*	eight tens
90	*gđébą-šǫ̀ka*	nine tens
100	*gđébą-hį̀wi*	a circle of tens
(101, 102, etc. are formed by adding, as with 21, 22.)		
200	*gđébą-hį̀wi-nampa*	two circles of tens
(300, 400, etc. are formed in a like manner.)		
1,000	*kokéwi*	one box

The term for one thousand is derived from the fact that the money which the Ponca received for treaty payments came in boxes which contained $1,000 each. Numerals above 1,000 were not secured. PLC stated that they were so rarely used that he did not know them. They could, however, be formed by combinations of the terms above, as *kokéwi-nampa*, 2,000. The numerals given by my informants correspond quite closely with those given by Riggs (1893, pp. xxiii-xxix).

"Four," "seven," and "twelve" were the numbers sacred to the Ponca, decreasing in importance in the order listed. PLC stated: "We use four a lot. Four is most important. I think we use it the most. Nearly everything we do is in fours. We use seven quite a bit too. There are seven sticks in the chief's fire." J. O. Dorsey (1890, p. 397) mentions "seven" as well: "Seven is the sacred number in the Omaha and Ponka gentile system, and is the number of the original gentes of the Dakota."

Some Ponca have told me that "four" is important because there are four winds or directions (PLC, WBB). "Seven" comprises these four directions plus zenith, nadir, and the locus of the individual, and is thus symbolic of his place in the cosmos. "Twelve" is said to be symbolic of the number of feathers in the tail of the war eagle. There has been some syncretism in this area on the part of Ponca peyotists. WBB stated that "seven" was important because "there are seven days in the week, the first being Sunday, the Lord's day." The same informant identified "twelve" with the Twelve Apostles.

Twelve moons or months were recognized by the Ponca. They were named after customary occurrences of the seasons. Apparently these terms went out of use many years ago, as only one informant, Leonard Smith, could supply the full set of names. They were as follows:

Month	*Ponca name*	*Translation of Ponca name*
January	*Má-spą̀*	Snow thaws.
February	*Míga-ìkįágđegđí-ke-mí*	Moon when the ducks come back and hide.
	or	
	Wažį́goma-waèke-mí	Water stands in ponds moon.
March	*Ištúkiaddà*	Sore-eyes (because of snow glare).
April	*Nąžįšta*	Rains.

Month	*Ponca name*	*Translation of Ponca name*
May	*Mé-pahą̀ga*	Summer begins.
June	*Maštė́-pahą̀gą*	Hot weather begins.
July	*Mé-oską̀ską*	Middle of summer.
August	*Waðápipìže*	Corn is in silk.
September	*Ą́pa-hòta-mí*	Moon when the elk bellow.
October	*Tą́de-màšąde-u-zi*	They store food in caches.
November	*Osní-ohą̀ge*	Beginning of cold weather.
December	*Má·de-ohą̀ge-sníade-aké*	Beginning of cold weather with snow.

Of the terms listed above, those for March and May were also known to PLC and OK; those for March, May, and July to AMC; and the term for May to Ed Primeaux. OK gave variant terms for January and February, the first being a recent term which was used only by the Northern Ponca. January was *Mí-nùxe-datéðe*, 'The moon when (even) kerosene freezes,' and February *Mí-mà-náska*, 'Moon when the snow melts.' AMC called December *Ma·ðe-oskąską*, 'Middle of winter.' Ed Primeaux called January *Dáxte-ma-nàga*, 'Deer paw the snow (in search of food).'

The Ponca divided the year into four seasons, according to PLC. The names of these were:

Season	*Ponca name*	*Translation of Ponca name*
Spring	*Mé-pahą̀ga*	Beginning of summer.
Summer	*Mé* or *Núge*	Summer.
Fall	*Tą́gą̀kðą̀*	When leaves fall.
Winter	*Má·de*	Snow.

The use of these terms was confirmed by AMC. Note that the term for spring is the same as that for the month of May.

Correlations between the growth of plants and the habits of the bison were noted. AMC mentioned an old Ponca saying: "When the shoestringweed is in bloom, the buffalo mate." Stages in the growth of plants also governed the activities of the tribe. Skinner writes that the buffalo hunt took place "when the squaw corn was about a foot high" (1915 c, p. 795). Ed Primeaux, a former participant in the Sun dance, said that this ceremony was held when the corn was in silk.

According to PLC the Ponca used the position of the sun and stars as a rough measurement of time. Adam Le Claire told me that the Peyote "fire chief" still keeps track of the time during a ceremony by noting the position of the stars. He keeps the "road chief" or leader informed, and this official regulates the ceremony accordingly.

Dorsey (1885 a, pp. 105–108) mentions that the Ponca of his day believed that the sun "went traveling across the sky each day." My informants did not know of this belief. Dorsey (ibid.) also mentions that the Ponca believed that if the "person in the moon" appeared to a youth in a dream, this caused the youth to become a homosexual. PLC and OK did not know of this belief.

Concerning the solar eclipse, PLC remarked: "The old Poncas thought that when an eclipse came the sun was dead. They called an eclipse *Mí-t'e*, which means 'dead sun.' Today we know that the sun never dies. It is just the moon coming between the sun and the earth."

AMC supplied the following:

> The old time Poncas paid a lot of attention to the stars, and had names for many of the constellations. The Ponca *Húđuga* or camping circle was based upon the circles of stars in the sky. The Milky Way we call *Waką́-ožą̀ge*, or "the holy path." Its movement was used for reckoning time. The North star is called *Miká-šką̀zi*, or "the star that doesn't move." It was used by hunters and travelers to find their way. The old time Poncas watched the moon too. In its last quarter the moon was called *Mí-t'e* or "dead moon." We look for signs of storm at that time.

J. O. Dorsey (1894, p. 379) writes: "That the Omaha and Ponka regarded the stars as Wakandas [gods or spirits] seems probable from the existence of *Níkie* [a name referring to an ancestor] names and the personal mystery decorations."

A Ponca thunder god called *Įgdą* is mentioned by Dorsey (1885 a, p. 105), but he goes on to say "They have no theories about the origin of earthquakes, rain, snow, or hail . . . ." I, too, was unable to secure from Ponca informants many explanations of meteorological phenomena which seemed to be of an aboriginal type. G. A. Dorsey (1905, p. 69), however, in writing of the Ponca Sun dance pole, states: "In the fork of the pole is the nest of the Thunder bird, sometimes spoken of by the Ponca as an eagle, sometimes as a brant or loon. This bird produces rain, thunder, and lightning." George Phillips, an Omaha, said that the members of his tribe call the nighthawk (*Chordeiles minor* subsp.) "Thunderbird" and believe that when they hear its cry a storm is near. They believe that the bird lives underwater in a spring about 1 mile north of Macy, Nebr. Phillips remarked: "We have seen them fly in there."

PLC said that the members of the *Núxe* clan "knew all about water and ice." He mentions this in his "History" (p. 19) as well. The *Hísada* clan are noted as "rainmakers" in the same source. He described the rainmaking ceremony of this clan as follows: "They make rains by rolling up bunches of redgrass, like is used in building earth lodges, and making a fire and burning some. Then some more is dampened, and this is put on top. This forms a gas and it explodes. This brings rain. It never fails. All of this is done with prayers." Fletcher and La Flesche (1911, p. 47), who mention the *Hísada* as a subclan of the "Wathabe," state that this group had charge of the rites relating to thunder, but do not mention the interesting bit of imitative magic given above, nor that the group were rainmakers.

Gilmore (1919, p. 132) records a Ponca belief that where pilotweed abounds, lightning is very prevalent. The dried root was sometimes burned during electric storms to avert lightning stroke.

Certain Ponca shamans were believed to have the power to control the elements. PLC recalled an occasion when Chief Standing-bear by praying outside of his tent averted a storm which threatened to stop a dance.

The Ponca had an intimate knowledge of the geography of the Central Great Plains region, as they hunted and traveled over a large part of it. The various topographical phenomena were noted and used as landmarks. PLC in his "History" (p. 20) mentions Wind Cave, in the Black Hills of South Dakota, calling it *Pahé-wađàhoni*, the hill that sucks in. The name derives from the fact that air inside the cave is usually of a different temperature from that outside, causing quite a noticeable draft at the cave entrance. The Dakota call the cave by a similar name.

The four directions are spoken of as the "four life-giving winds" by the Ponca. Directional symbolism is found in nearly all Ponca ceremonies. In some Ponca Peyote rituals an eagle-bone whistle is blown toward each of the four directions by the leader shortly after midnight.

The extensive knowledge which the Ponca possessed concerning the plants found in their territory is shown in part by Gilmore in his "Uses of Plants by the Indians of the Missouri River Region" (1919). This has been cited in many places in the present work. According to OK, PLC, WBB, and Joseph Rush, the *Makǫ́*, or Medicine clan specialized in herb medicines. This is noted by PLC in his "History" (p. 19). Fletcher and La Flesche (1911, pp. 41–47) list taboos for various Ponca clans and subclans. Several of these relate to plants. An idea of the Ponca concept of what happened to a person who violated such a taboo may be gained from PLC's comment that "Poison ivy was taboo to all of the clans."

Most Ponca education was informal. Girls learned from their mother and other female relatives and friends. Boys learned from their father and male relatives and friends. Occasionally some wise old man would gather a group of boys together and instruct them. Such a man was called a *wogǫ́ze*. *Wogǫ́ze* has become the word for "school" nowadays, being one word which is used by the Ponca but not by the Omaha. At the present time most Ponca attend school through the eighth grade. A few continue through high school and college. Many older Southern Poncas have attended Carlisle. At the present time higher education is often pursued at Haskell Institute, Lawrence, Kans., and Chilocco Agricultural School, Chilocco, Okla.

J. O. Dorsey (1885 a, pp. 105–108) describes several of the principal mythologic beings of the Ponca. Most of these were known to my informants as well.

Indáđịge, Dorsey writes, was a monster in human shape, with long hair. He hooted like an owl. VHM and PLC described the creature in much the same manner. VHM told of the creature attacking a group of hunters who were roasting a wild turkey. It was tall, with long hair, had bunches of grass tied to its upper arms and just below the knees, and carried a club. Its eyes were "pulled together" and continually watering. PLC showed me the place, in the hills west of Niobrara, Nebr., where *Indáđịge* was seen by the Ponca of his father's generation (pl. 18, *b*).

In all respects except size (i.e., forest habitat, long hair, owllike cry and characteristics, and club) this being is analogous to the Little-tree-dweller of the Dakota and the similar owllike forest men of the Ojibwa, Menomini, Potawatomi, Ottawa, Sauk, and Iowa. Unlike them, however, he never bestowed power upon individuals. Ponca mothers kept their children indoors in the evening by telling them that *Indáđịge* was about.

Dorsey (1894, pp. 386–387) mentions another creature, a water monster known as *Waką́dagi:* "These creatures have very long bodies, with horns on their heads." PLC gives a more detailed description in his "History" (p. 18), and he pointed out the place, approximately 3 miles east of Monowi, Nebr., where this creature was seen for the last time by the Ponca after it had crawled out of the Missouri (see pl. 18, *d*). PLC, reconciling tribal tradition with science, thinks *Waką́dagi* was a prehistoric monster which somehow survived into historic times. In my own opinion the Ponca *Waką́dagi* is clearly analogous to the "underwater panther" of the tribes of the Eastern United States.

Perhaps related is *Gisná*, which was described by JLR as like a leech or bloodsucker, but of such tremendous size that it was forced to lie "in a horseshoe shape" in the lake, which was its lair. This lake, near the present Monowi, Nebr., is reported never to freeze, even during the coldest winters. JLR mentioned that his brother had been magically "shot" by the *Gisná*, and through this acquired membership in the Ponca Medicine lodge society. This recalls Ojibwa and Dakota tales of persons being given power by the underwater panther.

Mąđážađịge (Mong-thu-jah-the-gah in PLC's syllabary) or dwarfs were said to live in the mountains. They are described by PLC in his "History" (p. 18). They led persons astray at night, but their power was dissipated by the rays of the morning sun. These may be the same as the creatures described by J. O. Dorsey (1885 a, p. 106) as follows: "There is a race of beings, having large heads and long hair, dwelling in solitary places, to which they entice unwary victims."

Fletcher and La Flesche (1911, p. 194) mention that "the *Nida* was a mythical creature, in one conception a sort of elf that crept in and out of the earth." These authors state that the term *Nida* was also applied to the bones of large extinct animals, and that it is still applied to the elephant (ibid.). PLC, however, in his "History" (p. 18) and in an interview, gives (and gave) the term *Pásnuta* (pa-snu-tah) for both the bones of extinct elephants and for the hairy mammoth allegedly seen by the Ponca near Butte, Nebr. He mentioned that this term was now used for circus elephants. Tales of "hairy elephants" are common in many Midwestern tribes, and I have personally secured them from Omaha, Ponca, Dakota, and Winnebago informants.

Dáxte-wàu or Deer-woman was mentioned by PLC, OK, WBB, and several younger informants. This personage is occasionally seen by the Ponca even at the present time. OK described her as follows:

> Say a young man is traveling alone at night. He sees a pretty girl and she makes him fall in love with her [by enchantment]. This girl is really the Deer-woman, and if he gives in, he will become a hermaphrodite [OK pronounced this "morphadite," and was probably using it, in the manner of local Whites, for homosexual]. Young men are warned that if they see this girl, they musn't give in to her, or something will happen to them.

J. O. Dorsey (1885 a, p. 107) in his discussion of Ponca mythologic beings, mentions the Deer-woman as well. He says, however, that men who had intercourse with her died rather than that they became homosexuals. At the 1961 Ponca powwow it was reported that Deer-woman appeared among the dancers at a "49" dance one night. A child noticed the deer feet beneath her skirts and screamed in fright, and a near-panic ensued. Though the young informant who reported this to me laughed at the whole affair, there seemed to be an undercurrent of nervousness about it.

Concerning the "Trickster" figure, J. O. Dorsey (1890, p. 11) writes: "*Makđįgeį* or *Makđíge*, the name of the mythical hero of the Ponkas and Omahas, answering to the Iowa and Oto *Mištšine*." This is undoubtedly the same as *Istʃ́nike*, mentioned by Skinner (1915 c, p. 779) and by my own informants (PLC, JLR, OK, AMC, WBB). Now called "Monkey" in English by both Ponca and Omaha, this creature is the central figure in a cycle of humorous tales. Alternating between good deeds and malevolent acts, he seems to represent the good and bad sides of man's character. Several of the Omaha and Ponca tales concerning *Istʃ́nike* have a wide distribution in North

America, such as the one which tells of his catching his paw between two tree branches which have been rubbing together and producing a squeaking noise, and in this way losing his roasted meat to a band of wolves.

Ghosts are still feared by the Ponca. Sometimes they cry; at other times they whistle. When traveling alone at night, present-day Ponca are terrified if they happen to hear a whistling noise.

Fletcher and La Flesche (1911, p. 49) record a Ponca myth in which *Wakǫ́da* gives the people a bow, a dog, and a grain of corn. They planted the corn "and when it grew they found it good to eat and they continued to plant it." This myth was unknown to my informants, and differs considerably from the legend found in PLC's "History" (pp. 20–21), which was also given by JLR.

The same authors (1911, pp. 47–48) record a myth in which the Ponca receive the feathers for the *Wá-wą* pipes. The same myth also tells how the clan pipes were made and distributed.

Decoration was formerly applied to nearly every article used by the Ponca. Tipis, clothing, and household utensils were all tastefully ornamented. On clothing the decoration, in the 18th century, was usually done with paint or with dyed and flattened porcupine quills. Gradually, in the 19th century, beadwork replaced the paint and quillwork in clothing decoration. Such decorative art was usually done by women.

Apparently the type of design was determined by the object to be decorated. Whitman (1937, p. xiii) mentions that all Ponca beadwork was geometric, but this statement is clearly in error. Most of the beaded designs on the breechcloths of the Sun dancers figured by G. A. Dorsey are stylized floral motifs (1905, pls. xv, xvi, xvii, xviii, xix, xxi, xxiv, xxvi, xxvii, and xxx). In present-day dancing costumes, both geometric and floral designs are used, with a few realistic motifs as well. In present-day "fancy dance" costumes, both geometric and floral designs are used, with a few zoomorphic motifs as well. The man's beaded breechcloth is usually done in a combination of floral and zoomorphic (usually horse) motifs. Moccasins, headbands, and "suspenders" most commonly have geometric designs. Gauntlets, armbands, and belts employ either floral or geometric patterns. The use of both floral and geometric designs holds true not only for the Ponca and other "Prairie" tribes, but for many "High Plains" tribes. The oft-reiterated statement that "Plains Indians always use geometric designs, Woodland Indians always use floral designs" is a standardized error in North American ethnology long in need of correction.

Some decorative art of the Ponca was highly symbolic in nature. Fletcher and La Flesche (1911, p. 45) write: "The people of the *Makǫ́* subdivision painted their tents with black and yellow bands."

They (ibid., p. 43) also mention that a subdivision of the *Đíxida* clan symbolically painted the "pipes" used in the *Wá-wą* rite. Little decorative art was observed among the Northern Ponca. The Southern Ponca, however, still make fine beadwork, and especially good work is done on Peyote "feathers," gourd handles, and staffs. Curiously enough, Peyote beadwork is done by men. However, the beadwork used on dancing costumes is still made by the women, as is traditional.

Representative artwork was usually done by men. Realistic designs of horses, bison, and dancing men were painted on tipi covers, shields, and robes. If, as often happened, a woman wished to use a representative design in her beadwork, she would ask a male relative to sketch it for her, then follow his sketch in her beading.

At least one Southern Ponca, Andrew Snake, was still doing silverwork in the old Woodland-Plains tradition in 1954. His principal customers were Osage "straight" dancers, for whom he produced armbands and neckerchief slides. He also informed me that he made an occasional "wedding bridle" for an Osage.

PLC mentioned that formerly children sculptured clay figures of horses, bison, dogs, birds, and humans, using clay from a slough located 2 miles west and 2 miles south of Niobrara, Nebr. Clay figures of this type have appeared in archeological contexts in Nebraska, one site being the Yutan site, 25SD1, which is identified with the historic Oto-Missouri. In these clay figures, as in the petroglyphs mentioned earlier, "visions" seem to have inspired the individual artist. Thus, one Ponca boy is said to have made a perfect model of an airplane many years before aircraft had been invented. This occurrence is still remembered and thought of as *xúbe* (supernatural) by some elderly Ponca.

Music was an art in which the Ponca excelled, and it is still a vital part of Southern Ponca culture. Ponca singers are in great demand at powwows throughout Oklahoma, and at least three Ponca men support themselves almost entirely by "following the powwow circuit" as singers. The musical instruments used by the Ponca aboriginally were drums of various sorts; gourd, rawhide, and deer-hoof rattles; eagle-bone and cedar whistles; and cedar flutes.

The drum was used principally in connection with the voice, to accompany dances and ceremonies. Rattles also were used in this manner, especially in sacred rituals. Whistles of eagle bone were used in the Sun dance, and, according to PLC, in the *Hedúška* as well, although cedar whistles were usually employed in the latter. Nowadays an eagle-bone whistle is used in the Peyote ceremony. The Indian flute was used in courting. It was the only Ponca instrument that was not connected with some dance or ceremony and was used solo. OYB was the last Ponca flute-maker and player among the Ponca. By 1954 he had ceased to play his instrument, though 2 years earlier I was privileged to hear the wonderful quavering tones of his instrument at a twilight concert.

The human voice was the Ponca musical instrument *par excellence*. Songs accompanied nearly every activity. There were songs to accompany various dances and ceremonies, such as the Sun dance, *Wà-wą*, and *Heđúška;* medicine songs which were thought to bear supernatural power and could call the spirits to heal the sick; vigorous Moccasin game and Hand game songs which were used to distract the players on the opposing team; love songs, some of which imitated the bell-like quavers of the courting flute, and mock love songs in which young men imitated lovesick girls. There were also lullabies which mothers sang to quiet their children and put them to sleep.

Fletcher (1900, pp. 90–91) writes that songs were sung by warriors as they left for battle, and Fletcher and La Flesche (1911, p. 442) mention that *Wétǫwą́*, or "brave heart" songs were sung by the women of the tribe to aid their absent warriors. One of J. O. Dorsey's Ponca informants told him (1890, p. 371): "My father went on the war path and he sang all the time. He was always singing as he walked. When he was a young man, he was always singing when he lay down at night." According to PLC, women formerly sang mourning songs or *Nágđe-wąųtà* when a relative died.

At the present time four classes of songs are still in use among the Southern Ponca: (1) dance songs, including those for the *Heđúška*, Round, "49", and other dances; (2) Hand game songs; (3) Peyote songs; and (4) church (White style) songs. The Northern Ponca are still very musical, but, with the single exception of PLC they have abandoned their native music and sing popular White songs instead.

SOCIAL ORGANIZATION

James O. Dorsey (1897, p. 213) calls the tribal organization, as existing among the Central Siouan tribes, a "kinship state" and points out that "the governmental functions are performed by men whose offices are determined by kinship . . . ." By this, Dorsey means that in aboriginal Ponca society the high status positions were almost entirely of the "ascribed" type, and not open to free competition among the tribal members. Instead, one's position in Ponca society depended upon his position in the family, his family's position in the clan, and his clan's position in the tribe. Certain clans outranked certain others socially, and had special rights and prerogatives not possessed by others. Marriage and the mutual rights and duties of the members of each clan were strictly governed by one's position in the system. In this respect the Ponca and other Central Siouan groups contrast strongly with their egalitarian neighbors to the north, the Dakota.

Eggan (1937, p. 93) classifies the Ponca kinship system as being of the "lineage" type and of the Omaha subtype. This system is generally found in groups which possess strong patrilineal clans like those of the Ponca. The chart (fig. 4) shows the Ponca kinship system from the viewpoint of the male EGO. It will be noted that in this system generation differences are ignored at certain points. The father's sister's children, for example, are classed with sororal nephews and nieces, and the mother's brother's children with maternal uncles and aunts. Hence, as EGO, I may have an "uncle" who has just been born and at the same time a "grandchild" my own age or older.

White has discussed this overriding of the generation principle in his article entitled "A Problem in Kinship Terminology" (1939, pp. 566–573). He demonstrates that in kinship systems of the Omaha and Crow types the principle of *clan affiliation* has become stronger than the principle of *generation difference.* Hence, since my mother's brother and all of his descendants in the male line belong to a different clan from my own, the members of which I owe a customary respect, thay are equated in the kinship system. Likewise, I am called "uncle" by my father's sister's children, and I call them niece and nephew in return.

The primary terms used by the Ponca are as follows:

Term	*Near English equivalent*
Indádi	Father
Inaha	Mother
Wiką́	Grandmother
Witígą	Grandfather
Wižį́ge	Son
Wižą́ge	Daughter
Witúžpa	Grandchild (either sex)
Wižį́de	Elder brother (male speaking)
Witínu	Elder brother (female speaking)
Witą́ge	Elder sister (male speaking)
Wižą́de	Elder sister (female speaking)
Wisą́ga	Younger brother
Wihé	Younger sister
Winégi	Uncle
Witími	Aunt
Witą́ska	Nephew (male speaking)
Witúška	Nephew (female speaking)
Witížą	Niece (male speaking)
Witúžąge	Niece (female speaking)
Witáhą	Brother-in-law (male speaking)
Wišíe	Brother-in-law (female speaking)
Wihą́ga	Sister-in-law (male speaking)
Wišíką	Sister-in-law (female speaking)
Witą́de	Son-in-law
Witíni	Daughter-in-law

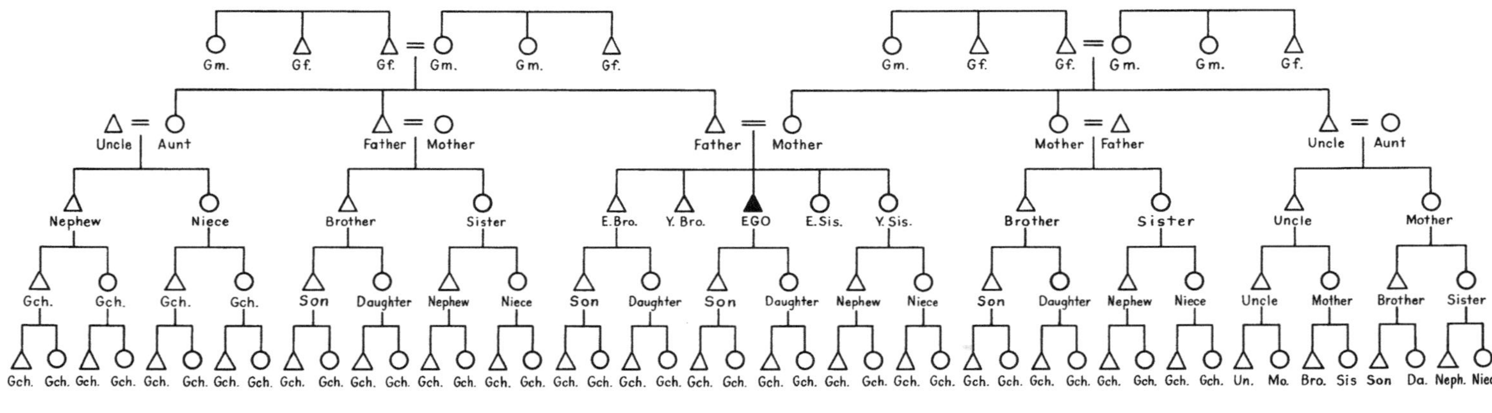

FIGURE 4.—Ponca kinship system, Ego male.

The prefix *wi-* signifies 'my,' i.e., *Winégi*, 'my uncle.' In direct address this is omitted, i.e., *Wíbđaha négi*, 'Thank you, uncle.'

At the present time the aboriginal kinship system is used only by older Ponca. Younger people, though they may know the terms, cannot apply them correctly, and use the Western European (Eskimo type) kinship system even when speaking their own tongue.

PLC stated that in aboriginal times a man, his wife, and their children occupied a dwelling, with perhaps the man's parents as well, if they were still alive. This is still largely true for the present-day Ponca. A large earth lodge might be occupied by two or three brothers and their families. A statement in a folktale recorded by Dorsey (1890, p. 91) indicates the presence, formerly, of communal clan bachelor quarters: ". . . Each of these married men had a skin tent of his own, but unmarried ones dwelt in communal lodges of their respective gentes [clans]." None of my informants had heard of this custom, which probably represents an ancient Southeastern Woodland pattern already abandoned by the Ponca in historic times.

The Ponca man "wore the pants" in his family. Dorsey (1897, p. 213) writes: "Among the Dakota, *as among the Đégiha* and other groups, the man is the head of the family" [italics my own]. The woman was the property of the husband, and should a man be dissatisfied with his wife he might "give her away" at the next *Heđúška* dance. A woman given away to the young men of the tribe in this manner had no recourse except to return to her parents' lodge (Skinner, 1915 c, pp. 784–785).

Apparently there was no hard and fast residence rule in the tribe. According to PLC newly married couples might go to live with either the groom's or the bride's parents, or set up a house of their own, depending upon personal choice and economic circumstances. Judging from the patrilineal kinship system, however, one suspects that residence was predominantly patrilocal in the past. It remains so today when economic circumstances do not permit a couple to establish their own household.

Adoption was commonly practiced to continue a family line. PLC remarked: "Sometimes, when the only son in a family died, the family would adopt some other child to take his place. This adopted son would be treated just like the little boy who had died."

Among the Ponca, husband-wife relationships were usually relaxed and easy. Now and then, however, it became necessary for the relatives of the bride to interfere. Dorsey (1884, p. 262) comments on this situation as follows:

> Among the *Đégiha*, if the husband is kind, the mother-in-law never interferes. But when the husband is unkind the wife takes herself back, saying to him, "I have had you for my husband long enough; depart." Sometimes the father or

elder brother of the woman says to the husband "You have made her suffer; you shall not have her for a wife any longer." This they do when he has beaten her several times, or has been cruel in other ways.

As mentioned earlier, the henpecked husband could divorce his wife by "giving her away" to the young men of the tribe at a *Hedúška* dance.

Husband-wife relationships which I observed, with but few exceptions, appeared to be very close, and often small signs of affection were exchanged by the two when they thought themselves unobserved. Nevertheless, quarrels do occasionally occur. The humorous term "coffee nerves," derived from comic-strip advertisements of the 1930's, is used to describe a man and wife who have been quarreling. When parents separated, the children were sometimes taken by the wife's mother, sometimes by the husband's (Dorsey, 1884 a, p. 262).

Very often, ceremonial obligations were undertaken jointly by a man and his wife. Skinner writes that a man and his wife usually joined the Medicine Lodge society at the same time (1920, pp. 306–307). This old *Đégiha* pattern has now been transferred to the Peyote rite. Thus, a Southern Ponca, upon learning that I had "eaten peyote" (i.e., was a member of the Peyote religion), immediately inquired if my wife also belonged, and was surprised when I informed him that she did not.

Relationships between parents and children of the same sex were very close. J. O. Dorsey (1890, p. 291) records, in the folktale "The Bear Girl," the following illustrative instance: "Her mother combed her hair for her, although she was grown. This was customary." At the present time when a Ponca girl decides that she wishes to dance in local powwows, she asks her mother to help her make a dance dress.

Whitman (1939, p. 187) describes the father-son relationship of Black-eagle and his father as quite restrained, but this was apparently a special case, for those father-son relationships which I observed, and which informants described to me, were very close. Most of the stories told me by JLR, PLC, and AMC had been learned from their fathers. Both sons and daughters were customarily disciplined by reprimand rather than by physical means.

The Ponca, like other Central Siouan tribes, honored the eldest child in the family above the rest. Whitman (1939, p. 182, note 14) writes: "Among the Ponca the Beloved Child was usually the oldest, either male or female. Such children were not scolded; they were given the best of everything." This child, if a boy, was the one who inherited the sacred bundles and ceremonial responsibilities of the father, and hence was given preferential treatment. That the special treatment of the Beloved Child was not considered quite fair by the younger siblings is indicated by WBB's statement, recorded by Whitman (ibid., p. 182): "He always scolded me, and never my older brother." Though the custom of honoring the eldest child was said by PLC and JLR to have lapsed, I noted that it was generally the eldest son who acquired the father's peyote "fireplace" (i.e., the right to conduct the ceremony) among the Southern Ponca.

A brother and his sister were allowed to play together until they were about 10 years old. At this time they separated and assumed the attitude of extreme respect and avoidance which they were to maintain toward each other for the remainder of their lives. They no longer played together and did not even speak to one another in public. If a brother wished to tell his younger sister to come home with him when they were visiting at someone else's home, he would ask a third person to relay the message. If no one was present whom he could ask to do this, he would announce in a loud voice "I am going home now." His sister, if she knew what was best for her, would take the hint and follow him.

At the present time this relationship has been relaxed, and I often observed brothers and sisters teasing one another, in the manner of Whites. Brother-brother and sister-sister relationships were, and still are, very close. The older brother or sister is frequently charged with the care of the younger one by the parents.

Concerning the relationship of grandparent and grandchild Whitman (1937, p. 47) notes: "The relationship between grandparents and grandchild is, among the Oto and the Ponca, a cherishing one." It was generally the grandfather who made a Ponca boy his first bow and arrows, and the grandmother who beaded his first dancing costume. Grandparents, also, could take the time to teach the children the tribal games and tell them the folktales which the parents, busy gaining a livelihood, did not have time to do.

A relationship of a different type pertained between an uncle (mother's brother) and his nephew, and an aunt (father's sister) and her niece. Such relationships were of the "joking type." This behavior applied not only to the mother's brother-sister's son and father's sister-brother's daughter but also, at least to some degree, to all other relationships where the kinship terms "uncle" and "nephew" or "aunt" and "niece" were used. The most obscene and cruel jokes were played upon a nephew by his uncle. It was considered bad form for the nephew to become offended, even if the uncle put a cocklebur under the boy's saddle blanket and thus caused him to be bucked off his pony. In return the nephew could appropriate any article belonging to his uncle without asking. Teasing of nieces by "aunts" was usually not so cruel. An "aunt" might chide her "niece" about boy friends or something of the sort (Skinner, 1915 c, p. 800; also PLC, JLR, and WBB). Whitman (1939, p. 183) records WBB's having received "squaw medicine" and sober advice from his mother's brother, showing that this relationship had a serious side as

718-071—65——7

well. The important consideration, however, is that this was a sort of thing which the boy's father, or his father's brother, would not have done.

Skinner (1915 c, p. 800) describes the brother-in-law/sister-in-law relationship as a joking one as well. This was confirmed by my informants.

J. O. Dorsey (1884 a, pp. 262–263), Skinner (1915 c, p. 800), and Lowie (1917, p. 91) all record the familiar mother-in-law taboo for the Ponca. It was mentioned by nearly all of my informants as well. Briefly, a man avoided his mother-in-law when it was at all possible, and she avoided him. The avoidance was phrased in terms of extreme mutual respect. The custom has now lapsed, but one Southern Ponca commented: "I still feel uncomfortable when my wife's old lady is around." A similar taboo obtained between a wife and her father-in-law.

Dorsey (1884 a, pp. 252–253) speaks of *Níkie* kinship, or kinship based upon a common mythical ancestor. Thus, the members of a Ponca clan and those in an Omaha clan with a similar name called each other by kinship terms because of their *Níkie* relationship.

Kinship terms, such as "grandfather" were used on ceremonial occasions to show respect to those officiating. Whitman (1939, p. 189) mentions that WBB had to use kinship terms in addressing the holy men in charge of the rites when he was undergoing a religious ordeal in the sweat lodge. At the present time Ponca peyotists customarily refer to one another as "brother" and "sister." This practice may have been borrowed from White churches, and is apparently universal in peyote-using tribes. Likewise, a Ponca peyotist always refers to his wife as "my companion" rather than "my wife."

There are several lists of Ponca clans in the literature, some of which differ quite widely from one another. In some instances the differences are so great as to present an impression of a rather transitory clan system in the tribe. I am inclined to believe, however, that this was not true. Many of the apparent differences result from different English interpretations of the *Đégiha* name. Others are seen to be the result of one author's calling a clan a subclan and vice versa. Interpretations of clan names might very well have changed through the years. The meanings assigned words have certainly changed elsewhere in the language. Likewise, the transformation of a subclan into a clan might reasonably have occurred with the extinction of other subclans in recent times. Therefore, since the differences shown may actually represent changes through time, and since no one source may be regarded as authoritative, several are presented below. The schemes are in chronological order, based upon the date of collection, beginning with Lewis H. Morgan and ending with the list secured from PLC, OK, JLR, LMD, OYB, AMC, and David Little-cook.

Dorsey and Thomas (1910, p. 279) quote Morgan's list of Ponca clans, giving Joseph La Flesche's interpretations in parentheses:

1. *Wasábe* 'grizzly bear' (properly black bear)
2. *Đíxida*, 'many people'
3. *Níkapàšna*, 'elk'
4. *Maką́*, 'skunk'; (*Maką́*, 'medicine')
5. *Wašábe*, 'buffalo'
6. *Wažáže*, 'snake'
7. *Núxe*, 'medicine'; (*Núxe*, 'ice')
8. *Wága*, 'ice'; (*Wága*, 'jerked meat')

In his own list, J. O. Dorsey (1891 b, pp. 331–332) gives several subclans, and divides the clans into phratries and moieties as well. Since Dorsey is the only author to mention phratries and moieties for the Ponca, and since my own informants vehemently denied any such arrangement, Dorsey's system should, I believe, be viewed with suspicion. Dorsey shows, in much of his work, a decided tendency to blend material from all of the Siouan-speaking tribes with which he was acquainted, such as the Ponca, Omaha, Osage, Winnebago, and Dakota. This may explain the disconformity between his scheme and the schemes presented by others. Dorsey (1891 b, p. 331) writes:

> The Ponka tribal circle was divided equally between the *Tšį́žu* and *Wažáže* half-tribes. To the former half-tribe belong two phratries of two gentes each, *ie.*, Nos. 1 to 4, and to the latter two similar phratries, including gentes 5 to 8.
>
> *Tšį́žu* half-tribe.—Thunder or Fire Phratry: Gens 1. *Hísada*, Thunder people, Subgentes not gained. Gens 2. *Wasábe-hitàži*, Touch not the Skin of a Black bear.
>
> *Tšį́žu* half-tribe.—Wind-makers, or War phratry: Gens 3 *Đíxida*, Wildcat. In two subgentes: 1. *Sį́de-àgđe*, Wears Tails or Locks of Hair; *Mágđe-itàži*, Touches no Charcoal and *Wasétʉitàži*, Touches no Verdigris. 2. *Wamí-itàži*, Touches no Blood. Gens 4. *Níkapàšna*, 'Bald Human Head', Elk people. In at least three subgentes: 1. *Tʰe-sį́de-itàži*, Touches no Buffalo Tails. 2. *Tʰe-đéze-đatàži*, Eats no Buffalo Tongues. 3. *Táxte-Ki-ąpa-đatàži*, Eats no Deer or Elk.
>
> *Wažáže* half-tribe.—Earth phratry: Gens 5. *Maką́*, Medicine, a buffalo gens, also called *Tʰe-šį́de-itàži*, Touch no Buffalo Tails. In two subgentes: 1. *Pą́kaxtì*, Real Ponkas, Keepers of a Sacred Pipe. 2. *Pą́ka-xúde*, Gray Ponkas. Gens 6. *Wađábe*, Dark Buffalo. In two subgentes: 1. *Tʰe-sį́de*, Buffalo Tail, *Tʰe-đéze-đatàži*, Eat no Buffalo Tongues, and *Tʰe-žį́ga-đatàži*, Eat no very young Buffalo Calves. 2. *Tʰe-pá-itàži*, Touch no Buffalo Heads.
>
> *Wažáže* half-tribe.—Water Phratry (?): Gens 7. *Wažáže*, Osage. In two subgentes at present: 1. *Wažáže sàbe*, Dark Osage, Keepers of a Sacred Pipe, or *Wasétu-itàži*, Does not Touch Verdigris, or *Nágđe-itàži*, Does not Touch Charcoal. 2. *Wažaže-xude*, Gray Osage, or *Wesá-wetàži*, Do not Touch Snakes. 3. *Necta*, an Owl subgens, is now extinct. Gens 8. *Núxe*, Reddish-yellow Buffalo (miscalled *Núxe*, ice). Subgentes uncertain; but there are four taboo names; *Tʰe-pá-itàži*, Does not Touch a Buffalo Head; *Tʰe-žį́ga-itàži*, Does not Touch the Yellow Hide of a Buffalo Calf; and *Tʰe-đéze-đatàži*, Does not Eat Buffalo Tongues.

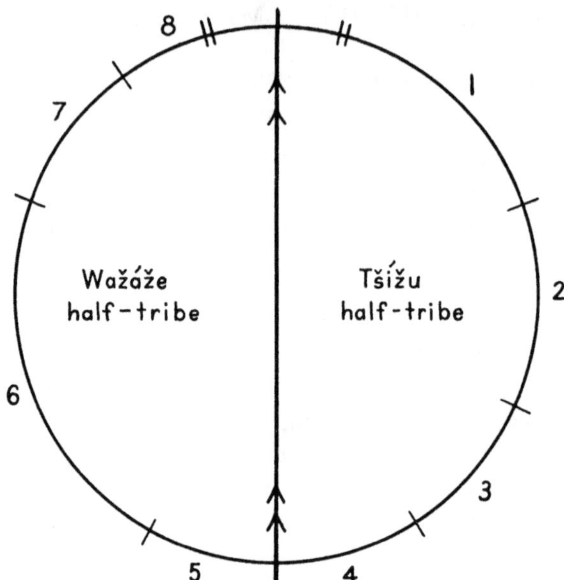

Fletcher and La Flesche (1911, pp. 41–42) write as follows:

There are seven gentes in the Ponca tribe, namely: *Wađábe, Điхida, Níkapàšna, Pǫ̀kaxtì, Wašábe, Wažáže,* and *Núxe.* These camped in the order indicated in the diagram . . ., beginning on the southern side of the eastern entrance of the tribal circle, to which the Ponca give the name *húđuga,* the word used by the Omaha also to designate their tribal circle.

1. *Wađábe,* Black Bear. Subgentes: (a) *Wađábe* (b) *Híđada* (stretched, referring to the stretch of the legs in running); . . . 2. *Điхida,* Meaning lost. Subgentes:

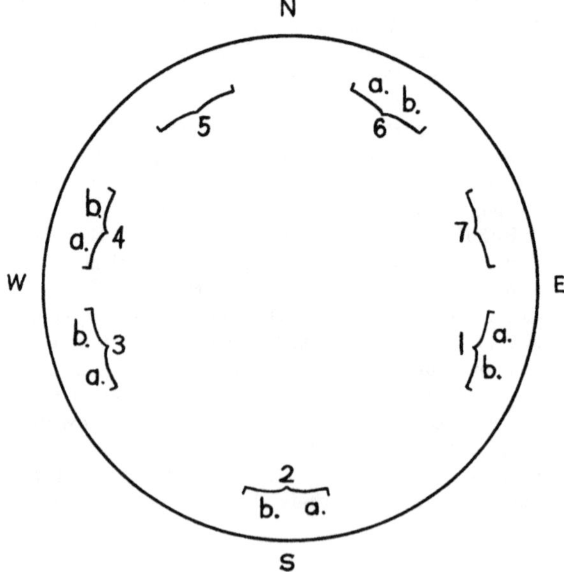

(a) *Đíxida*; . . . (b) *Įgdǫdį-dnèdeweti* (*Įgdǫdįdnède*, puma; *weti*, to dwell in); . . . 3. *Níkapàšna*, A man's skull. Subgentes (a) *Tʰáhatǫ-itàži* (*tʰa*, deer, *ha*, skin, *tǫ*, possess, *itàzi*, do not touch) . . . (b) *Tʰédįdeitàži* (*the*, buffalo, *dįde*, tail, *itàži*, do not touch); . . . 4. *Pǫkaxtì*: Real or original Ponca Subgentes: (*a*) *Pǫ́kaxti*; (*b*) Mą́ką́ (mystery or medicine). 5. *Wašábe*, a dark object, as seen against the horizon; . . . 6. *Wažáže*, an old term. Subgentes: (a) *Wažáže* (real *Wažáže*); name said to refer to the snake after shedding circle, old skin and again in full power. (b) *Wažážexùde* (gray *Wažáže*); refers to the grayish appearance of the snake's cast off skin; . . . 7.*Núxe*, Ice; . . .

Alanson Skinner (1915 c, p. 799) collected the following list of Ponca clans:

1. *Đíxida* (Do not touch blood)
2. *Wažáže* (Osage)
3. *Maką́* (Medicine)
4. *Núxe* (Ice)
5. *Níkapàšna* (?)
6. *Hísada* (Straight legs)
7. *Wasábe* (Black Bear)

He could learn of no subclans.

The list of clans which I secured, together with some of the clan duties and taboos, is as follows: There were seven clans, not counting the *Wá·ge-žįga* (Sons of White men clan). Starting with the clan at your left, as you entered the camp circle from the east, and proceeding clockwise around the circle, they were as follows:

1. *Wažáže* (Snake or Osage). This clan guarded the entrance to the *húduga*. They were reputed to be expert trackers. If a party left the village and did not return within a reasonable length of time, trackers from this clan were dispatched to search for them. Touching snakes was taboo to members of this clan. According to OYB the clan was divided into two subclans (*a*) *Wažážextì* (real *Wažáže*) and (*b*) *Wažážexùde* (gray *Wažáže*).

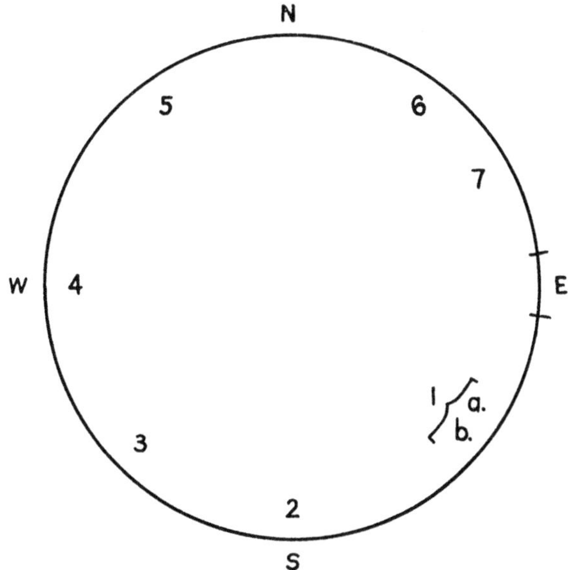

2. *Níkapàšna* (A skull or a bald head). Members of this clan were reputed to know "all about the human head," and as possessors of this knowledge were the tribal barbers and hairdressers. They also cured headaches. It was taboo for members of this clan to touch buckskin.

3. *Đíxida* (Blood). This clan performed imitative magic when the tribe was unsuccessful in finding game. They pointed their arrows and pretended to shoot some animal, saying at the same time "I'll shoot this fat one!" The *Đíxida* clan also officiated at the ceremony of installation of chiefs. It was taboo for members of this clan to touch either human blood or mice.

4. *Wašábe* (Meaning not known to my informants). The principal chief of the tribe was always selected from this clan. Members were forbidden to touch the head of any animal, since they were of the "head" (i.e., chiefly) clan.

5. *Makǫ́* (Medicine). This clan was reputed to contain the best herbalists in the tribe.

6. *Núxe* (Ice). Members of this clan "knew all about water and ice" (PLC). PLC told how the Northern Ponca chief White-shirt, a member of this clan, was able to cross Ponca Creek on thin ice because of his special clan knowledge of the properties of water and ice.

7. *Hísada* (The stretching of a bird's leg when running). PLC called this clan the most important because its members were the tribal rainmakers. The rain-making ceremony of this clan is described on page 75.

8. *Wá·ge-žįga* (White men's sons). This eighth clan was added to the list by LMD, who stated that he was a member of it and that it had been founded to accommodate the sons of White traders who took Ponca wives. Like the other Ponca clans, it was exogamous, although it had no clan rites or prerogatives. One of its taboos was the same as a taboo of the *Đíxida* clan, not to touch mice. If a member of either of these clans touched a mouse his hair would turn gray. This clan may very possibly be the *Waga* clan of Morgan (see p. 87).

OYB recounted an interesting legend to explain why the *Wažáže* clan is divided into two subdivisions. According to this legend the members of the clan were once conducting a tattooing ceremony. The hereditary chief of the clan, who was conducting the rite, had finished tattooing half of the members when an eagle flew out of the sky and, in spite of a fusillade of arrows, entered the lodge and blinded the chief by scratching his eyes out. The ceremony was thereupon discontinued. The members of the clan who had been tattooed before this event thenceforth called themselves *Wažážextì* (real or "complete" *Wažáže*) while those who had not been tattooed called themselves *Wažážexùde* (Gray *Wažáže*). This story is very interesting in that one meaning of the term *Wažáže* is apparently "snake." The powers of the air, symbolized by the thunderbird and eagle, continually wage war with the powers of evil, symbolized by the underwater panther and snake, in the mythologies of many North American Indian tribes. OYB said that formerly all of the Ponca clans had been divided into two or more subclans, but that these had been lost through time. PLC, until he heard this tale from OYB, had never heard of Ponca clans being subdivided.

Additional clan taboos, privileges, and duties, too numerous to include here, are found in the works of Dorsey (1894, pp. 381–382, 391, 411–412; 1897, pp. 214, 228–229); Fletcher (1896, p. 478); Fletcher and La Flesche (1911, pp. 42–48); Skinner (1915 c, p. 799); and Whitman (1937, p. 13). Special haircuts were given to small Ponca boys to show their clan affiliation. These are pictured by Fletcher and La Flesche (1911, pp. 42–46). Each clan likewise had a stock of names, both male and female, which belonged to it. Some of these alluded to animals important to the clan.

Clan exogamy was mentioned by all informants questioned on the subject. It still pertains to a degree, though breaches of the rule are apparently viewed with more leniency today than in the past. Even in aboriginal times intraclan liaisons took place. OK commented: "In the old days a man never married a girl from his own band (clan) . . . . Outside of marrying a girl, though, it was a different story. We have a saying in our tribe 'We are related only from the waist up.'"

Localization of clans in the permanent villages is suggested by Fletcher and La Flesche (1911, p. 51), describing the Ponca tribe as of 1874: "There were eight chiefs, each of whom had his 'band.' These bands were probably composed of persons from the gens or subgens to which the chief belonged." Such clan localization was not known to any of my informants, though they did state that each clan had a hereditary chief. There is certainly no clan localization among the Ponca at present, but it is said to occur among the Omaha.

Ponca government was of the very weak type which has sometimes been termed "tribal." Decisions were made by a council of chiefs, and enforced by a group called the "Buffalo-police" (because their period of greatest activity came during the tribal hunts). The chiefs attempted to act, at all times, in complete accordance with public opinion. Lengthy councils were held in which the head chief attempted to "feel out" each of the other leaders before proposing a course of action. Complete, or nearly complete, unanimity was necessary before any action would be taken. A chief who attempted to initiate a program without nearly unanimous backing, though he might not be challenged in the council, soon found himself without support.

White traders and explorers, accustomed to the hierarchical structure and "chain of command" of Western European government, found the Indian procedures hard to understand. Military men, in particular, were disgusted. James (1905 a, vol. 14, p. 313), writing of the Missouri tribes in general, states: "The Indian form of government is not sufficiently powerful to restrain the young warriors from the commission of many excesses and outrages, which continually involve the nations in protracted wars . . . ."

Even the Indians themselves realized that the usual lengthy deliberations were not appropriate during the tribal hunt. Here, decisions must be made and carried out swiftly, lest the entire tribe starve. Therefore, an almost dictatorial authority was temporarily invested in a single man for the duration of the hunt. This man, called the *Nudą́-hǫ̀ga*, which might be translated 'honored captain,' was in complete charge during his term of office. He could inflict severe punishments, even banishment from the tribe, upon persons who defied his rulings and thus imperiled the general welfare. Once the tribe had returned to its permanent villages, however, he became just an "ordinary citizen" again.

There were two principal classes of chiefs among the Ponca, the "big" chiefs, or chiefs of the first rank, and the "little" chiefs, or chiefs of the second rank. Persons selected for chieftainship in either of these groups were generally renowned warriors and statesmen, as well as members of "chiefly" clans. "Big" chiefs were generally older men who had served as "little" chiefs for a number of years and who, almost invariably, were the descendants of previous chiefs of the first rank in the male line.

The head chief of the tribe was the ranking chief of the "big" chief group. He was always of the *Wašábe* clan, the leading clan of the tribe. As custodian of the sacred tribal pipe he possessed religious as well as political authority, a situation strongly reminiscent of the priest-chiefs of the Southeast. He functioned as the chairman at council meetings, and installed all newly created chiefs.

Chiefs of the first and second ranks guided the tribe in peace and defensive warfare. They were also the religious leaders of the tribe. They convened in a special lodge pitched in the center of the *hú𝑑uga* to council and pray for the welfare of the people. According to PLC, LMD, LRL, AMC, David Little-cook, and David Eagle, there were seven chiefs of the first rank and seven of the second. Whitman (1937, p. 17) also gives seven as the number of Ponca chiefs. JLR and EBC, however, firmly denied this and insisted that the number in each group was 12. Fletcher and La Flesche (1911, p. 51) mention eight Ponca chiefs as of 1874, but it is not clear whether they mean tribal or clan chiefs. Each chief carried a pipe and a pipe bag as a symbol of his rank and wore, on ceremonial occasions, an otter-skin cap with a downy eagle plume erect in a socket at the back.

A third class of chiefs, apparently corresponding somewhat to the "pine tree" chiefs of the Iroquois, was mentioned by JLR. These men were called *Itúžpa* (literally "grandchildren"). They were successful warriors who had demonstrated that they were "not just interested in themselves, but in the tribe as a whole."

Not included in the above scheme were the clan chiefs. Each of the seven Ponca clans had a hereditary chief whose authority extended only to members of his own clan. A chief of the first, second, or third rank, however, might also be a clan chief.

A meeting of the "council of seven," that is, the "big chiefs," was sufficient to decide upon most matters. For more important business the "little chiefs" were called in as well. For really important affairs the *Itúžpa* and warriors were also admitted. JLR stated that the chiefs of the first rank often left minor matters to the "little chiefs." He also mentioned that many, if not all, of the chiefs of the first two ranks were assigned a special duty. One of the chiefs of the second rank, for example, was the tribal historian, and kept the tribal winter count or calendrical history.

Chiefs were expected to be circumspect in their behavior and to hold themselves above the passions of the ordinary people. They must not seek wealth, lest they be termed stingy. Neither must they invite reprisal by leading or even accompanying private war parties. Dorsey (1897, p. 214) writes: ". . . among both the Omaha and the Ponka the chiefs, being the civil and religious leaders of the people, can not serve as captains, or even as members, of an ordinary war party, though they may fight when the whole tribe engages in war."

Succession was apparently governed by both personal leadership qualities and by "noble descent." PLC said that: "Any man could become a chief if he was brave and generous. Usually, though, the son of a chief took his father's place when the old man died. If a chief was unworthy someone else took his place. He was put out." A man not from a chiefly line, of course, had a considerably harder time becoming a chief. Thus Skinner (1915 c, p. 783; author's italics) writes: "It was necessary for a person *not an hereditary chief* who was socially ambitious, and hoped for a chieftaincy, to join most if not all of the societies, preferably as a leader, and thus become known. He must feast them and lavish gifts on every one."

Theoretically, however, any man could aspire to all but the head chief's position, which always remained in the *Wašábe* clan. Unfortunately, we have no data to indicate how frequently men not of the high-ranking clans achieved high position in the tribe. According to PLC even women were not barred, and he recalled having heard of a great woman chief who led the tribe in the distant past. "She was made a chief because of her great supernatural power. She was a medicine woman and could do many good things."

Chiefs were installed in a solemn ceremony presided over by the head chief and conducted by the *Đíxida* clan. OK recalled the last chief-making ceremony of the Northern Ponca, in which he was created a chief of the second rank, as follows:

I remember the last time old man Birdhead made chiefs. I was made a chief that day, and I guess I am the only one left alive who was made a chief that time. The ceremony was held in a tipi. We all entered and went around to the left [in a clockwise direction] and took our seats. Then Birdhead, who owned the pipe and was head chief, made a speech. He told us that when we were chiefs we should always do good, and help the others in the tribe. Then the pipe was started around from the door, which was to the east, going around to the left. Each man took three puffs and then passed the pipe on to his neighbors. Prayers were interspersed with the smoking of the pipe. When the pipe got clear around to the door it was passed back around the way it had come. It was never passed over the doorway.

The head chief is the man who owns the pipe, and he is the only one who can make chiefs. He keeps the pipe wrapped up all the time except when it is taken out to be smoked. No man is a chief until he has smoked the sacred pipe. The right to the head chieftainship descends from father to son, and the pipe is passed along this way.

OK's account of the chief-making rite agrees quite well with that given by Dorsey (1884 a, pp. 359–360), but is much simpler. In OK's time the Ponca "tribal" pipe, together with the tribal chieftainship, had been removed to Oklahoma. Birdhead, the chief referred to in the account, was the last chief of the first rank in the Northern band, and as such, ranked as head chief of the Northern Ponca (pl. 21, *d*). The pipe he used was a clan pipe, which, by virtue of its being the only one in the north, had come to be regarded as the tribal pipe. The Ponca tribal pipe, as I learned in 1954, is still kept by Mrs. Grace Warrior, who lives near Ponca City, Okla.

In the southern band the last first rank chief was Horse-chief-eagle. His eldest son, David Eagle, would be the present chief if the former political system had survived. OK, as he indicates, was the last "little chief" in the northern band. Leslie Red-leaf, who died in 1955, was the last second-rank chief in the south. At the present time chiefs no longer govern the Ponca. In both bands a tribal council, whose members are elected by popular ballot, decides upon questions relating to the tribe. For several years Perry Le Claire, of Ponca City, has ably served as chairman of the Southern Ponca tribal council.

The tribal Buffalo-police or *Thé-wanǫ̀še* were the executors of the wishes of the chiefs. Each chief apparently had one or two of these policemen at his beck and call the year around. For special occasions, however, such as the tribal bison hunts or the Sun dance, additional police were recruited. Skinner (1915 c, pp. 794–795) writes: "As police . . . for any occasion the chief would appoint the bravest warriors of some society, but not the whole organization. For another occasion he would take men from another society." The duties of the tribal police on the bison hunt are described by PLC in his "History" (p. 19) and by Skinner (1915 c, pp. 796–797). In 1954 LMD and Charles Gives-water were the only Buffalo-police left in the Ponca tribe.

Being a chief or policeman in a small, highly interrelated tribe such as the Ponca was not easy, for right or wrong, the actions of these men were liable to earn them the ill will of not only the persons directly involved, but the clansmen of all those persons as well. No wonder, then, that chiefs hesitated to punish unruly young warriors.

Provinse, a student of Plains Indian government, has commented upon the subject as follows:

> Characteristic of Plains justice is the order-preserving nature of police activity as opposed to the idea of punishment for the sake of social vengeance. This is more clearly brought out by the attitude of the society toward the offender after punishment has been inflicted upon him. Conformity, not revenge was sought, and immediately after a promise to conform was secured from the delinquent steps were taken to reincorporate him into the society. [Provinse, 1937, p. 350.]

Provinse's remarks here concern the Plains tribes in general, but are particularly relevant to the Ponca. My informants stated that often after the Buffalo-police had whipped a man for violating the rule against individual hunting during the tribal bison hunt, they would give him gifts so that "his heart would not be bad." After all, on the next hunt this offender, or one of his clansmen, might be a policeman. That the notion of "reincorporating" the offender into society still survives to a remarkable extent among present-day Ponca, I learned from several chance remarks of my informants.

Provinse (1937, pp. 352–355) also notes the powerful force of public opinion toward social conformity among the Plains tribes. This, I would venture to state, is largely true of all tribal groups. To be spurned by one's tribesmen was a dreadful experience for the Ponca man or woman. Accounts of the public ridicule of leaders of unsuccessful war parties and the subsequent degradation of these men were secured from PLC, JLR, and OK.

Religious sanctions likewise acted as a powerful deterrent to illegal acts. Ponca beliefs regarding a murderer, recorded by Dorsey (1894, p. 420), include: ". . . he can never satisfy his hunger, though he eat much food; . . . ." JLR knew of this belief as well. OK cited the case of an Omaha Indian who, when given the wand or "pipe" to dance with in the *Wà-wą* ceremony, held it carelessly to show his disrespect for the proceedings, and was later killed by lightning.

As mentioned earlier, infractions of the customary tribal law were punished by the Buffalo-police. Provinse (1937, p. 351) summarizes this police function as follows: ". . . this was invoked most frequently and rigorously for the following purposes: (1) to regulate the communal hunt; (2) to regulate ceremonies; (3) to settle disputes, punish offenders, and preserve order in camp; and (4) to regulate war parties and restrain such at inopportune times." Though writing of the Plains tribes in general, Provinse's remarks need no qualification in their application to the Ponca.

When murder was committed, retaliation was left to the relatives of the murdered individual (Dorsey, 1897, p. 226). Fletcher and La Flesche (1911, p. 216) record the case of a Ponca who accidentally killed another man. His punishment was entrusted to the father of the deceased, who decreed that the offender be banished from the tribe for a period of 4 years. In connection with this tale these writers (ibid.) record the belief that the spirit of a murdered man would come back and spoil hunting parties by scaring off game. JLR mentioned this as well, and told of one such instance in which the murderer, desperate because the ghost had scared away all the game for several days, finally shot the specter with his rifle and was thereafter freed of it. This instance illustrates quite well the importance of supernatural sanctions in Ponca law.

The punishment of an adulterer was left to the injured husband. Skinner (1915 c, pp. 800–801) notes that: "A Ponca might kill, scalp, or cut the hair off a man whom he caught holding clandestine intercourse with his wife. A wife could kill another woman with whom her husband eloped. A husband could cut off the nose and ears of an unfaithful wife. Blood vengeance could not be exacted for these crimes."

At the present time the Northern and Southern Ponca are governed by the laws of the States in which they reside: Nebraska and South Dakota, the home of the Northern Ponca; Oklahoma, the home of the Southern band. In both areas I heard praise of the Ponca as "decent, law-abiding citizens" by local Whites, a rather rare situation for a minority group. There are, of course, a few delinquents, and one Southern Ponca family has been given the sobriquet "the James boys" by other tribesmen because of their reputation for petty thievery. The most common jail offense for members of either group is being "drunk and disorderly."

Concerning property among the Ponca, PLC commented:

> All of the property of the Poncas belonged to either families, individuals, or the tribe as a whole. Our community building belongs to the tribe as a whole. Individual property would be things like a man's gun, or his clothes. People would have to ask him if they wanted to use his stuff. The tent or house belonged to the family. If a member of the family left he lost his rights to the house. If a man left his wife, she kept the tipi. If she leaves him and runs off with another man, he keeps it.
>
> Anyone who stole property from someone else was whipped by the Buffalo-police.
>
> When a person died, some of his property would be given away to friends and relatives, but not all of it. Most of it would be kept by the husband or wife.

This last statement of PLC is at variance with Dorsey (1894, p. 374), who indicates that the Ponca practiced the complete "Give-away" at death. Perhaps PLC's statement reflects the usage of a later period in Ponca history, that of PLC's own lifetime.

According to PLC, ownership of the land rested with the tribe, and crops were worked and shared communally. JLR, however, stated that when the Mormon immigrants entered the Ponca country the tribe as a whole gave them the use of certain lands which were reserved by a clan then absent. When this clan returned, the Mormon pioneers were forced to vacate. This procedure seems to indicate that although the land was *owned* by the tribe, the rights of usufruct were distributed according to clan, and that certain clans, with the passage of time, had become identified with specific areas.

Property in movables was often identified by both clan and individual markings. Fletcher and La Flesche (1911, p. 42) write: "It was a custom in the Ponca tribe for each gens to have its peculiar manner of marking arrows, so there should be no dispute in hunting as to the gens to which a fatal arrow belonged. This mark, however, did not exclude or interfere with a man's private mark."

Certain incorporeal property was also "owned" by the clan and the individual. Each clan possessed, in addition to its clan ceremonies and traditional prerogatives, several personal names which often referred to the clan animals or clan taboos. These names were, in effect, "loaned" to individual clan members for their lifetime, but remained the "property" of the clan. When the holder of a certain clan name died, his name reverted to the clan "name pool," and could then be assigned to a newborn infant, not necessarily of the deceased man's family. The clan names thus became, in a sense, titles. It was usually possible to tell the clan affiliation of a Ponca by the name he bore, though the custom of "trading names" with other tribes, such as the Omaha and Dakota, provided a certain number of names which had no clan reference.

The esoteric knowledge of shamans and members of the various secret societies was also their personal property. If the owner wished to sell this information he might do so, though the price was usually high. Skinner (1920, p. 307) writes that members of the Ponca Medicine Lodge might pass on their knowledge, by purchase, to their eldest son or nearest relative. Otherwise these persons must purchase their memberships from the four leaders of the society at a much higher cost. The songs of these secret societies were also regarded as personal possessions of the members, and must be paid for should one desire to learn them. If a person learned such a song by simply overhearing it, and then proceeded to sing it himself without paying for it, he would be inviting bad luck.

At the present time many individual peyotists have their own personal songs, but these are free for anyone who wishes to learn them. The song may be referred to, however, as "so-and-so's song" if the composer who "made" the song is remembered. Songs of the *Hedúška* society are considered tribal property at present, and a young Ponca complained to the writer that the Kiowa were "great song thieves" because they have appropriated many Ponca songs and use them at their own gatherings. The same complaint was made of the

Winnebago. The Ponca also have "individual" *Hedúška* songs. When such a song is sung at a powwow, the man so honored, and his family, "give-away" to the singers and honored guests.

It was interesting to me to learn that the older Ponca have a strong interest in ethics. The following code of ethics was secured from PLC, and a slightly different one is found in his "History" (p. 19).

The Poncas have only seven little rules to follow. These are:

1. Have one God.
2. Respect the sacred pipe.
3. Be good to one another.
4. Do not talk about one another.
5. Be good to the old people.
6. Do not steal.
7. Do not kill.

To what extent this code of ethics reflects missionary teachings we cannot say. The rules certainly demonstrate the high value which the Ponca placed upon intragroup loyalty and cooperation. PLC also provided the following set of rules relating to the behavior of clan chiefs, and presumably applicable to the tribal chiefs of the first and second ranks as well:

1. Be good to the old.
2. Be good to orphans.
3. Be good to the needy.

This system clearly shows the function of the chief as a "provider" for his clan particularly, as in the case of orphans, of those not provided with close relatives willing to attend to their needs.

Ponca informants during the past 100 years have consistently combined ethics with religion. Since there was apparently little connection between religion and morality in many American Indian tribes, the Ponca are a bit unusual in this respect. Again, however, it is possible that much of this is due to missionary influences during the 19th century, though the Ponca deny this is true. At any rate Skinner (1920, p. 307) notes that: "The candidates [for the Pebble Medicine Lodge society] were instructed how to do things, and to live good lives." Likewise, Whitman (1939, pp. 190–191) tells of WBB's uncle lecturing him on the fact that if he leads a dissolute life he will later repent it: "What you have done is going to come back on you one by one. That is the time you are going to cry." I secured the same information from WBB 15 years later. Whatever the sources, it is clear that during the past century Ponca ideas of ethics and morality closely approximated those of the major culture.

OK stated that the women who were tattooed by the Night-dance society were supposed to be models of virtue and kindness thereafter, but that in later years they did not live up to this rule and were "too proud." Most of them, therefore, "came to a bad end, one way or another."

RELIGION, DANCES AND CEREMONIES, AND GAMES

An excellent summary of the basic religious attitudes of the Ponca was provided by PLC, who, when questioned on the subject, replied as follows:

> The Ponca religion is quite a simple one. We believe in only one God, and that is *Wakánda*. He tries to help us all of the time. We have a saying "*Wakánda-įdàdi bdogą́ gáxe.*" This means 'God our father has made everything.' A Ponca knows this and remembers it all of the time.
>
> The Poncas give thanks to God in their different ceremonies and religious worships. In the Sun dance, the *Wá-wą*, the *Hedúška*, the Peyote church, or in the Christian church, it is all the same God that we pray to and thank.
>
> *Wakánda-péži* is the same as the Devil to the Poncas. He is the bad god, and seeks to lead men into evil ways. There are other spirits or demons, but there is only one real God.
>
> After we die, we go to heaven. This is *Mą́gatà* in Ponca, and a man may say, just before he dies "I am going under the ground but I will be above you." This means that he believes that he will go to heaven.
>
> The chiefs were the main religious leaders among the Poncas in former days. They did the praying for the tribe.

PLC's statement, recorded in 1949, echoes information collected by J. O. Dorsey (1894, p. 366) half a century earlier. Dorsey writes: "In the *Đégiha*, the language spoken by the Ponca and Omaha, *Wakánda* means 'the mysterious' or 'powerful one,' and it is applied in several senses. It is now used to denote the God of monotheism. Some of the old people say that their ancestors always believed in a supreme *Wakánda* or Mysterious Power." In the same work Dorsey mentions *Wakánda-péži*, and says that the term was used for Satan after the Ponca had learned of him from the Whites (ibid., p. 371).

The Ponca conception of the supernatural might best be described as animatistic. Places, objects, and persons were considered *xúbe* or supernaturally powerful in various degrees. Whitman (1939, p. 180) writes: "*Xúbe* is the Ponca term for supernatural power. Anything animate or inanimate which is thought to possess supernatural power is said to be *xúbe*, and any man or woman who is thought to be able to control this supernatural power is said to be a *xúbe*."

Usually a Ponca boy secured his first *xúbe* on the vision quest, which took place at the age of puberty. With his face darkened with charcoal so that all would recognize his holy errand, he would go to some isolated hilltop to fast and pray for 4 days and nights, visited only by some older man who brought him a little broth and water after dark. If he were arduous and a bit lucky besides, the spirit of some bird or animal would appear to him and grant him power. Later, if he were both devout and lucky he might acquire more *xúbe* by fasting and praying, either in a vision quest or publicly in the Sun dance. *Xúbe* could also be bought and sold in the form of medicine packets.

The vision quest is no longer practiced and there has been a gradual erosion of belief in *xúbe* during the past 50 years. There are still many stories concerning it, however. PLC stated that when he was small he avoided the house of Shaky, a famous Northern Ponca shaman, because of this man's *xúbe*, and in his autobiography (1961, p. 18) he mentions his fear of the power of an old Dakota medicine woman who was *xúbe* from a mole.

Formerly this *xúbe* or medicine power was stored in medicine packets and sacred bundles. Medicine packets were generally individually owned and contained some small object or group of objects relating to the owner's vision, such as feathers from a bird, the skin or claws of an animal, or the powdered roots of plants. Bundles were usually larger in size, and made up of several such medicines, larger bird or animal skins, and the musical instruments and regalia used at the feast when the bundle was opened. Bundles were usually the property of a clan, a society, or even, as with the tribal pipe, of the tribe as a whole. There were, however, bundles which were individually owned.

Several types of bundles were used by the Ponca. Some related to war. These generally contained birdskins to which scalps were attached. They were carried by the leader of the war party, to be opened when the group was about to attack the enemy. Others related to hunting. Still others were used in curing the sick, and contained many herb simples. Some of the bundles of the Medicine Lodge society were employed to work black magic against the enemies of the owners. Formerly, sacred bundles were opened at least once a year, their contents ceremonially displayed and fumigated in cedar smoke, and their wrappings repaired or replaced. Such a bundle ceremony is described in Whitman's "*Xúbe*" (1939, pp. 180–181).

Bundles were usually hung in a safe place at the back of the tipi or earth lodge during the winter. In summer they were hung outside at least part of the time if the weather was good, but were removed indoors if it began to rain. When the tribe was on the move each bundle was transported on a separate horse, ridden by a young boy who had never had intercourse with a woman. The boy's job was to see that the bundle never touched the ground.

At the present time most of the old Ponca bundles are either in large eastern museums or have been buried with their keepers. However, there is still at least one bundle among the Southern Ponca. It is kept by Parrish Williams, who inherited it, as the eldest son in the family, from his father. Parrish, like most present-day Ponca, has an exaggerated dread of bundles. He has never opened the bundle, for fear of its power, and was loath to discuss it with me. John Williams, a younger son, was more cooperative, and commented that the bundle had been used in both hunting and war. After each successful employment of it, according to Williams, another piece was added to its contents. For example, after a successful hunt a buffalo tail might be added; after a war party, a scalp. He also believed that mescal beans were a part of the bundle's contents. The significance of these beans to the Ponca is discussed later in this chapter (pp. 121–124).

The Williams bundle, when I saw it in 1954, was kept on a specially constructed shelf in the Parrish Williams residence. It measured approximately 2 feet in length by 1 foot in thickness and was wrapped in a tanned animal hide secured with thick hide thongs. Several large gourd rattles tied to the outside undoubtedly provided rhythmic accompaniment to the ritual songs which were sung when the bundle was opened.

There are no longer any sacred bundles among the Northern Ponca. OK, JLR, and PLC all mentioned, however, that the late chief Whiteshirt kept a "pelican" (skin and head) which he used to "doctor" people. From the description of its use, it is evident that this was a personal doctoring bundle. OK, who was "doctored" with this bundle, described the ritual as follows:

> Once I asked old man Whiteshirt to come over and sing for me. I gave him something to eat and after we had finished he went to work. He had one of those big gourds and he shook it while he sang. After he sang a while he took up his pelican and began to hit me with the beak in different places on the body. It hurt! I hadn't figured on this. I just wanted to hear him sing.

PLC mentioned that Whiteshirt often wore a warbonnet made of pelican feathers to show his source of power (probably made of the wing feathers of the same bird as his "bundle"). He is shown wearing this bonnet in plate 21, *d*. George Phillips, an Omaha Indian, recalled that Whiteshirt used to bring his "pelican" to Peyote meetings when he was visiting on the Omaha reservation. When he sang he held the bird upside down, holding the tail feathers extended like Peyote "feathers." The Omaha peyotists were highly amused at this, partly because "medicine ways" (i.e., the Medicine Lodge and the animal cults) are not supposed to be mixed with the Peyote religion among the Omaha and Ponca, and partly because the pelican's tail was ridiculously short in comparison with the tails of other birds more commonly used for peyote "feathers."

PLC described another medicine bundle, used by the late Northern Ponca chief Broken-jaw. It consisted of a muskrat skin and a short, flat-ended, wooden paddle. In his curing rite Broken-jaw would first hold the muskrat skin, nose forward, to different parts of the patient's body. When he came to the part of the body where the malignancy rested, the muskrat skin would begin to quiver. Having completed his diagnosis, Broken-jaw would lay the skin aside, take up his paddle, and jab the patient with it in the area indicated. This would, ap-

718-071—65——8

parently, dislodge the foreign matter, which would pass out of the patient's body through the bowels and effect the cure. One hopes that none of Broken-jaw's patients was afflicted with appendicitis! In 1956 PLC made a copy of Broken-jaw's bundle and presented it to the Nebraska State Historical Society Museum in Lincoln.

The tribal pipe of the Ponca is considered the most powerful bundle. It is kept, at present, by Mrs. Grace Warrior (nee Standing-buffalo), a Southern Ponca. Ordinarily it is kept in a special room, reserved for this purpose, in the Warrior home. Because of the *xúbe* inherent in the bundle, this room is said to be continually foggy or hazy (Clyde Warrior). The pipe is, or at any rate should be, hung above the door of a special tipi during the annual Southern Ponca powwow, held in late August. Clan pipes, likewise, were held sacred, and Birdhead's clan pipe, which functioned for many years as the "tribal" pipe of the Northern Ponca, was treated with the utmost respect by PLC when he opened the bundle containing it for the University of Nebraska State Museum in 1951. Marvellously enough, just as PLC untied the wrappings of the bundle, there was a loud peal of thunder, although the day had been clear until that moment!

While on the subject of bundles, one should note in passing that while bundles and their attendant ceremonies are largely a thing of the past to present-day Ponca, the carved and painted boxes which contain the articles used in the Peyote rite are treated much as bundles were in the past. Likewise the "feathers" used in the rite are endowed with greater or lesser amounts of *waxúbe* or "power." Among the most powerful feathers are the scissortail flycatcher, "waterbird" (*Anhinga anhinga*), eagle, and flicker. Pheasant feathers, though attractive, have less power. The feathers of the owl are usually avoided, as their use marks the owner as a shaman.

Much of Ponca religion centered about various dances and ceremonies. The importance of such activity in Prairie and Plains Indian life has, in my opinion, been greatly underestimated by American anthropologists. This is probably due to the fact that both have become relatively unimportant in contemporary American culture. Thus, many ethnographers, while going into great detail concerning the political, social, legal, and economic systems of a particular group, gloss over the ceremonial life of the people in a few paragraphs. Yet ceremonial activity and dancing occupied most of a Plains Indian's spare time. Probably a third or more of a 19th-century Ponca's year was taken up preparing for or participating in such activity, and even today such activity looms large for many adult Southern Ponca.

In his Ponca "History" (pp. 19–21), PLC describes what are, to him, the three major Ponca ceremonials. These are the Sun dance, *Wá-wą* or Pipe dance, and *Hedúška* or "War" dance.

Concerning the Sun dance, George A. Dorsey states: "The name the Poncas give to the Sun Dance ceremony is Sun-Seeing dance; that is, the sun is a witness to the dance." This is from his monograph, "The Ponca Sun Dance," undoubtedly the most complete description of the rites (1905, p. 69). Readers interested in the many facets of this elaborate ceremony are directed to this work, a step-by-step account of one of the last Southern Ponca performances.

In his "History" (p. 19) PLC briefly characterizes the dance as follows:

> They have the Sun dance in midsummer when the corn is in silk. The dance lasts four days and four nights without drink, sleep, and without food, a real sacrifice. The dancers are in the shape of a wheel or representing the four winds they would swing every so often.

In an interview PLC commented further:

> The dancers are attached to the pole at the center with rawhide ropes, which are threaded through a gash in their breast. They swing on these ropes every now and then, trying to break the flesh. When they break the flesh they are finished dancing.
>
> The Sun dance is the biggest and most sacred ceremony of the Ponca. The Poncas used to have it when they were camped together as one tribe. Later, when the tribe split up, the Southern band still kept up the Sun dance. Some of the Northern Poncas would go down for it, because we are all one tribe.

Choreographically the Sun dance is quite simple. Dancers merely danced in place with a toe-heel step, gazing at the "thunderbird's nest," a bunch of boughs tied in the crotch of the center pole, and piping on eagle-bone whistles all the while. Occasionally a group of dancers, under the direction of their personal priest, would slowly dance toward the center pole a few feet and then retreat, maintaining a rough rank or line while doing so. Dancers equipped with "offering objects" such as sage wrapped hoops (emblematic of the universe) or cloth banners would hold them aloft, extended toward the "thunderbird's nest." These features of the dance are well illustrated in the plates which accompany Dorsey's monograph (1905); also in the old print of the dance reproduced in the present volume (pl. 17, *a*).

G. A. Dorsey obtained the following symbolic interpretation of the dance from Chief White-eagle (pl. 11), a longtime Sun dance priest:

> The lodge itself is typical of the circle of tipis overhead. The centre-pole seems to be symbolic of a man, an enemy, conceived of as naked, that the Great Medicine may see him. It is also conceived of as firewood, being of willow, which is said to be hard to kill and of a clean nature. In the fork of the pole is the nest of the Thunder-Bird, sometimes spoken of by the Ponca as an eagle, sometimes as a brant or loon. This bird produces rain, thunder, and lightning. The altar seems to be symbolic of a fireplace; it is also spoken of as the sun, which in turn is spoken of as the chief. According to Ponca mythology, in the beginning of creation was the sun or fireplace, and at that time it contained the four colors which are found in the four tipis of preparation. Next came the buffalo bull bearing a pipe, offering himself to the people. The bull came from the interior

of the earth and brought the people the paints of the lodge. Thus the exceedingly simple altar may be said to consist of the fireplace, or sun, the buffalo, and finally of the sage, which is symbolic of the people. [Dorsey, 1905, pp. 87–88.]

This interpretation of Sun dance symbolism, though it reveals many important Ponca concepts, fails to assign any overall symbolism to the rites. Nor could any of my informants do this, even those who had taken part in the dance. The true symbolism of the dance, it seems, has been lost by the Ponca and must be sought among other tribes which practiced the rites. Perhaps the most logical of the many interpretations of the Prairie-Plains Sun dance is that offered by the Assiniboin, Plains-Ojibwa, and Plains-Cree, Northern Plains groups whose performance of the dance is very similar to that of the Ponca. Their Sun dance is performed to call the thunderbird to bring rain for growing crops and to provide grass for the buffalo (or today, cattle). To induce this rainmaker to stop and "rest" in their territory a "nest" is provided for him in the fork of the Sun dance pole. The dancers are dressed to represent baby thunderbirds (i.e, naked and without plumage) and their piping on eagle-bone whistles imitates the constant chirping of nestlings.

There is much to be said for this interpretation. In addition to explaining the symbolism of the thunderbird's nest, the dancer's "naked" costume, and the whistle blowing, it also accounts for the use of willow (a tree which grows near, and is associated with, water) for the center pole and the performers' abstention from food and drink during the ceremony (i.e., they are waiting for the "mother" thunderbird to come and feed them). Perhaps the Ponca once held similar beliefs which have been lost through the passage of time, or, more likely, the Ponca adopted the form of the ceremony, without the underlying symbolism, from some other tribe, possibly the Dakota. In this connection it should be noted that the Omaha never performed the dance.

A recent Southern Ponca interpretation of the dance's meaning, interesting as an example of religious syncretism, was offered by WBB:

In the Sun dance the dancers imitate Our Lord when he was crucified. They dress in the same way he dressed, with just a wrapping around the waist. Instead of the crown of thorns we have wreaths of sage, because we are Indians. We pierce our bodies just like He was pierced when they nailed Him to the cross. The horsehair collars we sometimes wear [necklaces and bandoliers made of long red horsehair fringes] represent the blood flowing from the wounds in Our Lord's body.

G. A. Dorsey (1905, p. 88), in comparing the Ponca Sun dance with that of the Cheyenne and Arapaho, notes a few points of difference. In general, these hold true for other Plains tribes as well. He mentions that unlike the Cheyenne and Arapaho performances, the Ponca Sun dance was an annual affair, not dependent upon the vow or pledge of an individual. Neither did the dancers vow to dance or do so because they belonged to a certain warrior society. Instead, they were individually asked to participate by the priests.

The Ponca *Wá-wą* or Pipe dance is a version of the widespread Calumet ceremony. In his "History" (p. 19), PLC refers to it as "the next branch of the Sun dance." This does not indicate that there is any actual connection between the two ceremonies in PLC's mind, but merely that he would place it second in importance among the Ponca ceremonials.

In this dance the performer carries a beautiful feathered wand, fashioned like the stem of a calumet and called, in fact, a "pipe." This wand is carried in the left hand and a large gourd rattle, in the right. Waving the wand back and forth and shaking the gourd, he imitates the flight of the eagle. Whitman's description of the Ponca *Wá-wą* in "The Oto" has been termed the best in existence (1937, pp. 121–125). PLC in his "History" (pp. 19–20) gives the salient features:

> Anyone in the tribe that is needy makes a little bag of tobacco and hands it to anyone that has plenty to spare and if this man accepts this bag of tobacco the dance is given. A pipe and gourd is used. The gourd has a rattle, little stones inside it keeps time with the drum and the pipe on the left. While the dance is on, it is passed to anyone that wanted to dance with it and help give things away to the needy ones.

PLC's statement that only one pipe was used differs from the accounts of Whitman (1937, p. 282) and Skinner (1915 c, p. 789), both of whom note that two pipes were employed. James O. Dorsey (1884 a, p. 282), however, who observed the dance many years before these authors, says that the Ponca employed only one pipe. To further complicate matters, *all* of my Northern Ponca informants stated that only one pipe was used, whereas all of those in the south insisted that a minimum of two, and occasionally four, were employed.

The *Wá-wą* was extremely sacred, and involved the ceremonial "capture," adoption, and return of a person called the *hǫ́ga* or "honored one" by a ceremonial grandfather. This *hǫ́ga*, the child of the man who had accepted the gift of tobacco and who was to be honored in the ceremony, was usually a girl, though occasionally a boy. At one period in Ponca history the ceremony was used to cement peace treaties with enemy tribes. A member of an alien tribe, usually a chief or other influential person, was honored by the adoption of his child in the ceremony, and thereafter, at least in theory, labored to keep his people on terms of amity with the Ponca.

The ceremony also functioned, as PLC indicates and as Whitman notes in his account of the rite, as a means of redistributing wealth, both intratribally and intertribally. Most often the Ponca used the ceremony to secure horses from tribes which had an abundance when they were understocked, especially from the Teton Dakota.

Because the recipient of the pipe was always obliged to give the donor a large number of valuable gifts, certain unscrupulous persons, in the early reservation period, used the Pipe dance to live by the industry of others. Although in theory a man might refuse the gift of tobacco, most were in fact too proud to do so, even when they knew the donor was a rascal and they were too poor to accept. This fact was cited by EBC as one reason for the decline of the ceremony. It has not been performed since the 1890's in the Niobrara area. It persisted until about 1920 in Oklahoma. Though certain Southern Ponca talk of reviving the *Wá-wą* as a powwow attraction, it is unlikely that this will take place, as the fear of "doing something wrong" and thus incurring supernatural punishment is still strong among the older men, the only ones capable of reviving the ritual.

A very interesting fact not noted by the various writers who have discussed the Ponca *Wá-wą* is that the drum used to accompany the dance was a hollow-log water drum, of the type used by the Ojibwa and other Central Algonquian tribes in their Medicine Lodge rites. Parrish Williams, who mentioned this to me, stated that this type of drum was not used by the Ponca in any other dance or ceremony. Their use of the drum in this dance indicates either a considerable antiquity for the Ponca ceremony or that it was a more recent borrowing from some tribe in the Eastern Woodland area.

The last of the three Ponca dances which PLC considers most important is the *Hethúška* or "War" dance. In his "History" (p. 21) he writes: "The best dance is called Hay-thu-schka, known as the war dance; it is said that anyone that is not well and feeling bad and anyone that is mourning, the sound of the drum will revive them and make them happy." Skinner (1915 c, pp. 784–785), in his discussion of Ponca societies, gives an excellent description of the dance.

This dance, which was at one time merely one of several "owned" by Ponca warrior societies, was apparently borrowed from the Pawnee at an early date. It has now been a part of Ponca culture for so long, however, that they consider it their own, and even have an origin legend which explains its introduction. Skinner (ibid., p. 784) writes: "According to Charlie Collins, this society originated among the Ponca, and was founded by a woman who dreamed she went to another world where she saw Indians dancing." My own informant, Sylvester Warrior, was quite indignant when I suggested that the Ponca had borrowed the dance from some other tribe, saying: "There are too many songs in the dance which tell of Ponca being blessed by *Wakánda*."

As mentioned above, the *Hethúška* was originally a warrior's dancing society. Like other societies of this type, it had a roster of officers, including a drumkeeper, eight dance leaders, and two whip men who started each dance episode and who whipped reluctant dancers across the legs to make them get up and perform. The characteristic ornaments of the dance were the porcupine and deer-hair roach headdress and the "crow belt" or feather dance bustle. The latter was emblematic of a battlefield, and its use was restricted to certain officers of the society who were distinguished warriors. Both of these ornaments were ritually fumigated during the ceremony by holding them over a cedar needle smudge.

About 1880, with the decline of intertribal warfare, the *Hedúška* society began to take on a religious flavor. Instead of the war speeches and coup countings of the earlier dance there were long prayers for the benefit of the group by designated officials. Gift giving, rather than war honors, was the basis of admission. It was also about this time that women were admitted as dancers. Students of American ethnology will recognize this form of the dance as that which diffused from the Dakota tribe to the Central Algonquian groups as the "Dream dance" or "Drum religion." The *Hedúška* persisted in this form, in both Oklahoma and Nebraska, until about 1925, and is still retained by the Osage, who seem to have secured some of their ritual from the Ponca, as their ceremonial War dance or "Man's dance."

Today the Ponca dance has entered a third phase, which might be termed "Pan-Indian." Most of the religious elements (except for song texts) have been lost, and the dance is, for most participants and observers, merely a "big time." It is no longer the property of any organized group. Instead, any and all dancers are welcome, including visitors from other tribes. Gift giving, except for one afternoon performance, has been eliminated because it "slows down the program." The larger powwows feature specialty acts by visiting dance teams and a contest in which the prettiest Indian girl is crowned "powwow princess." There are also "championship" War dance contests for men. Costumes have become quite baroque, and the symbolism of the roach and crow belt have been forgotten.

Choreographically speaking, the *Hedúška* consists of individual dancers performing any steps they choose while circling the drum. The traditional progression around the drum was clockwise, but the Southern Ponca, as observed in 1952, 1954, 1959, and 1961 moved in a counterclockwise direction. PLC and older Southern Ponca attributed this change to the influence of Southeastern tribes, such as the Creek and Cherokee, whose dances progress in a counterclockwise direction. Many of the Ponca *Hedúška* songs refer to the exploits of Ponca heroes in the wars with the Dakota. A few have been borrowed from other tribes and some are slightly reworked versions of songs formerly used by other Ponca warrior societies, now obsolete.

Beginning in 1958 there was an attempt to revive the old *Hedúška* organization among the Ponca, and several performances of the dance in the old form have been held. Active in this revival were Sylvester Warrior and Clyde Warrior.

The annual Southern Ponca powwow, which features the *Hedúška* in its secular form, is held each year during the last week of August. It is one of the principal "Indian" events in Oklahoma, and draws large crowds. As many as three or four hundred dancers, representing a score of tribes, take part. Among the Northern Ponca the *Hedúška* has not been performed since about 1935. PLC, however, still owns a dancing costume and participates in the dances of other tribes on occasion.[38a]

Skinner (1915 c, p. 785) mentions a variant of the *Hedúška* called the *Šą́ Hedúška* or "Sioux *Hedúška*." It differed from the ordinary dance in that the performers shaved their foreheads and the sides of their heads and let their hair hang loose. This seems to represent a Ponca borrowing of the Dakota version of their own dance, for the Dakota admit that they learned the dance from the Omaha and Ponca (whom the Dakota regard as a single tribe, and call *Ómaha*). The Dakota of Pine Ridge and Rosebud Reservations still term the more formal version of their dance *Ómaha watšípi* or 'Omaha dance.' The *Šą́ Hedúška* is no longer performed by the Ponca as such, but one suspects that a great deal of the present "fancy dancing" style stems from this source.

OK and PLC both mentioned a dance called *Ohą́dize* or 'Reach-in-the-boiling-kettle.' This dance is known to the Dakota and certain other Prairie-Plains tribes as the "kettle dance." Dancers circle a pot of cooked dog meat four times, then, on a certain musical cue, the leader dips into the pot with his bare hand and arm and seizes a piece of meat. Usually this is a dog's head. PLC said that this dance was originally a part of the full *Hedúška* performance, but later evolved into a separate dance. The dance is still performed by the Teton Dakota and the Winnebago.

Another dance which was once a part of the *Hedúška* was described by PLC. It was called *Nudą́de-watšìgaxe* or "Going-to-war-dance."

First the dancers are all seated facing east. When the music begins they get up and dance forward with low, sneaky steps. After the first part of the song they go back to where they were. When the second part of the song begins they go forward again, then they go back once more. This is repeated a third time. Each time they go a little further ahead and straighten up a little more. The fourth time they break into a wild War dance, which is like the *Hedúška*. This last time the dancers move any which way, just as they please. This dance is a lot of fun. The Sioux still dance it now and then.

[38a] Since the above was written, PLC and the author, with the help of Omaha, Winnebago, and Dakota singers and dancers, staged two *Heduska* dances at the Northern Ponca Community Building (1963 and 1964). It seems unlikely that the dance will continue, however, as the Northern Ponca plan to sell the Community Building once they have been "terminated."

I have seen this dance performed on two occasions, once by the Teton Dakota at the Oglala Fair, Oglala, S. Dak., where it was called the "Sneak-up" dance, in 1960, and once by the Meskwaki at the Meskwaki powwow, near Tama, Iowa, in 1956. The announcer at the Meskwaki powwow called it the "Meskwaki dance."

The widespread Ghost dance did not reach the Ponca until about 1900, according to LMD. It came to them from the Pawnee, who had learned it from some tribe farther west.[38b] Among the Ponca there was only one leader, who was a powerful *xúbe* or shaman. He was assisted by two "prophets." Among the Ponca the dance was performed in order that the living might gain contact with deceased relatives and friends. Men and women danced in large circles, facing inward, their hands joined, in order that the "power" of the dance might pass freely from one to the other. The step was a simple step-drag to the left. The dance lasted 4 days. The first 3 days the group danced from noon until midnight, the last day from sunrise of that day until sunrise of the following day.

The leader and the two prophets danced inside the great circle, facing the dancers and watching for persons who were about to visit the spirits (i.e., collapse into a cataleptic trance). When the leader noticed such a person he would dance before him (or her) and project "electricity" into him by means of a small mirror which he carried in his hand. The person would then fall, and, according to the Ghost dance belief, his spirit would leave his body and travel to the spirit world where departed relatives and friends lived in a land of plenty. When his spirit returned to his body, which was still lying in the dance ring, he would tell the other dancers, through the leader and the two prophets, what he had seen and heard in the other world.

In connection with the Ghost dance a special form of the Hand game, known as the Ghost dance Hand game, was often played. The Pawnee form of the Ghost dance and its associated Hand game have been ably discussed by Lesser (1933) in his "The Pawnee Ghost Dance Hand Game." Since the Ponca practices were apparently borrowed from the Pawnee and remained virtually identical with those of that tribe, readers interested in a more complete description than that offered here are referred to this fine work.

The Ghost dance and Ghost dance Hand game never reached the Northern Ponca. Among the Southern Ponca the dance lasted until 1914–15. During the period of my fieldwork in 1954 the crow feather ornaments used in it were still preserved, according to WBB, by Mrs. Napoleon Buffalo-head, the daughter of one of the principals. The Ghost dance Hand game, which entirely superseded the older Ponca Moccasin and Hand games, is still played several times a year by the Southern Ponca.

[38b] James Mooney (1896, p. 159) states that "the Ghost dance was brought to the Pawnee, Ponca, Oto, Missouri, Kansa, Iowa, Osage, and other tribes in central Oklahoma by delegates from the Arapaho and Cheyenne in the west."

In connection with the present-day Ghost dance Hand game a dance, known simply as the "Gourd dance," is performed. Two persons, male or female, dance at a time, carrying large gourd rattles in the right hand. Choreographically the dance is much like the *Heđúška*, except that the dancers shake their gourds in time with the drum. This dance, according to LMD, was borrowed from the Pawnee at the same time as the Ghost dance Hand game. He mentioned, however, that the Ponca had previously possessed a Gourd dance of their own. This probably refers to the dance of the "Make-no-flight" society, mentioned below.

Another Ponca "Ghost dance," apparently a predecessor of that described above but not connected with it in any way, is described by James O. Dorsey (1884 a, p. 353). He writes: "*Wanáxe-iđàeđéma* are those who have supernatural communications with ghosts . . . . The dancers made their bodies gray, and called themselves ghosts."

The Ponca had many warriors' dancing societies besides the *Heđúška*. Since most of these are described at some length by both Dorsey (1884 a) and Skinner (1915 c) they will be treated quite briefly here. Each had its characteristic costume, songs, customs, and roster of officers. These warrior society dances, like the dances in present-day Western European society, were introduced, enjoyed a period of great popularity, and then were abandoned. Perhaps only two or three would be active at one time. There was apparently a rough sort of age grading in the societies, but it was not as clearly defined as in other Prairie-Plains groups. The *Tokála* dancing group was apparently made up of the youngest warriors, the *Heđúška* and Make-no-flight of slightly older, seasoned men, the *Mawádani* of middle-aged and older veterans, and the *Iská-iyúha* of old men and chiefs who had retired from military affairs.

The *Tokála* warriors' society or dance was described by Big-goose, one of Skinner's informants, as being, along with the Sun dance, *Heđúška*, and Not-afraid-to-die, one of the oldest Ponca dances (1915 c, p. 783). Dorsey (1884 a, p. 354), however, states that it was borrowed from the Dakota. Since the name means "kit fox" in Dakota and is meaningless in *Đégiha*, it would appear that Dorsey is correct.

Dorsey is the authority for the statement that the *Tǫkála* was composed of young warriors originally (1884 a, pp. 354–355). This group had a traditional rivalry with the *Mawádani* or "Mandan" warriors' society which sometimes resulted in wife stealing of the type so well known among the Crow (Skinner, 1915 c, p. 788). In later years the society disappeared, and its dance became a mere burlesque. PLC remembered it only as a "silly dance" performed to work up enthusiasm for the *Heđúška*. Choreographically it was much like the Round dance described below (pp.114–115). No animal mime was involved. The dance is no longer performed by the Ponca. It is still seen, but rarely, among the Yanktonai and Teton Dakota.

A dance called the *Míkasì* or 'Coyote dance' was also remembered by PLC. He stated that only men participated and that Give-away songs were sung in connection with it (i.e., songs in which the dancers give away gifts, as in the *Wá-wą*). It became obsolete about 1900. I strongly suspect that this dance is the *Đégiha* parallel of the *Tokála*, the *Tokála* having been merely a fashionable form of the dance which was adopted from the Dakota. Its choreography was identical with that of the preceding dance.

Both Riggs (1893, p. xxxii) and Dorsey (1884 a, p. 352) describe a warriors' dancing society called the "Make-no-flight." Dorsey (ibid.) writes: " . . . dancers hold gourd rattles, and each one carries many arrows on his back as well as in his arms. The members vow not to flee from a foe. They blacken themselves all over with charcoal." This is apparently the same dance which Skinner (1915 c, pp. 785–786) mentions as the "Not-afraid-to-die." He describes the society's dance: ". . . All [the dancers] stood in a row and danced up and down, remaining 'stationary.'"

I could learn nothing of this dance from my informants. The names of the society and their use of war bonnets with split horns at the sides, mentioned by Skinner (ibid., p. 785) suggest that this dance was a Ponca parallel of the Dakota No-flight and Strong-heart warriors' dancing societies, which were virtually identical with one another. The choreography suggests the Kiowa and Kiowa-Apache Blackfoot dance and the Plains-Ojibwa "One-legged" dance. The members of the Ponca Make-no-flight society, together with the members of the *Heđúška* group, seem to have been the military elite of the tribe, the "shock troops" in every battle.

The *Mawádani*, according to Dorsey (1884 a, pp. 354–355), was a warriors' society made up of "none but aged men and those in the prime of life . . ." This society performed a bravery dance, which functioned as a sort of "military funeral" over the bodies of warriors who had been slain by the enemy. Each body was placed in a sitting posture in the dance lodge, as if alive, with a deer-hoof rattle fastened to one arm. The dance was apparently identical with the *Heđúška* in its choreography.

Skinner (1915 c, p. 786) describes yet another warriors' dancing society called *Iská-iyùha*. This name means 'White-owners' in Dakota, and indicates the origin of the dance. He gives *Đáduxe* as another name of the society. Dorsey (1884 a, p. 355) gives *Gaxéxe* as still another synonym. This society was noted for the richness of its costumes, which were covered with many silver brooches.

PLC remembered the *Iská-iyùha* only as the "White-horse-dance." He described it as a lively dance much like the *Heđúška,* and stated that many gifts were given away at its performances.

In 1949 I saw this dance performed by a group of Teton Dakota at Trenton, Nebr. It resembled the *Ómaha* dance (the Dakota version of the *Heđúška*) so closely as to be indistinguishable from it, were it not for the lyrics of its songs. Among the Dakota, in the early reservation period, the members of this society all rode white horses, hence the name of the group. The Ponca name *Đáduxe* is merely the *Đégiha* equivalent of the Dakota *Iská-iyùha,* meaning 'White-owners.' Leonard Smith explained that the other Ponca name for the dance, *Gaxéxe,* referred to the noise made by the clashing metal ornaments and mescal bean bandoliers and bracelets worn by the dancers. Whitman (1939, pp. 186–187) gives a similar explanation. The group was made up of chiefs and older, respected warriors.

PLC described two other dances which seem to be of the warriors' dancing society type. The first of these is the "Big-belly" dance, in which buffalo bulls were imitated. According to PLC only older men, perhaps chiefs, participated. The dancers marked time in place during the first part of the song, then, on a musical cue, one man, a different person each time, would charge to the center of the lodge and pretend to hook something with his head, as if he were a bison hooking something with his horns. He would then give a present to someone in the audience and the dance would continue.

I observed this dance, performed by Teton Dakota, at the Milkcamp Community Hall, near St. Charles, S. Dak., in November, 1950. PLC participated with the Teton dancers on this occasion, wearing a buffalo headdress. In both the Ponca and Dakota tribes the dance is, in my opinion, a survival of the "Big-belly" or "Bulls" warrior society. This society was present in many Prairie and Plains tribes, and was composed of chiefs and old men. According to one informant, the *Iská-iyùha* and the Big-belly societies were the same, the one society performing two different dances. The name "Big-belly" attached to this society refers to the corpulency common to Plains Indian men of this age group.

The second of the previously unrecorded dances of the warriors' dancing society type described by PLC is the *Íkištàzi* or 'Not-ashamed' dance. The name referred to the fact that the participants were not ashamed to be seen taking part in an Indian dance. Only young men danced. They wore fancy broadcloth blankets as their distinguishing costume. As the song began they arose from their seats around the dancehall and danced to the center of the floor, in the *Heđúška* style but with shorter steps and subdued head and body movements.

PLC stated that this dance or society was originated by the young Ponca woodcutters who supplied fuel for the Missouri River steamboats. He considered it a strictly Northern Ponca dance, but in 1954 it was learned that the Southern Ponca also performed the dance at one time. It is now obsolete in both groups.

The Ponca chiefs formerly had a dance called *Ígazìge-wàą*. The dance was described by PLC as slow and dignified in character, in keeping with the high rank of the participants. On a certain musical cue the dancers all took four steps forward. Then they danced in place for a short time until, on cue, they took another four steps forward. The dance proceeded in this manner for the duration of the song.

The *Hąhé-watšì*, or 'Night dance,' the Omaha version of which is described by Fletcher and La Flesche (1911, pp. 493–509), was a prestige society. Men donated large sums of money and gave away large amounts of goods for the privilege of joining the group. This entitled them to have their daughters tattooed with the insignia of the society. The Night dance persisted until the 1930's among the Southern Ponca, and in 1954 I observed several Southern Ponca women who bore the characteristic blue spot of the society on their foreheads.

The Ponca women, like the men, had their dancing societies. The *Nudą́* was the woman's equivalent of the *Heđúška*. Skinner (1915 c, p. 790) states that its name was taken from the warpath songs composed by the braves, with which the women accompanied their dances. Its choreography is not known to me, though I suspect it was like the Soldier and Round dances.

Skinner (ibid., pp. 790–791) also describes a woman's dancing society called *Mazį́skàąpi* or the 'Medal dance.' The members of the society wore chiefs' medals around their necks.

Riggs (1893, p. xxvii) writes that: "The scalp dance is a dance for the women among the Ponca and Omaha, who call it *Wí-watšì*." According to Skinner (1915 c, p. 791) the dance was performed the day after the return of a war party. The women who danced bore the scalps, tied to short sticks. The *Wí-watšì* was also described by PLC: "Women form a big circle facing the center and move around the drum to the left." This dance was probably ancestral to both the Soldier dance and the Round dance, to be described below.

Dorsey (1884 a, p. 355) mentions two other women's dancing societies, the *Pa-đátą* and the *Gat'ana*. Neither was known to my informants. As with the men's societies, new groups were continually being formed and older ones passing out of existence. In a slightly modified form, this process has continued up to the present day. Following World War II several such women's groups were formed, each distinguished by its characteristic blanket or shawl with the group's name (i.e., "Ponca War Mothers") appliqued upon it. Usually the function of these groups is to honor the returning veterans of the tribe. At powwows the members of such a group, attired in identical blankets, often lead off in the Soldier or Round dance.

In addition to the dances described above, which were either sacred ceremonies or dances that were the property of organized groups, the Ponca had several dances which were open to all. One of these, which PLC saw in the 1890's, was called the *Gíani*. PLC (in a letter to me dated October 12, 1955) described the dance as follows: "Gee ah nee this they go around the drum in pairs and 4 of them facing each other and change, they just turn around and face others. This has died out in a very short years. I saw these in the 90s." Walter Hamilton, an Omaha Indian, stated that his tribe was also familiar with the dance. According to Hamilton, two men, dancing backward in *Hedúška* style, led the dance. They were followed by two women, facing forward, after which came two more men dancing backward, two women facing forward, etc. The women carried large eagle-wing fans, and fanned the men as they danced. At a certain point in the song the men would turn forward and the women backward, and the group would proceed in this manner for a while, then reverse, and so on. The double line proceeded clockwise around the drum throughout the dance. The name *Gíani* is said to refer to the fanning of the men by the women, the characteristic feature of the dance. Neither PLC nor Hamilton could explain the symbolism of the dance. It resembles, in its choreography, the Turkey dances of the Quapaw and Caddo.

Another dance open to all is the *Wanáse-watšigaxe* or 'Soldier dance.' It is a social dance at present, but has definite ceremonial overtones. It was witnessed at the Southern Ponca powwows in 1952, 1954, 1959, and 1961. On each of these occasions it was used to open the dancing program each night, and was identified by PLC as a "very old and honored Ponca dance." Men and women, interspersed, formed long lines, facing inward toward the drum, and circled the dance ground with a sidestep, moving in a clockwise direction. The best male dancers lifted their left knee with a slight snap as they stepped off with the left foot.

The Round dance, witnessed on the same occasions, was very similar, although the characteristic jerking of the left leg seen in the Soldier dance was not as evident in this one. I was told that the songs were slightly different as well. Both the Soldier dance and Round dances are accompanied by a pronounced loud-soft drumbeat. The Round dance is immensely popular among the Southern Prairie and Plains tribes at the present time, and the enthusiasm for it has spread to the Omaha in Nebraska and the Fox in Iowa. In 1952 a group of Omaha singers traveled to Oklahoma expressly to learn new Round dance songs. The origin of the Round dance is obscure. Some younger Ponca contend that it originated in Taos Pueblo, and is a secular form of the sacred Blue Lake Round dance of Taos. Others contend that it is merely a secular form of the old Ponca Soldier dance.

A secular Buffalo dance was performed once each evening at the Southern Ponca powwows I attended. It seemed to be purely social in nature. During the first part of the song the dancers, both men and women, moved about the arena in a counterclockwise direction, using *Hedúška* steps. On a musical cue, accompanied by a rolling of the drum, they turned toward the center of the dance ground, where the singers were seated around the drum. The drumbeat now changed to a heavily accented cadence and the dancers hopped in place, first on one leg, then on the other, at the same time "bunching up" like bison. On another musical cue they separated and continued around the arena in *Hedúška* style. The dance proceeded in this manner for the duration of the song. I am told that one of the songs used in this dance belongs to the now obsolete I*ská-iyùha* society.

Another dance which is performed at Southern Ponca powwows to break the monotony of the nearly continuous *Hedúška* episodes is the Snake dance. According to PLC and several Southern Ponca informants this dance was borrowed from Oklahoma tribes in recent years. It is performed by a long file of dancers, both men and women, led by two good male dancers, one at each end of the line. As the song starts, one of the men leads off with a brisk, trotting, "Stomp dance" type step, the long file of dancers jogging along behind him. He leads the queue in a serpentine path, sometimes coiling the whole line into a tight spiral. On a musical cue the dancers about-face and follow the leader at the other end. Thus the line of dancers twists, coils, and changes direction throughout the song, presenting a weird and beautiful effect. When viewed from the vantage point of the grandstand the line of dancers very much resembles a huge feathered serpent.

In its choreography this dance seems to be a variant of the "Stomp dance" of the Eastern Woodland tribes. The musical accompaniment, however, is provided by singers seated around a large drum, a feature more typical of the Prairie-Plains area.

The Stomp dance of the Eastern Woodland tribes is performed by the Southern Ponca on occasion. This dance, much like the Snake dance in its choreography, features antiphonal singing by a leader and a long line of dancers, both men and women, who follow him. Rhythmic accompaniment is provided by a "shell shaker girl," a woman who wears heavy terrapin shell or condensed-milk-can leg rattles, and dances just behind the leader.

According to Curtis (1930, vol. 30, p. 214), Henry Snake, a Ponca, brought the dance to his tribe from the Quapaw. Curtis also credits

Snake with having introduced the dance among the Osage, Oto, Cheyenne, Kansa, and Iowa. There are several "Stomp leaders" among the Southern Ponca at present, though these men are reluctant to lead the dance when more experienced Creek, Seminole, or Seneca-Cayuga leaders are present. Since the Stomp dance requires no particular costume, it is usually performed after the main part of the program at Ponca powwows (that is, after such dances as the Soldier, *Hedúška*, Buffalo, Snake, and Round dances). It is a great favorite of teenagers, who often "Stomp" all night each night of a powwow.

Another dance popular with the younger set is the "49." This dance, which seems to have originated among the Kiowa, is similar to the Round dance in its choreography, but has a much faster rhythm. Several circles of young people sidestep around the singers, who stand in the center of the circle holding a large drum. At times the singers pause and let the female dancers carry the refrain as they dance. The songs, I am told, are old Kiowa "war journey" songs. Like the Stomp dance, the "49" requires no special costume and is performed after the main program at powwows. A good "49" dance often lasts from 9 or 10 p.m. until dawn the following day.

Another dance recently imported from the Kiowa is the Brush dance. According to William Kimball this dance was once performed by the Kiowa as a part of their Sun dance rites. It was performed as an incidental daytime dance at the Southern Ponca powwow in 1952.

The group performing the dance was led by a middle-aged Ponca man wearing a mescal-bean bandolier and a "peyote blanket" of red and blue broadcloth. He carried a peyote gourd, which he shook in time with the drum, in his right hand, and peyote "feathers" in his left. A woman, probably his wife, wearing a buckskin dress and also carrying peyote feathers, danced beside him. These two were followed by a group of eight singers carrying a large *Hedúška* drum, beating it and singing as they proceeded. They were not in Indian costume. The singers were followed by a group of women, all wearing shawls or blankets and carrying green branches in the right hand. As they moved forward in the dance these women took care to maintain a crescent formation, the ends of the crescent pointing forward. The step was a simple advancing of one foot ahead of the other in time with the drum.

The party advanced, dancing and singing, for about half a mile through the powwow encampment, until they reached an open space, at which point the dance was ended and a Ghost dance Hand game was begun. PLC stated that he had never seen nor heard of the dance prior to this time. The date of the dance's introduction among the Southern Ponca is therefore post-1932, for PLC was then living in Oklahoma and would have been familiar with the Brush dance if it had been performed by the Ponca at that time.

At the present time the Northern Ponca retain only one aboriginal type dance, this being the widespread Rabbit dance. JLR said that this dance came to the Ponca from the Shoshone, but I am more inclined to credit its introduction to the Teton or Yankton Dakota. It is a purely social dance, and is probably the Indian adaptation of the square and round dances of the White pioneers. Couples, arm in arm in the "skaters' embrace" circle the drum in a clockwise fashion, stepping off with the left foot and bringing the right up with it in time with a heavy loud-soft drum beat.

During the period of my fieldwork the dance had not been performed for a number of years owing to the fact that the custodian of the Northern Ponca Community Hall, the only suitable place for holding such dances, refused to let it be used for "uncivilized" Indian practices, following the old-line "assimilationist" policy of the Indian Bureau.

A Begging dance is described by J. O. Dorsey (1884 a, p. 355), who writes: "The '*Waná-watšigaxe*' or *Begging dance* is not found among the Omahas; but among the Ponkas, Dakotas, etc." This "Begging dance," which I have observed among the Arikara, Dakota, Omaha, and Winnebago, is really not a dance per se but rather a dancing custom. Any suitable dance, such as the *Heđúška* or Round dance, may be used. A group of singers and dancers, usually composed of visiting Indians, gathers and moves about the camp of their hosts, stopping to sing and dance before the tent of every well-to-do person. At each tent, after an interval of song and dance, the owner appears and presents the group with a gift, whereupon they move along to the next one. After the entire camp has been circled an auction is held where single items donated to the group are sold to the highest bidder. The money from this auction, plus any loose cash contributed by the tent owners, is then divided among the group.

Among the Ponca, as in most Plains tribes, shamans were organized into groups on the basis of spirit helpers held in common. For example the *Matógaxe* or 'Bear doctor' society was composed entirely of medicine men who claimed to derive their powers from the bear, either directly, by means of visions, or indirectly, by means of purchase from other members of the group. Dealing primarily in herbal remedies, they were the physicians of the tribe. Another society, the "Buffalo doctors," which was devoted to the healing of wounds, was made up of shamans who had the buffalo as their tutelary deity. Its members were the Ponca "surgeons." [39]

---

[39] A bear-buffalo shaman dichotomy was present in many Plains tribes. Though shamans could, and did, receive power from many animals, these two were considered most powerful. They were, therefore, the two most often sought, and secured, as spirit helpers.

718-071—65——9

Skinner describes the Bear society as follows:

The *Matógaxe*, or bear dance, was one of the so-called mystery dances, and had four leaders, two waiters, and a herald. Before performing, a cedar tree was pulled up by the roots and set up in the center of the lodge. During the dance one of the participators would go up and break off a branch and scrape off the bark. Then he would circle the lodge four times, show it to the members, and announce that he would run it down his throat. He would then thrust it in until the tip barely showed. After a moment he would pull it out, and the blood would gush forth. One shaman had the power of thrusting the cedar through his flesh into his abdomen. After he pulled it out he merely rubbed the wound and it was healed. Still another would swallow a pipe, cause it to pass through his body, and then bring it out and lick it.

Big-goose once saw a man, who was performing in the bear dance, take a muzzle-loading rifle and charge it in everyone's presence. Another man circled the tent singing, and on the fourth round he was shot by the Indian with the gun; everyone thought he was killed, but he soon sprang up unhurt. Another performer took a buffalo robe, had a third man re-load the magic gun, and fired it at the robe. There was no hole visible, but the bullet was found in the center of the robe. [Skinner, 1915 c, p. 792.]

My informants AMC, Ed Primeaux, and Leonard Smith described the "magic musket" trick of the Bear society as well. Leonard Smith stated that when Shaky, the famous Northern Ponca shaman, performed the act he used bluestem grass to extract the bullet from the "bear's" body.

Though the Ponca Bear society no longer existed as an organized group there were, during the period of my fieldwork, a few Southern Ponca who claimed bear power and practiced as individuals. WBB was a bear shaman at one time, but he abandoned the practice when he "turned Christian" (i.e., joined the Peyote religion). He once stated that when he practiced as a Bear doctor he painted his hands black with yellow between the fingers in imitation of a bear's paws.

Likewise Henry Snake told me that he had once been offered bear power by an Omaha shaman while visiting near Macy, Nebr., on the Omaha Reservation. Snake expressed disbelief in the Omaha's power, so the Omaha told him, "Come down by the river tomorrow morning. Bring your wife and she can see it too." He then mentioned a certain place, quite secluded. Snake and his wife went to this location at the appointed time, and shortly after their arrival a huge black bear appeared, walked near them, and then disappeared in the brush. "It was that old man, disguised as a bear," commented Snake. In spite of this evidence of the Omaha's power, however, Snake did not take up the "bear way."

The *Tʰé-watši* or Buffalo "doctors" society, as indicated above, was devoted to the healing of wounds. Skinner (1915 c, p. 792) notes that—

. . . there were four leaders, two waiters, and a herald as officers. This society is now obsolete, as there is little call for the practice of surgery because there is no more war. If a man were wounded the buffalo doctors got together and squirted water on the wound. They would dance in imitation of the buffalo, wearing robes, buffalo horn caps, and tails. They painted only with clay which is the buffalo's pigment. They painted only the upper or lower halves of their faces. The buffalo dancers were very *waxúbe* or powerful.

I was unable to secure much additional information concerning this group. PLC, who wears a buffalo headdress similar to that of the Buffalo Doctors society when he dances the *Hеđúška*, stated that only red, yellow, and black face paint should be worn with this headdress. He criticized a Dakota buffalo dancer who used white paint for not respecting the "old buffalo ways."

The largest and most important of the Ponca medicine societies was the *Wašíška-ađè* or Medicine Lodge. This group, which is the Ponca equivalent of the well-known Ojibwa *Midéwiwin* and similar organizations of other tribes, was apparently a shamans' organization originally. In later years, however, like the *Midéwiwin* and the Omaha Shell society, it became a sort of "service club" as well. Though the leaders were still usually shamans, and practically all of the members of the Bear and Buffalo societies were *Wašíška-ađè* members as well, there were also many Medicine Lodge members who were not shamans at all. Even women and children, in fact, could and did belong. The professed goals of the society were the mutual benefit and prolongation of the life of the membership.

The name *Wašíška-ađè* may be translated 'White-shell-owners.' It refers to the "medicine arrows" (or better "medicine projectiles") used during a part of the ceremony known as the "medicine shoot." In historic times these were usually cowrie (*Cyprea moneta*) shells. Other items were also used as medicine arrows, however, one being a small, round stone. For this reason the group was sometimes called the Pebble society. Other projectiles, such as rooster spurs, fishbones, or mescal beans were sometimes used as well.

The Ponca believed that sorcerors could magically "shoot" or project these objects into the bodies of their enemies with their "medicine bows."[40] These medicine bows, which were one of the badges of membership in the society, were usually the decorated skins of small animals, such as mink, otter, weasel, or raccoon. Occasionally, however, an eagle's wing was used, and one account mentions a black silk handkerchief.

At meetings of the society, which were held in the type of structure called *diúđipu-snèdɛ*, members were lectured on morality, taught the legendary history of the order, and instructed in the use of various herbal medicines. There were also singing and dancing and magical performances by the Buffalo and Bear shaman contingents of the organization. However, the highlight of each meeting was the medi-

[40] This belief was very common throughout Northern Europe, Northern Asia, and North America. The German term *Hexenschuss* (lit. "witch's shot"), used in reference to a sudden sharp pain, usually in the back, seems to be a linguistic survival of this belief.

cine shoot, which followed the initiation of new members. These were contests in which the various shamans tested one another's "power" or *waxúbe*. One shaman, gasping the magic cry *Hex!*, *hex!*, *hex!*, would point the nose of his animal skin bag at another, thus "shooting" his "medicine arrow" into this person's body. The person "shot" in this manner would stagger and fall, apparently unconscious. Other shamans would then "doctor" this person, who would shortly recover. He would then "shoot" the first man, in turn, or another, until all members had participated. If a person "shot" in this manner was not immediately treated by other members of the society, or if they failed to retrieve the "medicine arrow" of his assailant, he would soon sicken and die.

Admission to the Medicine Lodge society was by purchase, and the price was high. If a candidate had relatives who were already members, however, the price was slightly lower. Skinner (1920, p. 307) also notes that: "a member possessed the privilege of passing on his knowledge, by purchase, to his eldest son, who might buy it of him instead of from one of the four leaders. If he had no son, he might sell it to his nearest relative. In any case, he had to inform the society of his intention."

Persons who had been "doctored" by the society were also eligible for admission at lower rates. The last Northern Ponca curing ceremony of this type was described by JLR, who had attended it as a small boy:

My brother was a great fisherman. He used to go out and fish all day. One night, after he had been fishing all day, he had a nightmare. He sat up in bed crying, "Daddy, save me, he's going to get me! Daddy save me, there he is!" My father went to his bed and shook him to wake him up. "There is nothing here to harm you," he said, "so don't be afraid." My brother had the same dream for four nights. The animal he saw was like a bloodsucker, only much larger. My brother was terribly afraid of this monster.

Then one day he went fishing in the lake near Monowi, the one that never freezes. This lake has a smell like sulphur, and steam comes off it. Even in winter it never freezes. This was the day my brother saw *Gisná*, the water monster. It was so big that it had to lie in a horseshoe shape because there was no room for it otherwise. The monster saw my brother and tried to hook him with his tail and drag him into the lake, but my brother fought his way back to shore. Seeing that he was escaping, the monster shot him with his tail and then disappeared under water.

Shortly after this my brother took sick, and we thought he was going to die. My father called in the Medicine lodge society doctors to see what they could do for him. Shaky was the leader of the society. My father said to him, "Come and examine my oldest boy." Shaky agreed to come. He instructed my father how to prepare the house for the ceremony. One night shortly after, Shaky and three other doctors came and put on their dance. They had my brother stand naked in the center while they danced around him. They asked my brother what the *Gisná* had told him when it shot him with its tail. My brother said, "It told me I was to be a doctor."

The first doctor danced around my brother. He suddenly stopped dancing right in front of my brother and took a big black water beetle from my brother's chest. This was part of what the *Gisná* had put there. I saw this bug myself as it was crawling away. Then the second medicine man danced around my brother. He took some green moss from the joints of my brother's arms and legs. [The joints were considered particulary vulnerable to medicine arrows, JHH.] He piled this moss on the floor. The *Gisná* had put this there too. Then the third medicine man danced around my brother. He found some of the round stones that we call "marbles" in my brother's hands. All of this stuff had been shot into my brother by the water monster.

Then Shaky came out to the middle of the floor. He asked each of the others if they had taken out everything they could find. "Try again, and see if you can find anything else," he said to them. Each of them tried again, but each found him empty. Then Shaky, the head doctor, said, "There *is* something else. I will try to get it out. If I can't get it out it will kill him." He went around and around my brother, without saying a word. Finally he stopped. "There is something else! He is standing on them!" He had my brother move each of his feet. From under each one he took a human eyeball.

"Now he is cleaned out!" said the doctors. Then Shaky said, "Don't take it all away from him. We must leave him some power to protect himself." So the doctor who had taken the marbles from my brother's hands gave him back one of these. After that he was considered a member of the Medicine lodge society, and was respected for having water-monster power.

After this, one time, we were visiting over at Macy. Those Omaha Pebble society people were having their ceremonies. As a joke they called my brother out to take part in their shooting ceremony. They were going to make a fool out of him. Just before they were going to begin the leader looked closely at my brother and then said. "Wait, we had better pass him by, he really has something [i.e., medicine power]."

The rhythmic singing for the dancing which accompanied the ceremony was provided, according to AMC, by a group of singers seated around a large drum. This is strange, for in most tribes possessing the rite a wooden water drum was used. The Ponca were familiar with the water drum but used it only in the *Wá-wą* ceremony.

Apparently the Medicine Lodge ceremony, unlike most of the old Ponca rites, persisted longest among the Northern Ponca. The ceremony described above took place about 1910, and Henry Le Roy, the boy "shot" by the water monster and cured by the shamans, was still a young man when he died in an automobile accident in 1926. Yet when Alanson Skinner (1920, p. 306) inquired about the ceremony among the Southern Ponca in 1914 he found that it had been "so long extinct . . . that practically nothing was remembered by the writer's [Skinner's] informants."

Another extremely interesting and perhaps significant medicine society was the Mescal Bean cult. The rites of this group centered around the mescal bean (*Sophora secundiflora*), the fruit of a leguminous shrub native to northern Mexico, Texas, and Arizona. The only mention of the Mescal Bean cult in the older Ponca literature is a vague statement by J. O. Dorsey (1884 a, p. 349), who, in discussing the Wichita dance of the Omaha, and the use of the mescal bean by this group, states: "Similar customs are found among the Pawnees and Ponkas." I am the author of a short paper on the cult (Howard, 1957).

LMD stated that the Mescal Bean cult had been a powerful organization in his father's time. He had heard a great deal about it, since his father was one of the leaders of the group and kept the sacred bundle of the society. He said that the Mescal Bean society was much older, with the Ponca, than the Peyote religion, which was acquired from the Cheyenne in 1902.

The Mescal Bean cult was secret, and even though his father had been a leader, LMD had never been allowed to witness the ceremonies. By hearsay, however, he learned the form of the ritual. He stated that the Mescal Bean society meetings were quite similar to present-day Peyote meetings. They were customarily held in a tipi, the entrance of which faced east. The leader of the rite sat opposite the door, in the place of honor. Another important officer, the fireman, sat across from him, just to the right of the entrance. Both of these officers have parallels in the Peyote ceremony. The leader held a staff as his emblem of authority, another feature also found in the Peyote ritual. (Fig. 5.)

Each member of the order owned an individual sacred bundle, but the principal bundle was kept by the leader. These bundles were opened during the ceremony and their contents displayed. The leader opened his bundle first, then the members. A tea was brewed

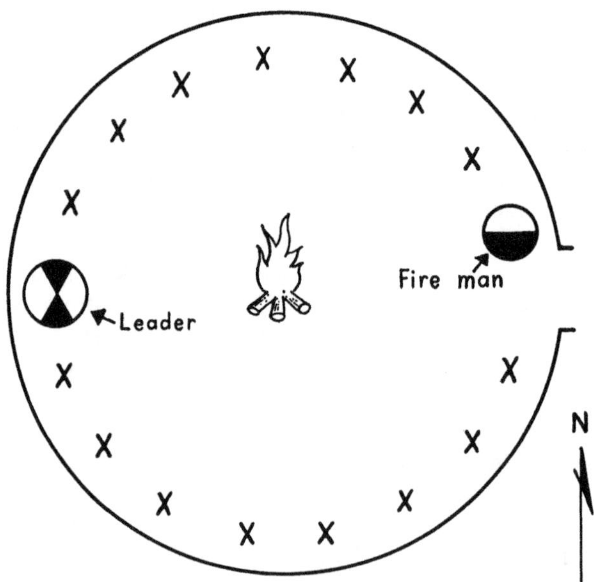

FIGURE 5.—Diagram of a Ponca Mescal Bean society meeting.

from mescal beans, which the members drank. Sometimes the participants secured visions after drinking this infusion. One sip of the decoction was said to be enough. Songs were sung to the accompaniment of a rawhide rattle which was struck upon a buckskin pillow filled with bison wool. Sometimes there was dancing as well.

"Yellow-hammer" (flicker) feathers were worn by the members of the Mescal Bean cult. LMD explained that the flicker was the "main bird" of the Mescal Bean group, just as the "waterbird" (water turkey or snakebird, *Anhinga anhinga*) is now the "main bird" of the Peyote religion—that is to say, this bird was believed to carry prayers of the members from earth to heaven. Many Oklahoma Indian groups share the Ponca respect for the flicker. An Arapaho, Jim Fire, explained the special importance of the flicker as follows: "We notice this bird is always able to find bugs and things under the bark of trees. That is why we Indian people associate him with doctoring. He can seek out hidden impurities." The Ponca Mescal Bean society members probably had a similar belief, as curing was quite important in their group.

In the old days of tribal warfare the mescal bean was used as a war medicine. LMD commented that "since the red bean is so very hard to crack, a man who carried it as his medicine would be hard to pierce with arrows or bullets." When used as medicines the beans were wrapped in a small circle of buckskin which was tied at the top with a buckskin thong. This buckskin wrapper was always perforated, since the bean "would die if it was not able to breathe." LRL was also familiar with the virtues of the mescal bean as a war medicine. He stated that warriors going into battle often put a mescal bean in either ear. If they did not fall out the wearer would be almost impervious to arrows and bullets.

The use of the mescal bean as a war medicine has not completely disappeared. When Parrish Williams, the son of James Williams (now deceased) went into the service in World War II, his father gave him a mescal bean to carry with him. Parrish still keeps this as a good luck charm, carrying it in an old-fashioned leather coin purse.

The mescal bean was also strongly identified with horses and mules, according to Ernest Blue-back, and he stated that these animals were given mescal bean tea to make them swift and to cure their infirmities. To illustrate this he told the following story:

> Once my granddad took part in a big buffalo run. A lot of other tribes took part too, some of them ancient enemies of the Poncas. The Sioux, Winnebagoes [sic], Omahas, and Pawnees were all there. Just before the hunt granddad went out to look at his buffalo runners and found that someone had shot them full of arrows for him. He had to shoot most of them to put them out of their misery. One mule that was down, though, had only been grazed. Now granddad used this mule to run buffalo sometimes. He painted the mule, gave it red bean tea to

drink, and sang over it. Pretty soon the mule got up and walked around. He rode that mule in the hunt and beat them all.

The mescal bean was sacred to many of the Prairie and Plains tribes, and several, including the Wichita, Pawnee, Tonkawa, Osage, Iowa, Oto, Kiowa, and Arikara also possessed cults centered about it in which mescal bean tea was drunk by the members. In view of the fact that the Mescal Bean cults are much older in the Prairie-Plains area than is the Peyote religion, and in view of the fact that some forms of the ceremony were very similar to the later Peyote rites, particularly those of the Ponca and Tonkawa, it is interesting to speculate that perhaps the Mescal Bean cult "smoothed the way" for the Peyote religion, and contributed much to the ritual form of the Prairie-Plains Peyote ceremony as well.

Fletcher and La Flesche (1911, pp. 490–493) mention a medicine society called *Ingđú̧-iđàeđè*, 'those to whom the thunder has shown compassion.' The society was open only to men and women who had been visited by thunder beings in dreams or visions. Members were believed to be able to control the elements, to bring rain or to drive storms away. Future events could also be foretold, and sometimes members pitted their power against one another.

There were two cults of ceremonial clowns among the Ponca. Both are described by Skinner (1915 c, p. 789). Concerning the *Heyóka* cult he writes:

Under this name went certain men who, because of some dream which I could not ascertain, danced in companies in the spring. [41] They used backward speech, and took food from boiling kettles. Some even poured boiling water over themselves. On account of the identity of the title of these clowns with the Dakota performers of similar antics, I suspect that the cult is of Teton origin.

He also describes a distinct clown cult called "Those-who-imitate-mad-men":

These people (called *Đaníbđađà*) are said to have been entirely distinct from the heyoka and the cult is perhaps not of foreign origin. They did ridiculous and foolhardy things, such as crawling up and trying to touch a woman's genitals in broad daylight; coming to a stream they would strip off one legging and moccasin and ford it by hopping on the clad leg and carefully protecting the bare one from moisture. They were looked upon as clowns and fun-makers and their antics are said not to have been significant.

Only the vaguest memories of these clown cults remained with my informants. JLR seemed to remember a *Heyóka* cult performance he had seen as a boy, but was not sure whether it was Ponca or Santee Dakota clowns. Clowns formed a popular diversion at the Southern Ponca powwows in 1952 and 1954. They were not part of any organized group, however, and appeared to be simply funmakers.

---

[41] Among the Dakota, men joined the *Heyóka* cult because of having dreamed of thunder. It was believed that if they did not dance as clowns they would be struck by lightning.

The Peyote ritual is the only religious ceremony of an aboriginal nature still performed by the Ponca. As noted earlier, it came to the Southern Ponca from the Cheyenne in 1902. Shortly thereafter the Southern Ponca carried it to the Northern band of their tribe. EBC stated that the Northern Ponca also had one "fireplace" or ritual which was introduced by the famous Winnebago leader, John Rave. This was a "cross" or "big moon" type ceremony. The Cheyenne ritual was the "half moon" or "basic Plains" rite which has fewer Christian features.

The general form of the Peyote meeting is as follows: About 8:30 p.m. the worshipers file into the tipi where the ceremony is to be held, and take their places. There is an opening prayer by the leader, then a general praying by all the members while smoking prayer cigarettes (cigarettes are not used in the Winnebago ritual). Peyote (*Lophophora williamsi*) is then distributed, usually in the form of dried "buttons." This is eaten, as a sacrament, by the peyotists. After this the singing begins. Each person sings four songs, accompanied by the gourd rattle, which he shakes, and the water drum, which is played by the man on his right.

At midnight there are prayers by the leader and a ritual drinking of water. The singing, interspersed with prayers, then continues until dawn, at which time a ceremonial breakfast of parched corn, fruit, and other native foods is eaten. The four closing songs are then sung by the leader and the meeting is ended. Most of the members loiter about the tipi until noon of the following day, at which time the host serves them a dinner.

Readers interested in a more complete account of the ceremony than it is possible to include here are referred to Weston La Barre's excellent work, "The Peyote Cult" (1938), in which both Peyote rituals used by the Ponca are described in some detail.

At the present time the Peyote religion is still flourishing among the Southern Ponca. Peyote meetings are usually held on Saturday night so as not to conflict with the workweek of those who have jobs. However, the Northern Ponca have not held Peyote meetings since the early forties. EBC, the last Northern Ponca leader resident in the Niobrara area, died in 1950. I am told, however, that another Northern Ponca, who lives among the Yankton Dakota, still runs an occasional meeting for that group's peyotists.

SPORTS AND GAMES

Next we turn to sports and games. It may seem odd to some that sports and games should be considered in the same chapter with religion, dances, and ceremonies. It will become evident in the discussion, however, that these sports and games were very often (though not invariably) connected with religion, and were regarded as ceremonies.

PLC mentioned that both footraces and horseraces were popular sports with the Ponca. On the morning of the third day of the Ponca Sun dance there was a ceremonial race by the dancers to the center pole (G. A. Dorsey, 1905, p. 76). The winner had the honor of counting first coup on a dead enemy.

The Ponca possessed several medicines which were used to make a horse fast during a race. The use of one of these was described by PLC:

> If you want to win a horse race you take the root of the *Pó-ipìye* [*Allionia nyctaginea* Michx.], cut a piece about two or three inches long, and chew it. While you are chewing it go and talk to your racehorse. Do this in secret just before the race. Tell the horse that he is going to win. Spit a little of the chewed root on your hands and rub the horse down with it, starting with the nose. Talk to the horse all the time. Grab his tail last. As you rub his tail say "You are going to have your tail up in the air." I used to use this quite a bit, and I always won the race. I hate to use it because it isn't fair to the others. For the best effect you should dig the root in the fall, when the power is going back into the roots. The name I gave you is the Sioux name; we Poncas call it *Maką-skìde* or "Sweet medicine."

AMC, LRL, and Ernest Blue-back also mentioned that mescal beans were sometimes ground up and given to racehorses to make them fast.

An old Ponca sport which is still popular with the Southern Ponca is shinny, or *Tabégasì*. Like the Southeastern Indian ball game, the Ponca game of shinny is in the nature of a religious observance, and certain rituals are performed in connection with it. The game has an appointed ritual custodian who is responsible for arranging for its play at the proper time. At the present time Ernest Blue-back "owns" the Ponca shinny game. He keeps the sacred ball used in it and announces the dates of the game each year. Shinny is played only in the spring. Blue-back stated that the game is played at this time so that the members of the tribe can "limber up" after the enforced inactivity of winter. Four games are played each spring, one game each day, spaced at intervals of a few days to a week. All of the men in the tribe who are able, participate.

The sticks are made of ash and have a slight bend at the end. They are about 3 feet in length at the present time, though they are said to have been slightly shorter a generation ago. The ball is of deerskin stuffed with horsehair, and each year the owner of the game makes a new ball. Ernest Blue-back showed me several which he had made. One had an interesting design upon it, a yellow cross with a red square where the arms of the cross intersected, flanked on either side by a design of crossed shinny sticks. Whitman (1939, p. 185) writes: "Among the Ponca the ball represented the earth and was mystically painted as such." I found no trace of such a belief, though I used many of the same informants as Whitman. Ernest Blue-back firmly denied any such symbolism.

The Ponca shinny game is played on a field a mile in length and about half a mile wide. At each end a goalpost about 6 feet tall is erected. The game is begun at a point half way between the goalposts. An official (formerly a shaman) draws a cross, representing the four winds (the same design painted on the ball mentioned above), on the ground and places the ball on it. Play commences in much the same manner as in a modern hockey game. The captains of each side raise their sticks above the ball three times, then the fourth time they attempt to drive the ball into the opponents' territory.

Play is fast and furious and often a player of one team mistakes an opponent's head for the ball. Each time one team works the ball to the opponents' goalpost one point is scored. The first team to score four goals wins.

LMD stated that formerly there was much more ceremony in connection with the shinny game than at present. Even the goalposts were in charge of special custodians. Before each game offerings of calico were tied to the posts and they were ceremonially marched to the ball field. There were four prescribed halts on this march at which the poles were lowered to the ground and the entire group raised a great war cry, drumming the palm of the hand over the mouth. After each game the posts were returned to the camps of their keepers.

Certain players possessed medicines or bundles which gave them ability in the game. Whitman (1939, p. 185) writes: "In his early youth Black Eagle's (WBB's) father gave him a good luck bundle . . . 'When I play shinny I use that medicine. You can't hit me.' " Ernest Blue-back commented that the Ponca believe that touching the ball in the shinny game is a cure for stiffness.

Ponca women had their own version of the game, according to J. O. Dorsey (1884 a, pp. 336–337). It was called *Wabáđade*.

Dorsey and Miner both mention a man's game is which arrows were first shot into the branches of a tree and then the players endeavored to dislodge them (Dorsey, 1884 a, p. 336; Miner, 1911, p. xxx). Another game played with arrows is described by Dorsey, who writes:

> *Mą́gadĕze* is a game unknown among the Omahas, but practiced among the Ponkas, who have learned it from the Dakotas. It is played by two men. Each one holds a bow upright in his left hand with one end touching the ground and the bow-string towards a heap of arrows. In the other hand he holds an arrow, which he strikes against the bow-string, which rebounds as he lets the arrow go. The latter flies suddenly towards the heap of arrows and goes among them. The player aims to have the feather on his arrow touch that on some other arrow which is in the heap. In that case he wins as many arrows as the feather or web has touched; but if the sinew on his arrow touches another arrow it wins not only that one but all in the heap. [Dorsey, 1884 a, p. 339.]

The widespread bowl dice game was known to the Ponca. J. O. Dorsey (1890, p. 617) gives an origin legend for the game in which Ukiaba (?), "a tribal hero of the Ponca," sends five plum stones, the counters in the game, to a young woman he has seduced, afterward telling her "Keep the plum stones for gambling. You shall always win." The game was played only by persons of the same age and sex. Two players made up a side. Five marked plum stones were placed in a shallow wooden bowl and this bowl was struck against a pillow. Certain combinations of marked stones indicated a winner. (Dorsey, 1884 a, pp. 334–335.)

Another game of chance, the well-known moccasin game, was also played by the Ponca. A player from one side hid a stone under one of four moccasins, singing all the while to distract the opposing players. A member of the opposite side then guessed the location of the stone. PLC, who described the game, had seen it played only once, when he was a small boy.

Very similar to the moccasin game is the hand game, a variant of which is still popular with the Southern Ponca. Two players from one side hide two pieces in their hands while a member from the opposing side attempts to guess their location. The present form of the game, which came to the Ponca from the Pawnee in connection with the Ghost dance, is described by Lesser (1933) in "The Pawnee Ghost Dance Hand Game." The game still has religious overtones for the older Ponca, and until fairly recently the gaming implements of a successful player were buried with him because his children feared the *waxúbe* or "power" which they carried.

It is very common for a Southern Ponca family or organization to sponsor a hand game in honor of a visitor from some other tribe. The various donations made by losers during the game are then presented to this visitor as a mark of esteem.

PLC, LMD, and Parrish Williams all told the same origin legend for the old, pre-Ghost dance, hand game. A Ponca war party of about 20 warriors left to raid an enemy tribe. Months passed, but no word of the departed men reached their anxious relatives. Finally they were presumed to have been ambushed and were given up for dead.

A year or two later a young Ponca was hunting in the region where the war party had disappeared. Night fell and he wrapped himself up in his robe and went to sleep. In his sleep he began to dream. A wolf howled four times, each time coming closer. Finally it was only a few feet from him. The wolf spoke to the young hunter, telling him that the missing war party was nearby. The wolf then taught the young man a medicine song and vanished.

The young man rose and walked in the direction the wolf had indicated. He saw a light in the distance, and as he came nearer he noticed that it came from a fire burning in a large grass lodge. Indians were playing some sort of game inside, near the fire. It was the hand game.[42] They sang as they played and seemed to be having a wonderful time. The young hunter recognized the players as the members of the lost war party. He spoke to several of them but they ignored him, absorbed in their gambling. He stayed with the group most of the night, watching the game and learning the songs used to accompany it. Just before dawn he left and returned to the main camp of the Ponca.

He informed the head chief that he had located the missing warriors. The chief and his Buffalo-police went to investigate. When they arrived at the spot which the young man had described they found only the ashes of a campfire and various scattered human bones. When the young man was informed of this he realized that he had been watching ghosts play the hand game. From that time on the Ponca played the game as their own.

Ponca boys had many sports and games of their own. As we would expect, these lacked the ceremonial associations of the adult games. J. O. Dorsey (1884 a, p. 340) describes a variant of snow-snake known as *Mąíbagi*. This was also known to PLC: "A game that the Ponca children used to play was called *Mąíbagi*. This means 'Slide-a-stick-on-the-ground.' The stick was held at one end and thrown underhanded along the ground. The boy whose stick went the farthest was the winner. The game was played in the summer." According to PLC the Northern Ponca used fossil ivory from "elephant" (mammoth or mastodon) remains found at the mouth of Ponca Creek for the tips of the game sticks used in the *Mąíbagi* game.

J. O. Dorsey (1884 a, p. 341) describes two other children's games which resemble games played by White schoolchildren. One was a game of tag: "Children strike one another 'last,' saying 'Gatša,' i.e., 'So far.' " The other he describes as follows:

> *Taháđize* is played by two persons. A's left hand is at the bottom, the skin on its back is pinched by B's left hand, which, in turn, is pinched by A's right, and that by B's right. After saying "*Taháđize*" twice as they raise and lower the hands, they release them and hit at each other. . . . These two customs were observed among the Ponka children.

PLC described a Ponca boys' game called *Maníkađèđe* or 'Mud-on-a-stick':

> This game was played by two opposite sides. They would go down by the river where each player would cut himself a willow stick. Then they would mold a ball of mud on the end of the stick. The two sides would pretend to be warriors from two different tribes, and throw mud at each other from the end of their sticks. This was great sport. Both sides would be covered with mud at the end of the day.

[42] Parrish Williams stated that these warriors were playing the moccasin game rather than the hand game, and that the hand game had developed from the older moccasin game. If so this "origin legend" is an interesting example of syncretism.

PLC also mentioned popguns of clay which were made by the Ponca children:

> You went down by the river and got some good sticky clay. This clay you could make into a hollow ball by rolling it on your elbow. When you had a good round ball you threw it out in the water. Then you took a stick, put a ball of mud on the end of it, and threw this at the floating clay ball. If you hit the ball it exploded with a loud pop. This was one of my favorite games when I was a boy. It is called *Ní-ìkatùši.*

PLC and Leonard Smith both mentioned that Ponca boys used to slide downhill on sleds in the winter. The sleds were made of flat bison ribs lashed together with sinew.

At the present time the favorite pastime of many Southern Ponca adults is playing cards. Several of the Southern Ponca homes I visited had a raised wooden platform, covered with canvas or rugs, in the front yard, shaded by overhanging trees. Here the long summer afternoons are whiled away with Poker, Hearts, or other games. Apparently card games have been popular for many years, for certain typically Indian practices have developed by which the players may increase their luck. Thus Gilmore (1919, p. 82) states that the fruit of the long-fruited anemone was chewed and spit on the hands, or burned and the hands rubbed in the smoke, as a charm in card playing. The name of this plant is *Wađíbabà-maką́*, or "playing-card-medicine."

WAR AND PEACE

All of my informants stressed the fact that the Ponca were not a warlike people, and were content to live in peace with other tribes. They also pointed out, however, that the Ponca were quick to resist any incursion upon their tribal domain. At this late date it is quite difficult to ascertain just what the extent of the Ponca territory was in the late prehistoric and early historic periods, or how well the tribe defended it.

In 1954 I spent considerable time attempting to determine the boundaries of the traditional Ponca domain. Though they differed in minor details, the accounts of the various informants were remarkably consistent. The area delimited, however, seems far too large to have been used or defended by a tribe as small in numbers as the Ponca were in the 18th and 19th centuries. The informants insisted, however, that this was true, and that the tribe had been much larger formerly. For what it is worth, then, a consensus of their statements on the subject is presented below.

The eastern boundary of the Ponca territory, according to most informants, was a line extending south to the Platte River from a place on the Missouri called *Ní-àgatšàtša*, 'The-place-where-water-splashes-on-the-chalk-cliffs.' Most informants thought that this

Ní-àgatšàtša (or *Ní-àgatšàki*, as some pronounced it) was the site of the present Sioux City, Iowa. J. O. Dorsey's "Omaha Indian Map," however, which was compiled from data furnished by Omaha and Ponca informants in the period 1877–92, locates it near the present Homer, Nebr.[42a] The Omaha, according to my informants, had their villages east of this line. Though they hunted west of the boundary they acknowledged that they were doing so as guests of the Ponca. The Omaha insist, of course, that the Ponca were *their* guests.

The southern boundary of the Ponca domain was the Platte (North Platte west of the fork). All informants agreed that the Pawnee villages were south of the Platte and that that tribe customarily hunted south of that river.

The western boundary of their territory was vaguest in the minds of most informants. Some stated that it extended from a point "just west of the Black Hills" in South Dakota south to the North Platte River. Others mentioned an even vaster domain with *Páhe-žè-egą́*, 'The-hill-that-resembles-an-erect-penis,' the present Pike's Peak, as the western boundary marker.

Most informants agreed that the northern boundary followed the Missouri west from *Ní-àgatšàtša* to the mouth of the White River in what is now South Dakota. From the mouth of the White River the boundary line continued straight west through the Black Hills to meet the western boundary. PLC remarked that the Ponca also claimed a strip of land north of the Missouri "a day's hunt" or about 30 miles in from the river in the present Bon Homme and Charles Mix Counties, S. Dak. This was confirmed by VHM.

PLC stated that the Ponca had hunted in this strip for many years prior to the time that the Yankton Dakota, recent arrivals from Minnesota, asked the Ponca if they might settle there. In return for land on which to live, the Yankton offered to help the Ponca when the latter tribe was attacked by its enemies. The Ponca agreed to these terms and the Yankton built their villages in the vicinity of their present reservation. However, PLC pointed out that the Yankton failed to live up to their agreement, for when the Teton Dakota attacked the Ponca the Yankton did not come to their aid. Nevertheless the Yankton Dakota and the Ponca always remained friendly, even when the Teton from the Rosebud and Pine Ridge Reservations were constantly raiding the Ponca.

Ponca relations with the Omaha, their neighbors to the east, were generally quite friendly. The two tribes often joined for the summer bison hunt and there was some interchange of personnel, through marriage and adoption, a pattern which continues up to the present time. Relations became somewhat strained, however, in 1864, when

---

[42a] Blueprint copies of this map are on file at the Nebraska State Historical Society, Lincoln, Nebr., and at the Laboratory of Anthropology, University of Nebraska, Lincoln, Nebr.

the Omaha, under their chief Logan Fontanelle, ceded a large tract of land to the Government. Part of this land, which lay south of an east-west line drawn through the mouth of the Iowa River, was claimed by the Ponca, who were not a party to the treaty. When the Ponca chief *Wégasàpi* or "Whip" learned of this cession he was furious, and prepared to lead a war party against the Omaha, saying "When the Omaha have defeated the Ponca in battle, *then* they can sell our land!" At the last moment, however, *Wégasàpi* was turned from his purpose by Government promises of annuity payments. Nowadays, though the Omaha and Ponca visit freely with one another, a few Ponca still harbor resentment against their sister tribe because of "Fontanelle's crooked deal."

Ponca relations with the Pawnee, who were south of the Platte, were also good, as a rule. Occasionally, Pawnee horsethieves would enter the Ponca country. If caught, these horsethieves were killed on the spot, and this sometimes led to reprisals. Nevertheless, there was much visiting and a great deal of cultural exchange between the two tribes. Both the *Wá-wą* and *Heđúška* dances probably came to the Ponca from the Pawnee. According to PLC, the Ponca also maintained friendly relations with the Arikara or "Sand-Pawnee" when that tribe lived in South Dakota, and intermarried with them to some extent.

To the southwest of the Ponca, at one time, lived the *Pád.ka* or Padouca tribe. The Ponca identify these people as Comanche, but recent ethnohistorical and archeological work has shown that they were Lipan Apache (Champe, 1949; Secoy, 1951). Relations with this tribe were never friendly, and warfare was continuous until the Padouca were finally broken and driven from the land. PLC mentions the Ponca wars with the Padouca in his "History," and most of my other informants also mentioned them. The Padouca were skilled horsemen, and savage opponents. LMD had heard that they often used long lances with loops at the end with which they could snare and decapitate their enemies.

The West was apparently an empty waste as far as the Ponca were concerned. There seem to be no tales of contacts with tribes to the west, though many stories tell of long hunting trips in this direction, some as far as the Rocky Mountains, where the Ponca made hide "moccasins" to protect their dogs' feet, and hunted the Rocky Mountain goat.

To the north of the Ponca were the various bands of the Dakota nation. East of the Missouri were the semisedentary Yankton. West of this river were the warlike and nomadic Teton. We have already noted that the Ponca and Yankton Dakota were good friends. Relations between the Ponca and the Teton seem to have been amicable also, until shortly after the middle of the 19th century. Several of the travelers who journeyed up the Missouri found Ponca visiting in the Teton villages. Maximilian (1906, vol. 22, p. 160), for example, mentions a young Ponca named Ho-ta-ma, among the Dakota at Fort Pierre: "Frequently he was seen with his comrades playing what was called the hoop game, at which sticks covered with leather are thrown at a hoop in motion."

From about 1850 on, however, the Teton became increasingly belligerent. After the Ponca settled on their reservation, in 1858, the Teton found it quite convenient to raid them. This situation was made considerably worse by the Sioux Treaty of 1868, in which the United States, by error, ceded to the Dakota the reservation which had been guaranteed to the Ponca. Young Dakota braves who were seeking war honors now had a good excuse for attacking the Ponca—the Ponca were intruders on Dakota territory! Their raiding was intensified until the Ponca could scarcely venture outside their villages to till their land. It was this situation which finally prompted the Federal Government to remove the Ponca to the Indian Territory.

The Santee Dakota, who became neighbors of the Ponca following the Minnesota Uprising of 1862, and now occupy a small reservation adjoining that of the Northern Ponca, were apparently friendly with the Ponca from the first. The Teton recognized this fact, and when they raided the Ponca they often shot up the Santee settlement just for good measure. Relations between the Northern Ponca and the Santee are very good at the present time and there has been a great deal of intermarriage and cultural exchange through the years.

The Ponca were, of course, familiar with many other tribes with whom contacts were less extensive than for those listed above. PLC and Dave Little-cook (a Southern Ponca) supplied the following list of tribes with which the Ponca were acquainted.

English name	*Ponca name*	*Translation of Ponca name*
Arapaho	*Maxpíato*	Blue cloud.
Arikara	*Páđį-pìza*	Sand Pawnee.
Blackfoot	*Sí-sàbe*	Black foot.
Caddo	*Páode*	------------------------------
Cherokee	*Tšéđʃkì*	(Ponca version of the English name for the tribe—used only by the Southern Ponca.)
Cheyenne	*Šahíeđa*	(Ponca version of the Dakota name for this tribe—meaning "Red speakers," i.e., People of an alien [non-Siouan] speech.)
Comanche	*Pádǫkà*	(Believed by some Omaha and Ponca to have to do with the head, or hairdress.)
Dakota (Sioux)	*Šą́*	------------------------------
Santee Dakota	*Isą́-atʰì*	(Ponca version of the Dakota name for the Eastern Dakota, meaning "Dwellers at the knife.")

718-071—65——10

English name	*Ponca name*	*Translation of Ponca name*
Yankton Dakota	*Ihą́tąwì*	(Ponca version of the Dakota name for this band of the Middle Dakota, meaning "Dwellers at the end of the circle.")
Iowa	*Má-xùde*	Thought by some Ponca to be a corruption of *Pá-xùde*, "Gray heads."
Kansa or Kaw	*Ką́se*	------------------------------
Kiowa	*Kaǧéwa*	(Ponca version of the English name of the tribe.)
Mandan	*Mawádani*	------------------------------
Nez Perce	*Pegą́sąđè*	Braided forelocks (said to refer to a customary Nez Perce male hair-dressing).
Ojibwa	*Wáxtawį̀*	------------------------------
Omaha	*Umáhą*	Upstream people.
Osage	*Wažáže*	An ancient *Đégiha* term having reference to snakes.
Oto	*Wađótadą̀*	Lechers.
Pawnee	*Páđį*	------------------------------
Potawatomi	*Wahíđaxəm*	------------------------------
Quapaw	*Ugáxpe*	Downstream people.
Winnebago	*Hótą̀ga*	Big voices.

Names given by Fletcher and La Flesche (1911, pp. 101–103) which were not mentioned by my informants are:

Bannock	*Bánikì*	[Appears to be the *Đégiha* version of the English name for the tribe.]
Caddo	*Páđį-wasàbe*	Black Pawnee.
Oglala band of Teton Dakota.	*Ubđáđa*	[Ponca version of the Dakota name.]
Kickapoo	*Hígabu*	[Appears to be the *Đégiha* version of the English name.]
Kiowa	*Maxpíato*	Blue clouds. [I am certain that this is incorrect. Note that it is the same as the term given by PLC and Little-cook for "Arapaho." The Dakota have the same name, *Maxpíato*, for the Arapaho.]
Missouri	*Niútatšì*	Those who came floating down [the river] dead.
Sauk	*Đáge*	[Appears to be the *Đégiha* version of the first part of this tribe's name for themselves *Qsákiək*.]
Wichita	*Witšitá*	------------------------------

Ponca terms which Fletcher and La Flesche state were different from the Omaha terms, or were not used by the Omaha, are:

Crow	*Ką́ǧí-witšàša*	Crow people [a term adopted by the Ponca from the Dakota without modification].

English name	*Ponca name*	*Translation of Ponca name*
Crow (variant)	*Húpatȟda*	[Perhaps a *Đégiha* corruption of the variant Dakota name for the tribe, *Psalóka*. This, in turn, is a corruption of the Crow name, for themselves, *Apsáruke*.]
Dakota of Lower Brulé Reservation.	*Kúda-witšàša*	Lower people [a term adopted from the Dakota without modification].
Dakota of the Rosebud Reservation (Brulé band of Teton Dakota).	*Šą́xti*	Real or pure Sioux.
Dakota of Pine Ridge Reservation (Oglala and Brulé bands of Teton Dakota).	*Sitšą́xu*	Burnt-leg [the Dakota term for the Brulé, adopted without modification by the Ponca].
Tonkawa	*Níkađatè*	[Not given by Fletcher and La Flesche, but translated "Cannibals" by George Phillips, Omaha.]

To Army officers and others accustomed to Western-European techniques, the American Indian manner of waging war seemed unorganized and the "troops" lacking in discipline. Thus J. O. Dorsey (1884 a, p. 312), commenting on the military organization of the Omaha and Ponca, writes:

> War was not carried on by these tribes as it is by nations of the Old World. The *Đégiha* and other tribes have no standing armies . . . . no militia, ready to be called into the field by the government. On the contrary, military service is voluntary in all cases, from the private to the commanders, and the war party is usually disbanded as soon as home is reached. They had no wars of long duration; in fact, wars between one Indian tribe and another scarcely ever occurred; but there were occasional battles, perhaps one or two in the course of a season.

In spite of Dorsey's statement that the Ponca maintained no militia, in a later work he (1897, p. 214) indicates that the *Đíxida* and *Níkapàšna* clans served in somewhat such a capacity: "The *Đíxida* gens and part of the *Níkapàšna* gens of the Ponka tribe are considered to be the warriors of the tribe, though members of other gentes have participated in war." The names of these two clans, which mean "Blood" and "Bald Head" (i.e., a scalped head) are certainly appropriate for warrior groups.

Defensive warfare was the only type sanctioned by the tribe, and chiefs were forbidden to engage in any other form of warlike activity. Raids on other tribes, even though these groups were traditional enemies, were undertaken solely upon the responsibility of the leader who had organized them, and leaders of unsuccessful war parties were held accountable for the deaths of their followers. Whitman (1939, p. 180) writes: "If a man tried to lead a war party without adequate supernatural aid, the proof of which would be the failure of the expedition, he was liable to be severely flogged by the Buffalo Soldiers of the tribe."

In spite of the penalty for failure, however, warfare was an important avenue to success, and renowned war leaders seldom lacked followers. The various warriors' dancing societies, with their emphasis on military virtues, spurred the youth of the tribe to seek fame on the warpath. These societies vied with one another, each attempting to gain more war honors than the others. Generally each society maintained a fierce competition with one other rival group. Members of the society which had been more successful than its competitor in the most recent engagement could steal the wives of the members of the other group (Skinner, 1915 c, p. 692).

Dorsey (1884 a, p. 352) mentions "no retreat" obligations in connection with the Make-no-flight society, and Skinner (1915 c, p. 78) notes them for certain officials of the Not-afraid-to-die and *Iská-iyúha* groups. Men who had such obligations usually wore a bandolier with a long slit tail, and carried a lance. In an advance they led the charge. If the tide of battle began to turn, they passed their spear through the slit in their bandolier and literally staked themselves in place, making retreat impossible. Thus anchored, they stood and fought until their comrades could rally and save them. Needless to say, it was often difficult to find men willing to fill the offices of spearmen in the various societies.

War honor feathers and other war honor decorations and privileges of the type so well known for other Prairie and Plains tribes are mentioned for the Ponca by a number of writers (McGee, 1898, pp. 156–157; Fletcher and La Flesche, 1911, p. 440; Skinner, 1915 c, p. 794). I also collected the following list of war honor decorations and their symbolism from LRL:

1. One feather worn erect at the back of the head: Wearer has killed an enemy.
2. One feather worn horizontally at the back of the head: Wearer has captured an enemy.
3. Two feathers worn in the roach headdress: Wearer has counted first coup on an enemy.
4. One feather worn hanging over the forehead in front: Wearer has scalped an enemy. (This decoration has become a standard item in the present-day "straight" dancing costume.)
5. A red feather worn in any manner: Wearer has been wounded in battle.

On the basis of internal evidence I am personally inclined to take the various war honor feather systems with more than a grain of salt, not only in the case of the Ponca, but for the Prairie and Plains tribes in general. Every ethnographer, it seems, secures the "correct" war honor feather symbolism for the tribe he is studying, which he duly reports. The "rub" is that each system collected is quite different from those collected previously from that group.

Thus, the system which I collected for the Ponca does not match any of those previously described, nor, in fact, do any two of these agree! Symbolism probably did exist, but of a very loose and individual character, the wearer assigning the symbolism after he had made his favorite ornament. After all, in small tribes such as the Ponca and Omaha, it was quite easy to keep one's heroes straight even without distinctive ornaments.

At the present time the porcupine and deer-hair roach headdress, the crow belt, and various "war honor" type feathers are worn indiscriminately by all dancers in the Southern Ponca *Hedúška* dance. PLC, the only Northern Ponca dancer, sometimes wears such regalia in the dance as well. His favorite headdress, however, is a buffalo-skin cap, with horns, of the type worn by the Buffalo shamans and the Big-belly warrior society. Attached to this headdress are crow feathers, owl feathers, an eagle feather, and a coyote tail. PLC explained that the creatures represented by these decorations were all "takers of the meat" (i.e., scavengers on the battlefield), and were thus considered the guardians of warriors. The same creatures were represented in the original form of the crow belt or dancing bustle (Fletcher and La Flesche, 1911, pp. 441–442). Another dance headdress occasionally worn by PLC is a red-fox-skin turban with an erect golden eagle tail feather at the back. Leonard Smith stated that this headdress was formerly the insignia of the Ponca warrior. Chiefs wore a similar headdress but of otterskin, with a downy eagle plume in the back.

Actual "wars" of long duration and involving large numbers of men were not common with the Ponca, as we have noted above. The most common type of warlike endeavor, according to PLC, JLR, OK, LMD, LRL, and Lea Peniska, was the small raiding expedition which went in search of scalps and horses. Such war parties were led by an experienced man who owned or could borrow a sacred war bundle which guaranteed success to his venture.

The procedure followed on such a raid is succinctly described by Skinner, as follows:

The war leader, who carried a sacred *waxúbe*, or war bundle, and went ahead of the party could neither turn back nor go aside. If the party saw the foe, or desired him to turn off, they pulled him back, or turned him in the direction they wanted to go. He slept by himself, and all his cooking was done for him. Buffalo meat was prepared, and an attendant offered it to him in his hands on a bunch of sagebrush. The leader might only take four bites.

Scouts were sent out to all four points of the compass and told to watch, or, at night, to listen for the enemy. They went wrapped in white or gray blankets and acted like wolves, stooping over and trotting and signaling by howling. If they saw anything they came in trotting together, then apart, then coming together. At night, when the leader wanted them to return, generally about midnight, the party would howl like wolves to call them in. The scouts went as far as they could, and the one who went in the direction the party was traveling, left an arrow where he had been to be picked up as the party went by.

If a foe were seen and the war bundle was "opened on him," he must be killed, even if a mistake had been made and he turned out to be another Ponca and a relative.

When an enemy was killed, the Ponca scalped him, then cut off his head and threw it away. The sign for Ponca in the sign language indicates this custom. They also severed a dead enemy's hands from the wrists and threw them away. They also slashed the slain foe's back in checker board style. This was called "making a drum of an enemy's back." All these deeds were considered brave and could be boasted about. [Skinner, 1915 c, p. 797.]

Several such raiding expeditions were described by my informants. Accounts of two of these, which I consider typical, are presented here. The second describes an unsuccessful raid and the treatment accorded its leader.

A PONCA HORSE-STEALING RAID

As told by PLC

Now I will tell you a story that I heard from one of the oldest men in the tribe when I was a little boy. This story took place just before the Poncas were moved to Oklahoma. They needed horses so some of the men decided to go and capture them from the Sioux. Seven men started from the Ponca camp, which was right by the monument [the monument to the Mormon pioneers, approximately 3 miles south and 2 miles west of Niobrara, Nebr. This was the "Gray Blanket" village]. The whole Ponca tribe was camped there.

They were carrying ropes to lead the horses that they captured. They went west. They traveled quite a while before they saw any sign of the Sioux. Finally they found a big Sioux camp. The Sioux were dancing. The leader of the Poncas said, "We must hide until after dark."

They found a big log of driftwood and hid behind it. They stayed there all day. Once they were nearly spotted by a woman who came to gather wood. The leader whispered "Don't shoot unless they see you." The woman turned away before she saw them and went back to the village.

The Sioux danced until dark. The Poncas waited until the camp had quieted down, and then the leader said, "Now I am going to get the horses. You wait on that high spot over there." He left them and crept toward the Sioux camp.

The Sioux had their horses picketed near the tents so that if a horse made a noise its owner could hear it. Finally the Ponca leader reached the Sioux camp. He crept from one bunch of horses to the next, looking them over. Finally he came to an especially nice bunch. He found a wonderful speckled horse there. He picked out six other horses and put ropes around their necks. He led these seven horses out of the camp, and all the other horses followed.

Soon the Sioux found out what had happened and came in pursuit. "He! he! he!" they were yelling as they came after the Poncas. The six other Poncas were waiting in the place where the leader had told them to. They all got on the horses the leader had brought. By this time the whole Sioux camp was awake and coming after them fast. Dogs were barking and the men were getting their weapons ready in the Sioux camp. The Ponca scattered, each man going his own way. They thought they would have a better chance that way.

The leader of the war party, the man with the speckled horse, was the first man to return to the camp here. He came riding down between those two hills over there [two hills about 1 mile west of the Mormon monument]. All the people came out to greet him. They asked for the others and he told them what had happened. "I don't know what happened to the others," he said. The families of the other warriors thought that their boys had been killed and they all mourned.

The next day the second rider came in. He too had no news of the others. On the third day another warrior came in. He didn't know anything about the others. He hadn't seen them. The fourth day they finally all returned. The leader gave the wonderful speckled horse that he had captured to his brother. It was the fastest buffalo runner the Poncas ever owned.

NĄ́ŠKI-TĄ̀GA'S WAR PARTY
As told by JLR

Once there was a Ponca war party of seven men. Their leader was a man called *Ną́ški-tą̀ga,* which means "Big-head." They called him this because he had a big funny-shaped head. This war party traveled several days and didn't see the enemy. They traveled until their moccasins wore out. They came to some timber and went into it. They went to a clearing and began to mend their moccasins.

They had just begun to sew when they were attacked on all sides by the enemy. *Nąški-tą̀ga* escaped by running faster than the enemy. He ran as hard as he could, but the enemy were right behind him. They had horses and he knew they would soon catch him.

He was running across a flat place when he noticed a prairie wolf hole. He quickly jumped into this hole and covered himself with weeds. These holes are quite large, big enough for a man to hide in. He waited a short while, and suddenly he heard a roar above him. The horses were going right over the place where he was hidden!

He waited in the wolf hole until dark, then he got out and began to run again. He ran all that night. The next day he hid under a cutbank. Finally he got home safely.

He waited for the others to come back to camp, but they never showed up. They were all killed by the enemy. Because of this the people of the tribe turned against *Ną́ški-t̄ ga* and called him a poor war leader. They said that he always managed to get back safely himself, but the men who went with him never did. He was finished.

Only when the Ponca had been attacked in their villages or when their territory had been invaded in force did the Ponca tribe fight as a unit. On such occasions all of the men of the tribe, including the chiefs, entered the conflict. Sometimes even the women took part. J. O. Dorsey writes:

> When the foe had made an attack on the Omahas (or Ponkas) and had killed some of the people it was the duty of the surviving men to pursue the offenders and try to punish them . . . . When the Ponkas rushed to meet the Brulé and Oglala Dakotas, June 17, 1872, *Hudą́gi-hų̀,* a woman, ran with them most of the way, brandishing a knife and singing songs to incite the men to action. The women did not always behave thus. They generally dug pits as quickly as possible and crouched in them in order to escape the missiles of the combatants. [Dorsey, 1884 a, p. 312.]

JLR also described a defensive battle:

A BATTLE BETWEEN THE PONCA AND THE SIOUX

Once six Sioux came to attack the Ponca when they were camped on the Niobrara here. The Ponca didn't want to fight, but the Sioux kept firing into the camp until finally the Ponca got mad enough and chased them. They chased the Sioux across the Niobrara and beyond.

It was terribly hot day, and finally the Sioux horses, which were already tired, gave out. The Poncas saw the horses where the Sioux had turned them loose and cried, "There are their horses! Now we will catch them for sure!" All but two of the Sioux were run down by mounted Ponca and killed.

These last two Sioux barricaded themselves in some rocks. One of the Sioux held back the Ponca while the other dug for water, as they were both suffering greatly from thirst. The Poncas had dismounted, and were trying to crawl up on the Sioux where they had barricaded themselves. The Sioux who was holding the Ponca back was a good shot, though, and held them off. Once he cut the feather in two that a Ponca was wearing on his head.

It was plain that the Poncas couldn't get the Sioux in this way. Finally the Ponca leader said "Let's rush them." The Poncas remounted and rode down the two Sioux, killing them both.

The one Sioux who was such a good shot they mutilated and cut into pieces. Each warrior took a piece back. One warrior took his head, another his hand, and so on. They took them back to the village and rode around with them while the women danced the Scalp dance.

Later one old woman gathered up the pieces where they had been thrown in the dirt and buried them, so the children wouldn't see them lying around. She told the people who were watching her: "They deserved this for attacking us when we wanted no war, but they are humans after all."

Concerning the return from war, J. O. Dorsey (1884 a, p. 270) writes: "When men return from war the old men, who act as criers, halloo and recount the deeds of each warrior, whom they mention by name." Scalps taken by the party were turned over to the women, who stretched them over small willow hoops and painted the backs red. They were then attached to poles for the scalp dance. Warriors who had been killed by the enemy were danced over by members of the *Mawádani* warriors' dancing society and then buried in full battle regalia.

Captives were apparently well treated by the Ponca. Dorsey (1884 a, p. 332) writes: "Captives were not slain by the Omahas and Ponkas. When peace was declared the captives were sent home, if they wished to go. If not they could remain where they were, and were treated as if they were members of the tribe; but they were not adopted by any one."

Trophies of war were often kept by the Ponca and shown at parades and dances. Both PLC and Andrew Snake (a Southern Ponca) told of a Dakota warrior who used an Omaha dance (*Hedúška*) whistle as a war signal. However, he gave away his position by his whistling, and was found and killed by the Ponca. Later the Ponca composed a *Hedúška* song describing the incident, which is still a favorite among the Southern Ponca. The whistle which the Dakota was blowing when he was killed was displayed whenever this song was sung. This famous whistle, the end of which is carved to resemble a crane's head, is now on display in the Ponca City Indian Museum, Ponca City Library, Ponca City, Okla.

Fletcher and La Flesche (1911, pp. 439–441) describe the Ponca ceremony of conferring war honors, in which the sacred bundles figured prominently. Warriors were required to tell of their warlike deeds in the presence of the entire tribe and the unopened war bundles. Persons who lied or exaggerated concerning their deeds were threatened with supernatural punishment.

Peacemaking between the Ponca and other tribes, according to J. O. Dorsey (1884 a, p. 332; 1890, pp. 399–401), was usually effected by sending an envoy bearing a peace pipe to the enemy. Hyde (1934 a, p. 53) writes of a tradition mentioning that a *Wá-wą* ceremony was performed at a great peacemaking council attended by the Ponca, Omaha, Arikara, and Cheyenne.

At the present time, of course, tribal warfare is a thing of the past. Present-day Ponca know some tales of the old tribal wars, however, and are very proud of the tribe's military tradition. Veterans of World War II were highly honored on their return from the service, and pictures of veterans in uniform are found in many homes. One Southern Ponca family visited in 1954 had even built a small indoor shrine to honor the servicemen and servicewomen of the family. This consisted of small flags, pictures of members of the family in uniform, and religious and patriotic mottoes, all arranged artistically over the fireplace.

LIFE CYCLE

According to my informants, sexual intercourse was treated quite openly by the Ponca in aboriginal times. Since privacy was virtually unknown in an Indian camp or village, children at an early age probably observed their parents and others engaged in the sexual act. Two positions were commonly employed by the Ponca and Omaha in sexual intercourse; in the first the man lay above the woman, in the other their positions were reversed. Foreplay consisted in rubbing the genitals in the case of the male and rubbing the breasts and genitals in the case of the female.

Several philters or "love medicines" were used by Ponca men to seduce women who were cold to their advances. A small amount of this substance, usually plant material, was brushed on the girl's clothing, put in her food, left where she would step over it, or otherwise brought into contact with her. A favorite trick was to open a moistened packet of the medicine upwind of the girl. Once she tasted or smelled the medicine it acted as a powerful aphrodisiac and drove her to her would-be lover in spite of her inclinations.

Gilmore (1919, pp. 80, 82–83, 107, 134) lists meadowrue, bloodroot, wild columbine, "love seed" or *Cogswellia daucifolia,* and "fuzzyweed" or *Artemisia dracinculoides* as plants used in this manner.

Usually such love medicines were secured from an old shaman. Shamans renowned for particularly potent philters amassed considerable wealth from their manufacture and sale. Whitman (1939, pp. 190–191) notes that WBB secured such a "squaw medicine" from his mother's brother. At the time he was given the medicine he was warned that if he did not use it correctly (i.e., to secure a wife; not to seduce one woman after another) his misdeeds would "come back on him." This is a common concept among both the Ponca and the Omaha.

Sexual abstinence was observed before and during ceremonies. G. A. Dorsey (1905, p. 71) writes that participants in the Sun dance abstained from women, fearing a serious accident if they did not do so. Whitman (1939, p. 192) notes that ". . . married men were supposed to stay away from their wives four days before a peyote meeting."

Like his war honors, a Ponca man's record with women was a prestige factor in Ponca society. Skinner (1915 c, p. 788) tells of a men's society, the members of which publicly boasted of their conquests in love. He also notes that the Ponca women got together and boasted of their lovers, but there seemed to be no definite society established for this purpose.

Though chastity in unmarried girls was rare, complete promiscuity was frowned upon. Whitman (1937, p. 48) notes that if a girl denied a suitor and was not circumspect in her conduct thereafter she was liable to be raped. Apparently rape and seduction were common, as Whitman (1937, p. 72) later notes that Ponca girls were sometimes laced up in bison hides at night to protect them.

Harlots were rare in the tribe, though there were always one or two women in the tribe known as "run arounds." At the present there are two or three "toughies" in the Southern band. Though such women were frowned upon by the tribe, under certain conditions their conduct was excused. Whitman (1937, p. 86) writes: "Among the Ponca, it was said that a woman might become a run-around through a vision. In such a situation her conduct would be condoned." Just how many women availed themselves of this excuse for promiscuous behavior is not mentioned.

The familiar institution of the *berdache* or transvestite was found among the Ponca. As among the Dakota and other neighboring tribes, these men were sometimes taken as wives by warriors. They were reputed to make the best quillwork and beadwork. The condition was attributed to at least two causes. J. O. Dorsey (1894, p. 379) writes: "A Ponka child once said to the author, . . . 'If boys make a practice of playing with the girls they become . . . *Mi-xuga* [berdaches].'" PLC and OK held this belief as well. They also stated that if a man permitted himself to be seduced by the Deer-woman the same condition would result.

Extramarital sex relations on the part of a married woman were met with drastic punishment. Skinner (1915 c, pp. 800–801) writes: "A Ponca might kill, scalp, or cut the hair off a man whom he caught holding clandestine intercourse with his wife. A wife could kill another woman with whom her husband eloped. A husband could cut off the nose and ears of an unfaithful wife. Blood vengeance could not be exacted for these crimes."

JLR told a folk tale concerning a young woman, married to a man several years her senior, who had been having intercourse with her lover "under the tipi cover." Her husband, learning of her activities, traded places with her the following night. When the lover came and made his advances, the husband cut the lover's penis off and tied it to his wife's hair while she slept. The next morning when a crowd had gathered about the slain lover, the wife was identified as being the cause of his death by this singular hair ornament.

According to Jones (1890), the Ponca practiced wife lending when they visited, or were visited by, their friends from other tribes. This is, however, the only mention of this custom for the Ponca in the literature.

PLC made the following remarks concerning birth and its attendant customs among the Ponca:

> Births just came naturally among the Poncas. There was no birth control. In the old days, they tell me, a woman gave birth to her baby in a kneeling position. She was on a hide. Sometimes her female relatives would come and help her. Nowadays a bed is used, just like the White folks.
>
> In the old days you never saw any deformed children like you do now. The reason for this was that no one ever married any possible relation of his. They were also more careful about keeping away from a woman when she was having her turn [i.e., during menses].
>
> Births didn't come very close together in the old days. A woman wouldn't have her second child until the first one could walk around and take care of itself. The man and woman stayed away from one another unless they wanted a baby.

One wishes that there were more information available concerning the vital statistics of groups such as the Ponca. In such an economy, children are a handicap much longer than they are in a fully agricultural society. Lactation is prolonged and a woman cannot easily handle more than one infant at a time when the tribe is on the move, as on the tribal hunt. In spite of PLC's statement, there seems to be considerable evidence that infanticide has been general among food-gathering peoples and groups which, like the Ponca, had a mixed economy but were on the hunt for months at a time.

Dorsey (1884 a, p. 263) notes that the "Couvade is not practiced among the *Đégiha.* Foeticide is uncommon."

The umbilical cord of the child was commonly placed in a buckskin amulet made especially to preserve it. These amulets were still being manufactured by Ponca mothers for their children in 1954. These fetishes were usually in the shape of a horned toad for boys and in the shape of a turtle for girls. The horned toad symbolized endurance and longevity, the turtle fertility. In earlier times such fetishes were worn on the clothing of the child until puberty, but at the time of my fieldwork they were wrapped in cloth and secreted by the mother in a bureau drawer or other hiding place.

Concerning infancy, PLC stated:

> Ponca children were very carefully brought up in the old days. At first the mother carried the child around on a cradleboard that was fastened to her back. This could be set up against a tree when she was working around the camp. It had a wooden bow in front so that if it fell over the baby wouldn't fall face down in the dirt.

The down of the cattail was used by Ponca mothers as a talcum for their babies, as a padding for cradleboards, and in quilting baby wrappings. Newborn infants were also laid in it (Gilmore, 1919, pp. 64–65).

Most Ponca mothers of both bands still breast feed their babies if it is physically possible. Gilmore (1919, p. 136) mentions the use of an infusion of skeletonweed stems by mothers having a scanty supply of milk in order to increase the flow.

PLC mentioned that "when babies' teeth began coming in, they were given a piece of dried meat to chew on to help this along." All informants, when questioned as to the age of infants at creeping, standing, walking, and talking, stated that it was "just the same as White people." Although no detailed study was made in this area, I observed nothing which would negate this statement.

Unfortunately, early European explorers generally had little to say about child development in such groups as the Ponca in early post-contact times. Some interesting information concerning stages in development recognized by the aboriginal Ponca is contained in the Ponca folk tale "The Rabbit and the Grizzly Bear," which was recorded by J. O. Dorsey (1890, p. 47):

> (1) He commenced talking, saying words here and there, not speaking plainly or connectedly. (2) Next, he spoke without missing a word or syllable. (3) He became like boys who pull the bow and shoot very well, and who run a little now and then, but not very far. (4) He was as a youth who can draw the arrow, and who runs swiftly for some time. (5) He became a young man, one of those who carry the quiver and take wives.

Little information was secured concerning child care. Dorsey (1885 a, p. 107) mentions Ponca mothers scaring their children by telling them stories of *Indáđinge,* and thus making them behave. JLR mentioned, in a story, a woman putting her niece outside the tipi because the child would not stop crying. Jealousy of the woman's own daughter, possibly the Beloved Child, was implied.

I was impressed, while living among the Ponca, at the small amount of physical discipline used with children. Now and then a parent would scold a child for "getting into things," but this was all. No temper tantrums were observed, and little crying.

A Ponca child's education began as soon as it was able to imitate and learn adult patterns of behavior. Respect for sacred objects was inculcated at an early age. Whitman (1939, pp. 181–182) quotes WBB to the effect that: "Children were taught to respect the bundle. 'When we wanted to play or scuffle, we couldn't do it in the tipi on account of what hung in it.'" He later notes that WBB's father scolded his son for not listening to the father's prayer before breakfast (ibid., p. 182).

PLC made the following remarks concerning children's education and upbringing: "Some older man or woman taught the children how to act, and told them stories about famous people and battles. There was one thing that they always said to children. They told them 'Get up at daybreak. Go to bed with the sun.' "

Besides the games mentioned in an earlier chapter, the following children's activities are mentioned by Gilmore (1919, pp. 68, 72–73): Red hay stems were used by little boys as arrows; little girls used cottonwood leaves to make toy tipis and toy moccasins; whistles were also made of cottonwood leaves on occasion.

Children had contests involving the eating of unripe wild gooseberries without grimacing (ibid., p. 34). Spiderbean pods were used by little boys to imitate rattles, as were black-rattle-pod and little-rattle-pod pods (ibid., pp. 89–91). Wild sweetpea pods were roasted and eaten in sport by children (ibid., p. 98).

Violets were used by children in a game of "war," the heads of the violets being snapped by one person at his opponent (ibid., p. 103). This was apparently similar to the game played by contemporary White children in which dandelion heads are snapped. Elderberry stems were used by small boys for making popguns (ibid., p. 115).

J. O. Dorsey (1885 a, p. 108) notes that: "The Omaha and Ponka boys catch an insect called the *teatata* which resembles the 'hobby horse,' or praying insect. After saying certain words over it, they think that it turns its head in the directions of the buffaloes, or else in that of the Dakotas. . . . The whippoorwill . . . was often addressed by the children, who thought that it repeated their words."

An important childhood rite, the ceremony of "Turning the Child," is described by Fletcher and La Flesche (1911, pp. 44–45). During this ceremony a child was led into a sacred tent in which a stone, representing long life, had been placed. The child was led to the stone, made to stand upon it, and then turned by the hereditary priest to each of the four lifegiving winds or directions. During this ceremony a child's infant name was "thrown away" and a new name, having clan significance, was bestowed. A lock of hair was cut from the heads of boys who were "turned" but this was not done to girls. This ceremony was last performed in the 1930's. Perry Le Claire was the "child" turned and LRL the officiating priest.

The vision quest was an important part of a Ponca boy's training in former years. The boy went to a secluded place, his face painted with charcoal, and fasted for a number of days, in hopes that some "spirit helper," usually an animal, would "pity" him and give him supernatural power or knowledge. Whitman (1939, pp. 184–185) notes that WBB was sent on the vision quest by his father. The vision quest is no longer practiced by either band of the Ponca.

There was no puberty ceremony for boys in the Ponca tribe. PLC commented that when a boy became old enough to start being interested in girls he began braiding his hair. This was a sign that he was beginning to think of himself as a man.

OK remembered a sort of girl's puberty ceremony in which the Northern Ponca chief Birdhead gave away a horse in honor of the fact his daughter had become a woman. The horse was highly decorated, with quilled leg ornaments and a beaded bridle. It was led into the dance ring and given to an old woman with appropriate speeches. This was considered a great honor for the daughter.

Concerning menstruation, J. O. Dorsey (1884 a, p. 267) writes:

> Among the Omahas and Ponkas the woman makes a different fire for four days, dwelling in a small lodge, apart from the rest of the household, even in cold weather. She cooks and eats alone, telling no one of her sickness, not even her husband.

Lowie also mentions this custom, and it was mentioned by all of my informants as well (Lowie, 1917, pp. 92–93). Women were considered very dangerous during their period, and were carefully excluded from ceremonies. JLR attributed much of the disease of present-day Indians to the fact that the menstrual taboo is no longer strictly observed. His opinions on this matter were echoed by WBB and other Southern Poncas.

Ponca boys began going on the warpath at what would be considered, in our culture, a very early age. PLC and JLR stated that it was not uncommon for boys 12 or 13 years old to accompany war parties, and this statement is confirmed by that of J. O. Dorsey (1890, pp. 372–377) concerning young *Nudą́-axa*. Such boys secured water and firewood for the older warriors and performed other camp drudgery.

Present-day Ponca youths usually attend school until they are 16 or 18; they then travel about the country for a year or two before they settle down and marry. The traveling around period is spent in visiting other tribes, following rodeos, visiting large cities, and visiting places of unusual interest. They support themselves during this time by working on and off for eating money and by staying with other Indians. Young men from other tribes visit the Ponca in the same manner, often from such distant groups as the New York Iroquois and the Plains-Cree of Saskatchewan. Most adult Ponca men have a large fund of stories relating to their wanderings at this stage of life which are recounted in much the way the old tales of war expeditions would have been told a few generations back.

Concerning marriage customs of the Ponca, A.D. Jones, Superintendent and Clerk of the (Southern) Ponca Agency, in a letter to J. M. Wood, the Agent, dated November 12, 1890, writes as follows:

> Girls married at 14 to 16 years of age. Often a man "bought" a girl with ponies when she was very young, then married her later. In this case she might live with him in his camp if he were already married to her older sister, otherwise she would remain with her parents until of marriageable age. Wives who were not sisters often refused to live under the same roof. The mother-in-law wielded great power. If the husband mistreated his bride the mother-in-law would fetch her home.

Jones' comments on the early age of Ponca girls at marriage are confirmed by Dorsey (1884 a, p. 259), who writes:

> It is now customary for girls to be married at the age of fifteen, sixteen, or seventeen years among the Omahas, and in the Ponka tribe they generally take husbands as soon as they enter their fifteenth year. It was not so formerly; men waited until they were twenty-five or thirty, and the women till they were twenty years of age.

PLC commented on Ponca marriage customs as follows:

> When a boy wanted to marry a girl, he could do it in one of two ways. The first way he gave lots of presents to her family, such as horses and buffalo robes. This was the most common way. If her family kept the presents, it meant that they approved the marriage, and the girl would come and live with the man.
>
> The second way was by arrangement. A boy would go to his parents. He would tell them that he was interested in a certain girl, and ask them to help arrange a match. If they were willing, they would go and talk with the girl's parents. After four days, if the girl's parents didn't complain, the boy's parents collected a large number of gifts and took them over. Four days later these gifts were returned.[43] This made the marriage good.

These two forms of marriage may reflect the mixed cultural heritage of the Ponca. The first form is quite typical of the High Plains area (i.e., Cheyenne, Teton Dakota) while the second is the usual form in the Eastern Woodlands (i.e., Ojibwa, Potawatomi).

James (1905 b, p. 25) refers to young Omaha men eloping with married women and coming to live with the Ponca. Perhaps, in like manner, Ponca couples eloped and went to live with the Omaha to avoid the censure of their tribe.

[43] By "these gifts" PLC actually means gifts of comparable value, not the same items.

At the present time the Ponca customarily contract marriages in the manner of the major White culture, i.e., in either a church or a civil ceremony. Common law marriages are also quite common.

Courtship was sometimes a bit difficult for the Ponca youth in aboriginal times, since maidens, though usually quite willing to come at least half way, were closely chaperoned by older female relatives. With a strong will, however, the Ponca boy usually found a way. PLC commented as follows:

> When a boy wanted to impress a girl he would wear his best clothes and parade in front of her whenever he could. At dances he would try to talk to her alone. Girls would walk under a boy's blanket for a while, and the boys would talk to them.
>
> It was usually quite hard for a boy to talk with a girl alone. Wherever a girl went, some female relative would go along. Boys sometimes found opportunities to speak with girls when the girls went after water. When a girl was interested in a boy she would make it easy for him to see her. Sometimes a boy would court a girl by playing his flute outside her tent at night. She would know who it was, and if she could, she would go outside and speak with him.

Little information could be secured on Ponca nuptials. One gains the impression that there was slight formal ceremony. PLC commented merely that a Ponca bride braided her hair and put on her best clothes for the marriage feast. This feast was attended by the families of the bride and groom and a few of the couple's friends.

As I have indicated earlier, the Ponca practiced polygyny. PLC commented: "Usually the old-time Poncas only had one wife. Sometimes, though, a well-to-do man would take two wives. If he did this he usually took the younger sister of the first wife, because they could get along better if they were sisters. Standing-bear, the chief, had two wives, and they were sisters. A woman never had two husbands."

At the present time monogamy is the only form of marriage in the Ponca tribe.

Divorce was simple in Ponca society. PLC stated: "If a man and wife didn't get along, or weren't satisfied, they just split up." Skinner (1915 c, pp. 784–785) writes of men giving away their wives in the *Hedúška* dance, and Whitman (1937, p. 41) notes that: "For prestige fathers gave up their sons to war; husbands gave away their wives."

There was no fixed rule regarding the disposition of children of a divorced couple. J. O. Dorsey (1884 a, p. 262) writes: "When parents separate, the children are sometimes taken by their mother, and sometimes by her mother or their father's mother. Should the husband be unwilling, the wife cannot take the children with her. Each consort can remarry."

Separation and desertion are the common forms of ending a marriage among the present-day Ponca. Though legal divorce is recognized as the "right way" of doing things, few Ponca bother with it. Cost is undoubtedly a factor, but the fact that the old pattern of divorce was simple separation is probably more relevant.

Dorsey (ibid., p. 260) mentions a widow remarrying in a rather unusual manner. She ran a race with her suitors and the one who caught her became her husband. This "reverse Sadie Hawkins" procedure was considered loose conduct on the part of the widow by Dorsey's informants.

PLC commented as follows on the status of the aged in Ponca society:

> The Poncas took care of their old people as best they could. They tried to treat the old people as good as possible, because everyone gets old sooner or later. In the old days, if the tribe was going on a long journey, the old people were sometimes left behind. It was said that nature would take care of them. The old people were well loved because they knew the stories and history of the tribe.

J. O. Dorsey (1885 a, p. 107) states that the old were "addressed reverently when alive" and in another work (1890, p. 29) he mentions a certain corrupt form of speech "used by old women and children," which indicates that the aged were treated with indulgence. In yet a third study (1884 a, pp. 274–275) he writes:

> The Omahas and Ponkas never abandoned the infirm aged people on the prairie. They left them at home, where they could remain till the return of the hunting party. They were provided with a shelter among the trees, food, water, and fire . . . . The Indians were afraid to abandon (*wagdá*) their aged people, lest *Wakąda* should punish them when they were away from home.

An interesting comment upon Ponca acculturation and how it affected the old men's position in the tribe is contained in Whitman's "Xúbe, A Ponca Autobiography":

> In a society in which the goals could best be reached by the young, the practice of *xúbe* [the use of supernatural power, JH] gave to the older men the necessary instrument of control by which they could maintain their ascendancy over an ambitious younger generation. *Xúbe* kept the young in their place. As a man grew older he acquired more and more power. As his physical vigor slowly diminished, he took on supernatural strength. Only at the end of his life did a man give up his power, usually to a receptive and selected son. By this act he was thought to kill himself; his life was ended; and he died.
>
> Now that the white man has shattered *xúbe* with his superior power, the Ponca father has little left to hand on to his son; the old man can no longer maintain his ascendancy, because today the young have lost faith and interest. They no longer fear their elders who have become an economic burden instead of a source of spiritual and economic strength. The effect on Ponca society of this loss of respect has been one of rapid and tragic disintegration. [Whitman 1939, pp. 192–193.]

With the foregoing statement in mind, I discussed *xúbe* with some of the younger Ponca. Though a few could "speak the language" of *xúbe*, that is, knew how it was supposed to operate, it was very clear that to most of them the various sacred rites in which this sacred power figured, together with their bundles and paraphernalia, were something one spoke of with respect only out of consideration for the feelings of the older people. Though one young man remarked, "It sure would have been wonderful if the old folks had passed that stuff down to us," even this individual had made no effort to learn what little sacred lore remains in the tribe.

Turning next to the subject of sickness, we note that to the Ponca there were two principal types of illness: the type which resulted from natural causes and the type which was caused by sorcery or the displeasure of the spirits. Diseases or injuries of the first type were generally treated therapeutically (i.e., herbal teas for stomach disorders, splints for broken limbs, etc.). Diseases of the second type, since they were caused by magical or supernatural means, could be combated only by means of a stronger counter magic. Often one could not be sure which type of disease had come, and it was therefore thought best to take no chances. Thus, many Ponca remedies combined therapeutics with magic.

The following cure for snakebite, given by Fletcher and La Flesche (1911, p. 46), illustrates this well:

> When any one in the tribe chanced to be bitten by a snake, he sent at once for a member of the *Wažáže* [Snake, JH] gens, who on arriving at the tent quickly dug a hole beside the fire with a stick, and then sucked the wound so as to draw out the blood and prevent any serious trouble from the injury. The purpose in digging the hole could not be learned from the writer's informant.

To the Ponca, magical methods were as reasonable as splints for a broken leg. For example, Fletcher and La Flesche (1911, p. 43) mention that members of the *Đíxida* clan cured pains in the head by wetting an arrow with saliva, setting it in position on the bow string, and then pointing the arrow at the sick man's head four times. Then the *Đíxida* rubbed the afflicted person's head with the arrow, and so effected a cure for the pain.

The Ponca possessed numerous herbal remedies, many of which were recorded by M. R. Gilmore (1919). The following have been abstracted from his work:

Puffballs were used as a styptic for any wounds, especially for application to the umbilicus of newborn infants (p. 62).

Cedar fruits and leaves were boiled together and used internally for coughs. For a cold in the head, twigs were burned and the smoke inhaled (pp. 63–64).

Cattail down was used as a dressing for burns and scalds (pp. 64–65).

Calamus was used as a carminative, and the rootstock was chewed as a cough remedy and as a remedy for toothache. For colic an infusion of the pounded rootstock was drunk. As a remedy for colds the rootstock was chewed or a decoction was drunk, or it was used in the smoke treatment (pp. 69–70).

Blueflag rootstock was pulverized and mixed with water or saliva and the infusion dropped into the ear to cure earache; it was also used to medicate eyewater. A paste was made to apply to sores and bruises (p. 72).

Oak and red elm bark were boiled in water and the decoction given for bowel trouble (p. 75).

Wild four-o'clock root was chewed and blown into wounds (p. 78). Windflower also was used for wounds, externally or internally, and was also used as a wash for sores (p. 82).

The root of the blue cohosh was boiled and used as a fever medicine (p. 83).

For kidney trouble a decoction of wild black currant was used (p. 84).

A wash for the inflammation of the eyes was made by steeping the fruit of the wild rose (p. 85).

Chokecherry bark and fruit decoctions were used as diarrhea remedies (p. 89).

The root of the Kentucky coffee tree was pulverized and mixed with water and used as a rectal injection in cases of constipation. A syringe made of an animal bladder and a bird leg bone was used in connection with this (pp. 89–90).

Shoestringweed was used as a moxa in cases of neuralgia and rheumatism. The stems were attached to the skin after having been moistened at one end, and were then fired and allowed to burn down to the skin (p. 93). Rabbitfoot was used similarly (pp. 97–98).

Chamaesyce serpyllifolia (Pers.) Small was boiled and the decoction drunk by young mothers whose flow of milk was scanty or lacking (p. 99).

The raw root of the pleurisy root was eaten for bronchial or pulmonary trouble. It was also applied to wounds and sores (p. 109).

The root of the tall milkweed was eaten raw as a remedy for stomach trouble (p. 110). Wild mint tea was used as a carminative (p. 112).

Prairie groundcherry root was used in the smoke treatment. A decoction of the root was used for stomach trouble and headache. A dressing for wounds was also made from it (p. 113).

Hot plantain leaves were applied to the foot in order to draw out a thorn or splinter (p. 115).

Coralberry and buckbrush leaves were steeped to make an infusion for weak or inflamed eyes (p. 116).

Wild gourd was highly regarded as a medicine. It was called "human being medicine" from its shape. Gilmore (p. 117) notes that "as a remedy for any ailment a portion of the root from the part corresponding in position to the affected part of the patient's body is used—for headache or other trouble in the head some of the top of the root is used; for abdominal trouble a bit of the middle of the root; and so on."

Combplant was used as an antidote for snakebite and for other bites and stings. It was also used in smoke curing. As a remedy for toothache a piece was kept on the painful tooth. Burns were bathed in the juice of this plant, and it was said that shamans bathed their arms and hands in the juice so that they could take a piece of meat from a boiling kettle without suffering pain (p. 131).

Angle stem root was commonly burned in the smoke treatment for a cold in the head, neuralgia, and rheumatism (p. 132).

A tonic for horses was made of pilotweed (p. 132).

Ragweed was used to cause nosebleed, being snuffed up the nostrils. This was done to relieve headaches (pp. 132–135).

Sticky head was used by the Ponca for consumption (p. 135).

Beaverroot was boiled and the decoction was taken for intestinal pains and as a physic (p. 107).

Skeletonweed stems were made into an infusion for sore eyes. Mothers having a scanty supply of milk also drank this infusion in order to increase the flow (p. 136).

Present-day Ponca still use many herb remedies, but the services of White docters are employed in cases of serious illness. A few plants of medicinal use were collected from PLC, who also described their uses.

Artemesia glauca, or green sage, is made into an emulsion which is taken both internally and externally for burns. PLC described a case in which a woman had been badly burned with lye and had been "given up" by White physicians. PLC's brother Henry, aided by PLC, cured the woman with decoctions of this plant, forcing her to drink large quantities of it and covering all but a small part of the burned area with cloths soaked in the fluid. The small area was left exposed to "let the poisons out."

Prairie cone flower is made into a tea which is taken for kidney trouble, sore back, gallstones, and general aches and pains. PLC was using this when visited in 1951, having recently hurt his back.

Lygodesmia juncea, or skeletonweed, mentioned previously as having been used in an infusion applied to sore eyes and to increase the flow of milk in a mother's breasts, was given as a diarrhea remedy by PLC. The stems are cut into 1-inch lengths and soaked in a quart of water until they have imparted a definite greenish hue to the liquid. Doses of this infusion are taken by the patient every half an hour until he is cured.

Members of the Peyote religion in the Southern band tend to regard their ritual plant as a catholicon, or cure-all, and tell marvelous tales of patients cured by it, including persons suffering from tuberculosis.

PLC described the proper way to dig a medicinal plant:

> Before you dig the plant, stand over it and pray. This plant belongs to Mother Earth, and we must thank her for it. After you have prayed, dig the plant very carefully. Cut the stem off over the hole, and throw the top part of the stem, the

part you aren't using, back in the hole. Then sprinkle tobacco in the hole, praying again. This is to thank Mother Earth for her gift. After you have dug the root, scrape it very carefully, and thread it on a string to dry.

PLC remarked that dried Mayflies and the bladder of a young rabbit had been used by Whiteshirt, the Northern Ponca chief and shaman, in his "doctoring way." PLC had learned this when he was a young man, from a chance remark made by Whiteshirt, but had failed to ask for further information. Had he done so, Whiteshirt would have taught him their uses. "I was foolish not to ask him when I had the chance."

Adam Le Claire, a Southern Ponca, is known as a "bleeding doctor." Persons who are not feeling well go to him to have their blood "thinned." He taps a vein in the arm with a small steel lancet (formerly a flint knife was used) and removes a quantity of blood. May Kimball, also a Southern Ponca, stated that when she was a girl she had been doctored in this way by having cuts made in her temples. It is not known whether "bleeding" of this sort is an aboriginal practice or, one acquired from the major "White" culture where it was extensively practiced until about one hundred years ago and is still used today for the treatment of high blood pressure and certain heart ailments. At any rate it was, and is, practiced by a number of American Indian tribes of the Prairie and Plains region as far north as the Plains-Ojibwa.

Some Ponca ideas concerning death are recorded by J. O. Dorsey (1894, p. 374), who writes:

About eighteen years ago, the author was told by the Ponka, . . . that they believed death to be caused by certain malevolent spirits, whom they feared. In order to prevent future visits of such spirits, the survivors gave away all their property, hoping that as they were in such a wretched plight the spirits would not think it worth while to make them more unhappy.

Here we have an excellent explanation of the Prairie and Plains custom of the "give-away."

Whitman (1939, p. 184) notes that: "Xubes were said to have short lives. They were also liable to lose their children." He (1937, p. 97) also records the Ponca belief that a medicine man could prevent sickness, so that when it came time to die, he suddenly dropped dead.

After a person died, his spirit continued to exist. Dorsey (1894, p. 419) writes:

They have a very crude belief. Each person is thought to have a *wanáxe* or spirit, which does not perish at death. According to Joseph La Flèche and Two Crows, the old men used to say to the people . . . i.e. "If you are good, you will go to the good ghosts. If you are bad, you will go to the bad ghosts." Nothing was ever said of going to dwell with Wakanda, or with demons.

Also (p. 421):

There has been no belief in the resurrection of the body, but simply one in the continued existence of the ghost or spirit.

Fletcher and La Flesche (1911, p. 310) also record a belief in the continued existence of the soul. In describing the Ponca chief-making ceremony they cite the speech of an old man, who remarked: "The chiefs, although long dead, are still living and still exercise a care over the people and seek to promote their welfare; so we make the offering of food, the support of our life, in recognition of them as still our chiefs and caring for us." PLC also mentioned an old Ponca, stating that after he died he would be "above," or in heaven, looking down upon his people.

Occasionally spirits hovered about on the earth as ghosts and there are several Ponca tales concerning encounters with them. Whitman (1939, p. 193, footnote 60) writes that: "Black Eagle was afraid of ghosts. Power, it was thought, might also be handed on after death if the recipient came to the grave after dark immediately following burial. When a man dies, the heart and eye are thought still to possess life until the spirit passes to the spirit world."

Ghosts sometimes tormented the living: "The spirit of a murdered person will haunt the people, and when the tribe is on the hunt, will cause the wind to blow in such a direction as to betray the hunters to the game and cause the herd to scatter, making it impossible for the people to get food" (Fletcher and La Flesche, 1911, p. 216). This belief was also mentioned by JLR, who told of a murderer shooting a ghost with his gun and thus freeing himself from the curse.

Shamans were thought to be able to predict their own deaths. J. O. Dorsey (1888 a, p. 73) records that: "Bare-legs had a presentiment of his own death. He saw his spirit covered with blood upon a hill; four days later, May 3, 1872, he was slain." Whitman (1939, pp. 192–193) likewise records WBB's father predicting his own death by the fact that his spirit helper, a mescal bean, had become cracked.

PLC described Ponca mortuary customs as follows:

> When someone died, the relatives would cut off their hair and mourn for a long time. Both men and women would cut off their hair and cut their arms and legs with a knife. They wouldn't eat for four days afterwards.
>
> A body was buried in the ground and a roof was made over the grave. This roof was made of logs in a Λ shape. This was then covered with dirt.
>
> The people often thought of the dead. Sometimes they will throw away a little piece of food when eating, for a dead person's spirit, or set a glass of water out for it. When a crying is heard outside people throw a little food out. They think maybe it is the spirit come back.
>
> People were usually buried in some of their best clothes, and sometimes a little food and water was placed with them.

Special painted designs, denoting the clan of the deceased, were applied before burial. In some cases other special insignia were added as well. Fletcher and La Flesche (1911, p. 44) write: "When a member of the subdivision *Táhatȯ-itȧži* [of the *Níkapȧšna* gens] died, moccasins made from the skin of the deer (which was taboo to the living) were put on his feet that he might not 'lose his way,' but go on safely and 'be recognized by his own people' in the spirit world."

Concerning Ponca graves Maximilian writes: "Towards evening we were near the Assiniboin steamer, which lay before us, and halted in the vicinity of Basil Creek, where the Poncas formerly dwelt, numbers of whose graves are seen upon the hills" (Maximilian, 1906, vol. 22, p. 290). We are not told how these graves were built. At a later period Alanson Skinner (1915 c, p. 801) described the graves as follows: "Now the Ponca bury their dead in the ground altogether, but formerly they used scaffolds and trees." Bushnell (1927, fol. p. 52) shows two illustrations of Ponca burials, one of the scaffold type, the other of the log-roofed type mentioned by PLC (see pl. 14, the present volume).

JLR commented upon Ponca burial customs as follows:

> The old time Poncas used to use both scaffolds and graves to put the dead in. In winter, when the ground was frozen solid and they couldn't dig a grave, they buried the person on a scaffold. In summer they dug a grave. Ponca graves were quite shallow. Various gifts were placed with the dead person.
>
> Sometimes, in the old days, the man's family would tie his favorite horse to the grave. This is not done any more. We don't ever bury on a scaffold any more either.

Dorsey mentions a complete give-away at death as the Ponca custom, but PLC stated that only a partial give-away was practiced in his day. He also mentioned that the Ghost Lodge or Spirit-keeping ceremony of the neighboring Dakota was unknown to the Ponca. Mourning feasts did occur, however, and G. A. Dorsey (1905, p. 71) witnessed one at the Ponca Sun dance which he attended. Presents were distributed in the name of the deceased on this occasion. A similar custom is mentioned by J. O. Dorsey (1894, p. 148): "If the deceased was a male and a member of an order of young men, all who belong to it are invited to a feast where they sing songs." Skinner (1915 c, p. 785) notes that: "The *Heđúška* helps people mourn for their dead, and makes collections of gifts for bereaved people to help dry their tears."

Deceased persons could be referred to by name (J. O. Dorsey, 1883, p. 273). Indeed, it was common for a Ponca to assume the name of a deceased ancestor (J. O. Dorsey, 1894, p. 371).

At certain times the spirit or soul of a dead person would be reincarnated. When this occurred, the child in which the soul was reborn often grew up to be a shaman. In 1954, while visiting the Southern Ponca, I was shown such a child. This boy, it was reported, knew things which he could not possibly have learned except in a previous life. He could speak in great detail of events which had taken place long before his birth and he could also look into the future. Mrs. Wilson D. Wallis reports a similar belief among the Canadian Dakota (personal communication, 1954).

NORTHERN PONCA–SOUTHERN PONCA: DIFFERENTIAL ACCULTURATION

In the preceding chapters Ponca culture has been described as fully as the information available and my own abilities allow. I have also attempted to show, when the information permitted, changes through time and the present differences between the cultures of the Northern and Southern bands. Thus far, however, the possible causes of these differences have not been treated at any length. It is the purpose of this final chapter to consider what factors might have been responsible for the existing differences, especially the differential acculturation.

It was noted in the Preface that early Ponca culture was very close to that of the Central Algonquian and Central Siouan tribes. This culture developed in, and was primarily adapted to, a Woodland and Prairie environment. The Ponca have retained elements of this Woodland-Prairie culture up to the present. After reaching the Niobrara region, however, the Ponca gradually began to assume more and more traits characteristic of the tribes of the High Plains.

In the early period the Ponca seem to have borrowed extensively from the Caddoan-speaking tribes to the south and west, the Pawnee and Arikara. The *Hełúška* complex is very likely Pawnee in origin and the *Wá-wą* may be as well. Both Omaha and Ponca traditions state that the art of building earth lodges was learned from the Arikara (Fletcher and La Flesche, 1911, p. 75).

In historic times, however, borrowing was heaviest from the Teton and Yankton Dakota, neighbors of the Ponca to the north and northwest since about 1750. Various costume styles, military and medicine societies, games and social customs are undoubtedly Dakota importations. Of course we must not infer that this borrowing was a one-sided affair. The Dakota secured their *Ómaha* or Grass dance from the Omaha and Ponca, and many other traits and complexes which have come to be considered "typically Dakota" may ultimately prove to have stemmed from the *Đégiha*. Nevertheless, it seems quite likely that the Ponca, being the smaller group, were more often the recipients of Dakota customs than the reverse.

By 1877, the year of the Ponca Removal, the "Dakotaization" of the Ponca had reached such a point that it is often difficult, when one is presented with a series of old photographs showing both Dakota and Ponca, to separate the members of the two tribes by their dress and equipment. Likewise, most of those traits which distinguish the Ponca of this period from their close linguistic and cultural relatives, the Omaha, are features which the former tribe had borrowed from the Dakota. Examples are the Plains style woman's dress, hard-soled Plains moccasins, and geometrically designed beadwork in the "lazy stitch" technique. It may be assumed that this borrowing was not limited to items of dress and personal equipment, and that other, nonmaterial, traits were borrowed as well.

With the division of the Ponca tribe into Northern and Southern bands after the Removal, the situation was altered. Those Ponca who chose to remain in the Indian Territory were now no longer in face-to-face contact with the Dakota. Among their new neighbors in the south were various Northeastern, Southeastern, and Central Siouan groups whose influence cannot but have tended to reinforce or revive Woodland elements in Ponca culture. Likewise certain new Eastern complexes, such as the "Stomp" dance, were introduced.[44] New Plains elements, not of Dakota origin, were introduced as well, such as the Ghost dance, Peyote religion, and Brush dance.

In the north, the process of assimilation to Dakota culture continued. There was a great deal of intermarriage with the Santee and Yankton Dakota, and, after the cessation of hostilities, with the Teton Dakota as well. This intermarriage, of course, led to increased cultural exchange. Members of both bands, in discussing recent Ponca history, acknowledged that the Northern Ponca had "picked up a lot of Sioux ways" in the years since the Removal. This was particularly evident, according to EBC, in the last *Heđúška* dances held in the Niobrara area. The Northern Ponca dancers "dressed and danced like the Sioux, bending down and shaking their heads Sioux style."

At the same time these differing tribal influences were affecting the cultures of the two Ponca bands, White acculturation was proceeding apace. In the preceding chapters the reader will have noted that in nearly all respects the culture of the Northern Ponca more closely approximates that of the Whites than does that of the Southern band. In their economy, technology, social organization, and ceremonialism, the Southern Ponca have retained much more of the aboriginal pattern.

The only striking exceptions to this general rule are in the areas of traditional history and mythology, where the Northern Ponca are the more conservative. The reasons for this are immediately apparent. The Southern Ponca, in their new environment, were no longer reminded of past events by geographic landmarks (i.e., the site of the Ponca fort, the den of *Wakądagi*, etc.); hence the stories connected with these landmarks were forgotten. This was clearly demonstrated to me when I was gathering data in connection with the Ponca land claims litigation in 1954. It was very important, in this work, to secure descriptions of the tribal domain in terms of recognizable geographic landmarks. Almost all Northern Ponca informants over

[44] According to Curtis (1930, p. 214) it was Henry Snake, a Southern Ponca, who introduced the Stomp dance to the Osage, Oto, Kansa, Iowa, and Cheyenne. I was present when Henry's brother, Andrew, introduced the Creek style Stomp dance among the Omaha, in 1949.

35 years of age were able to supply data of value, while in the Oklahoma group only a very few old people were able to do so.

In my opinion the three principal factors responsible for this differential proportion of White acculturation are:

(1) The difference in the size of the two bands.

(2) The large percentage of White intermarriage in that portion of the tribe which became the Northern Ponca band.

(3) Reinforcement of certain Indian traits among the Southern Ponca through their participation in Pan-Indianism.

The very considerable difference in the size of the two Ponca bands is perhaps the main reason why the Northern Ponca have approximated White culture more closely than have their Southern kinsmen. According to Dorsey and Thomas (1910, p. 279) 225 Ponca returned to Nebraska, while 600 remained in the Indian Territory. Obviously, all other factors being equal, the culture of a small group would tend to be swallowed up by the dominant culture more quickly than that of a large one.

All of the other factors were *not* equal, however, even at the start, and this brings us to the second point. Although Chief Standing-bear and a few of his close relatives were unmixed, many of those who returned to Nebraska with him were of mixed Indian-White descent. Also, the percentage of individuals of mixed Ponca-White descent in the Northern band was considerably augmented at the time the Northern Ponca reservation was created.

The circumstances of this event, one of the "hidden pages" of Ponca history, were explained by PLC and JLR in 1954. It seems that in order to secure a reservation from the Government, Chief Standing-bear needed considerably more personnel than had followed him from Indian Territory. He therefore sought to enroll in his band as many persons as possible of Ponca or part-Ponca descent in order to qualify it as a "reservation size" band. Thus, many persons of mixed descent, who before that time had formed a sort of "fringe group" in the area and had, in fact, not even been moved to Indian Territory with the main body of the tribe, were now enrolled as Ponca. These individuals, mixed both biologically and culturally, were gradually absorbed into the Northern Ponca band.

The third factor listed, the influence of Pan-Indianism, is more difficult to assess. One might begin by defining terms. By Pan-Indianism is meant the process by which certain Indian groups are losing their tribal distinctiveness and in its place are developing a generalized nontribal "Indian" culture. Some of the elements in this culture are modifications of old tribal customs; others seem to be innovations peculiar to Pan-Indianism. The Southern Ponca have participated in this phenomenon from the start, which I would place somewhere between 1915 and 1925.

To date there are few accounts of Pan-Indianism in the anthropological literature. Petrullo was the first to touch upon the subject:

> The reservation system has caused the old tribal animosities to disappear, and there has arisen a sympathetic attitude of the various tribal units toward each other, with the result that intercourse between them has become common, and each other's rites are observed and studied with the avowed purpose of comparison. This constant interchanging of ideas is giving rise to a novel feeling for Indian nationality. As welcome as this may be to one interested in the progress and development of the Indian, it must not be underestimated as being of prime importance in the disintegration of tribal culture patterns. The Delawares are actively participating in this, and as a result not only have they assimilated many of the ideas emanating from other tribes, but have disseminated their own widely. [Petrullo, 1934, p. 26.]

Herskovits, in his "Acculturation," also touches upon the subject. In commenting upon Margaret Mead's study of the Omaha, "The Changing Culture of an Indian Tribe" (1932) he states:

> The great emphasis placed in this study on the impact of white culture on the "Antlers," furthermore, tends to obscure the effect on the same people of a highly significant process of inter-tribal acculturation that the book implies is going on among the Indians themselves. It would undoubtedly have been very illuminating if the fact that the "Antler" takes refuge from his sense of a loss of tribal dignity through identifying himself with the larger group, "the American Indian," had been further probed. [Herskovits, 1938, p. 50.]

In his concluding chapter he elaborates upon his earlier statement:

> The mutual give-and-take that results when American Indians of many different tribes come together in rodeos and exhibitions of various sorts is well worth the attention of ethnologists. Such an obvious example of intertribal acculturation as the spread of the war-bonnet, now the authenticating label of a "true Indian" no matter what his tribe, comes to mind as a rough illustration of this sort of borrowing; but one can only speculate whether the obviously foreign elements seen in the performances of the various tribes of Southwest Indians at such a gathering as the Gallup Festival, assumed for purposes of show in the presence of a white audience, are carried home to invade tribal rituals. [Ibid., pp. 124–125.]

The late Karl Schmitt, of the University of Oklahoma, was much interested in the subject of Pan-Indianism, and read a paper entitled "A Possible Development of a Pan-Indian Culture in Oklahoma" at the 1948 meetings of the Central States Branch of the American Anthropological Association. He intended to publish on this subject, but his untimely death halted the project.

William Newcomb, Jr., has published a brief study of Delaware participation in Pan-Indianism (1955), and his "The Culture and Acculturation of the Delaware Indians" (1956) also contains excellent material on the subject. I have a short paper on the general subject of Pan-Indianism as well (1955 b).

Both Newcomb and I have observed that the powwow, centering around the modern form of the *Heđúška,* or War dance, is the prime secular focus of Pan-Indianism in Oklahoma. In addition to the

War dances, which occupy much of the time at powwow, there are other Indian dances and activities. Among the Plains Indian elements are Round dances, the Buffalo dance, and the Ghost dance Hand game. From the Eastern Woodlands come the "Stomp" and Snake dances; from the Southwest comes the Eagle dance. Of non-Indian origin are championship dancing contests and "powwow princess" events. The "Indian Cake-walk," a version of musical chairs accompanied by Indian singing and drumming, is of mixed derivation.

In the large tent villages surrounding the powwow arena, a Southern Ponca, Choctaw, Delaware, or any other tribesman can associate with other Indians in an "Indian" atmosphere. In the evening he may reaffirm his Indian ethos by actively circling the big drum or by passively identifying himself with the dancers from the sidelines. What matter if he is a Cherokee, yet dances Plains Indian dances in a Plains Indian costume? It is all recognized as being part of an *Indian* whole, and this is the essential point.

The Southern Ponca are ardent powwowers, and furnish singers and dancers for the celebrations of many surrounding tribes. Their own annual "Ponca powwow" is likewise a Pan-Indian affair, and draws its participants from many tribes. Costumes, dancing styles, and music, are rapidly becoming standardized throughout the State of Oklahoma.

The "Pan-Indianization" of the Southern Ponca has effected many changes in what little remains of the aboriginal culture of the band. For example, the fact that a premium has been placed on the ability to sing *Hed̶úška* songs, which are the accompaniment of the Pan-Indian War dance has brought about a mild revival of this musical form. Likewise, since Ponca singers are called upon to sing for other tribes quite frequently, the Ponca have felt compelled to learn the favorite songs of other groups. Nowadays we even find Ponca who can lead (i.e., sing for) the Southeastern "Stomp" and Alligator dances, and teams of Southern Ponca dancers perform the Pueblo-derived Eagle dance at various powwows.

The degree to which Oklahoma Indian dance costumes have become standardized is immediately apparent, even to the untrained observer. The "feathers" style costume is now worn by nearly all male participants in the War dance, regardless of which tribe. In the case of the Southern Ponca this has meant that older, more characteristically tribal, costume styles have been abandoned. Younger Southern Ponca, lacking the perspective time gives, often do not realize that things have not always been so, and consider the rather baroque "feathers" outfit, with its fancy butterfly bustles, to be the same costume their ancestors wore two or three hundred years ago.

Some Southern Ponca girls, apparently resenting the relatively restricted role that tribal tradition and the heavy woman's dress assigned them in the dance, have now taken up the man's style of dancing, wearing a slightly modified version of the man's "feathers" costume. Although some of the older people object, the innovation is spreading.

Just as the War dance-centered powwow is the most important secular focus of Pan-Indianism, so the Peyote cult is its prime religious expression. This form of worship, the Indian feels, is really his own. Since the unifying effect of Peyotism has been discussed at some length by others, particularly La Barre (1938) and Petrullo (1934), I shall not enter into great detail here. Worthy of mention in passing, however, is a Peyote meeting which I attended in the summer of 1954. Though technically a "Ponca" affair, since it was sponsored by a Ponca family and held on the Ponca reservation, the meeting was led by a Comanche, and attended by Kiowa, Comanche, Sauk, Delaware, Oto, Pawnee, Southern Cheyenne, and Omaha adherents. Southern Ponca peyotists present at this ceremony assured me that the large number of tribes represented was not unusual.

Like the powwow, the Peyote religion has affected the remaining aboriginal culture of the Southern Ponca. The tipi and the costume blanket, once everyday parts of Ponca culture, have become symbols of peyotism, and in this manner have been retained by the tribe longer than would probably have otherwise been the case. "Peyote beadwork," the Southern Plains technique which came to the Southern Ponca on the gourds, feathers, and other ritual equipment of the religion, is now used quite often on dancing costumes and souvenirs made by the Southern Ponca in place of their older lazy-stitch and spot-stitch work.

Having described some of the principal features of Oklahoma Pan-Indianism, let us now consider some of the social factors which seem to have played a special role in its growth.

One of the principal factors fostering this intertribal solidarity is undoubtedly ethnic discrimination. Although the Indian slums found in the cities of other States with large Indian populations are not common in Oklahoma, some discrimination in employment and housing does exist. Many Oklahoma Whites tend to lump all tribes together, merely as "Indians." This, of course, elicits a complementary reaction.

The common low economic level of most Oklahoma Indians, partially a result of the ethnic discrimination just noted, is also a major contributing element. Most Oklahoma Indians lease what little land they have and supplement the income thus derived with wage labor performed for Whites. The common poverty of the members of different tribal groups, by its contrast to the position of the surrounding majority, undoubtedly fosters a strong feeling of unity. This is well illustrated in the traditional remark of the Indian host to his mealtime guests: "We don't have much; we're just Indians."

In this connection it should be noted that the oil-wealthy Osage, although geographically in the vortex of Pan-Indianism, participate in it much less than their poorer neighbors. In their version of the *Hedúška* or War dance, the long prayers and other religious features which have been discarded by other groups are retained. The Pan-Indian "feathers" costume is viewed with disapproval by most Osage, and the more traditional "Straight dance" costume is worn, even by the younger men. Some of these younger dancers, however, have now adopted the "feathers" style of dancing and costume, but use it only when they attend the more Pan-Indian powwows of the Ponca, Quapaw, and other tribes. In the same vein, it should be noted, the Osage are also resistant to the Pan-Indian "half-moon" Peyote ritual, preferring the older (with them) "big moon" variant. Apparently the relative wealth of the Osage, which automatically distinguishes them from neighboring tribes and gives them a greater opportunity to identify themselves successfully with the non-Indian community, removes their incentive to sacrifice tribal distinctiveness for the sake of solidarity with the larger minority society of Indians at large.

The use of the English language as a lingua franca has likewise been instrumental in the growth of Pan-Indianism. Indeed, many younger Indians do not understand an Indian language. At all Oklahoma powwows that I attended, except those of the Osage, English was used by the announcer. In 1954 a young Pawnee dancer admitted to me that he could not tell a Pawnee song from a Ponca song by its text. He was, in fact, observed dancing vigorously to a Ponca tune which told of the killing of a Pawnee horsethief, much to the amusement of certain Ponca present. Recently many "Stomp" dance and Round dance songs have been composed which have English words. These are great favorites among the younger people. Likewise, English is now the language spoken at Peyote meetings, although now and then a worshiper, after first excusing himself to the members of other tribes present, will pray in his native tongue.

Intermarriage between members of different tribes may be regarded as both a cause and an effect of Pan-Indianism. The announcer at a "Stomp" dance "shell shaker" contest held in connection with the annual Quapaw powwow in 1954, was often hard put to identify, by tribe, the girls participating, although he was obviously acquainted with them or with their families. One contestant was identified as a Shawnee-Delaware-Wyandot. The winner of the War dance contest at this same gathering was part Osage and part Quapaw, and the winner of the "Straight dance" contest was a Creek-Osage.

Increased geographic mobility is another prominent factor facilitating the intertribal exchange of ideas and promoting a feeling of

Indian "nationalism." Although Indians have always been fond of visiting one another, until recently the mere limitation of transportation made it difficult to go far from home. With the advent of the fast car, however, such desires could be more easily indulged. Now it is common for Oklahoma Indians to make short visits to tribes in Nebraska, Iowa, and even Wisconsin at powwow time. The 1952 Ponca powwow was attended by delegations of Omaha and Winnebago from Nebraska, not to mention groups from almost all of the larger Oklahoma tribes.

Finally, I might mention Indian school contacts as a source of much Pan-Indian feeling. Certainly the "Indian" clubs at schools such as Haskell and Chilocco, with their multitribal membership, have been responsible for a great deal of the intertribal exchange of songs, dances, and costume styles. La Barre (1938) has discussed the role of Indian school contacts in the diffusion of the Peyote cult.

In summary, we may say that all of these situations and pressures lean in one direction, creating a cumulative pressure which Pan-Indianism attempts to relieve. Ethnic discrimination, in effect, is the mark of the refusal of the larger society (White) to permit complete merging in it of Indians who, by merging, would lose separate identification either with specific tribes or with Indians in general. Because identification with "Indians" makes one a member of a larger peer group than identification with a tribe, this is the usual choice. The low economic status of Oklahoma Indians, because it stands in contrast to that of most Whites, also prevents the development of a sense of identification with White society, and fosters a we-group sense among Indians at large (the Osage excepted).

The use of the English language works against tribal exclusiveness, but is equally appropriate to Pan-Indian identification or to identification with Whites. Intermarriage between members of different tribes works in the same manner, but there is less tendency toward identification with Whites. Increased geographic mobility could work in either way as well, except where ethnic discrimination makes it harder for Indians to merge with Whites in the use of motels, restaurants, etc. while en route, and makes points of rest during travel more apt to have Indian associations. Indian school contacts, multitribal in nature, definitely work against tribal exclusiveness and for Pan-Indian identification. Because they occur in special Indian schools, identification with Whites is less likely to occur.

Having discussed these social factors which seem to have fostered Pan-Indianism, we turn now to the question of Pan-Indianism as a part of the larger phenomenon of "nativistic movements," and the significance to be drawn from considering its nativistic aspects. Linton (1943, p. 230), in his article on the subject of nativism, defines such a movement as "any organized attempt on the part of the society's members to revive or perpetuate selected aspects of its culture." He offers a typology of such movements based upon an end-means formulation.

Linton approaches nativistic movements in the social context of dominance-submission. For the subordinated groups there is a sense of deprivation and frustration, and this leads them to nativistic protest. Unhappy in the present, they seek to restore at least a part of the past. For a number of years Linton's view expressed in his paper (1943) reflected the opinion of most students in this area. More recently, however, Voget (1956) and Wallace (1956) have approached these phenomena on a slightly different tack.

Voget (1956, p. 259), under the rubric "reformative nativism," discusses three charismatic movements: the Iroquois *Gaiwiio* (better known as the Handsome Lake religion), Peyotism, and the Shaker Church of the Northwest. He sees all three as movements which "pave the way for a more secular, pragmatic, and accommodative adjustment." He discusses Pan-Indianism (p. 259) but refuses to admit it as a reformative movement because of its largely secular nature (p. 260, footnote 9). For some reason he does not consider Peyotism a component of Pan-Indianism (p. 260, footnote 9).

Wallace (1956, p. 265) titles his paper "Revitalization Movements." He defines such a movement as a "deliberate, organized, conscious effort by members of a society to construct a more satisfying culture." Important points brought out by Wallace which, in my opinion, make his concept more useful than either Linton's or Voget's, are found in his discussion of the "Varieties and Dimensions of Variation" which a movement may have (pp. 275–279). Points two and three seem particularly relevant to a discussion of Pan-Indianism. For one thing, a movement may be *more* or *less* religious, and Wallace notes a trend away from religious bases of action (p. 277). In point three, "Nativism," he points out that the amount of nativistic activity in a revitalization movement is likewise variable. Some movements, for example, are antinativistic from a cultural standpoint, though quite nativistic as to personnel (p. 278). Mead's (1956) recent study of the Manus "New Way" illustrates this very well. Rather than attempt a revival of their old culture in the face of deprivation and frustration, the Manus have made a heroic attempt to discard as much as possible of both their material and nonmaterial past. At the other end of the scale we might place the Iroquois *Gaiwiio*, which retained great amounts of the existing culture pattern unchanged. Most movements, including Pan-Indianism, fall somewhere in between, retaining those elements of the old considered useful or attractive, adapting others, and casting aside the rest. The culture, through the revitalization movement, thus is reshaped to fit the altered conditions faced by the society that bears it.

In Oklahoma Pan-Indianism the elements selected for perpetuation, namely the powwow, with its associated dances and activities, the Ghost dance Hand game, and the Peyote religion, are all symbols not of the *old* but of the *new* Indian way of life. Although all of these elements existed before Pan-Indianism, they have recently been developing as fixed and ever-enriched complexes, and have been getting more and more widely adopted as overt expression of "Indian-among-Indians" self-perception.

Pan-Indianism is thus seen as a revitalizing movement that provides Oklahoma Indians with a fund of common knowledge and experience that sets them off from other ethnic groups, maintains the dignity of the group through intertribal solidarity, and at the same time permits accommodative adjustment to the dominant American culture.

Although Pan-Indianism is, at present, largely limited to the social (powwow and Ghost dance hand game) and religious (Peyote religion) spheres, the potential economic and political advantages of larger size may be realized in future years by Indians in Oklahoma. Indeed, the common support and mutual encouragement for the Peyote religion in the face of opposition, without which the church groups of the various individual tribes would have been outlawed long ago, have shown what can be achieved through intertribal cooperation. Discussion of common problems, such as land-claims cases, termination, etc. in seminars such as are held in connection with the Gallup Ceremonial in New Mexico, or as were held at the American Indian Chicago Conference, loom ahead. At the present time participation in such conferences is limited to only a few of the more articulate and acculturated Indians, but will undoubtedly become increasingly important in future years.

LITERATURE CITED

Andreas, A. T.
1882. History of the State of Nebraska. Chicago.

Anonymous.
1907. Kansa. *In* "Handbook of American Indians north of Mexico." Bur. Amer. Ethnol. Bull. 30, pt. 1, pp. 653–656.
1952. South Dakota physical types. Univ. S. Dak., W. H. Over Mus., Museum News, vol. 13, No. 5, p. 1.

Atkinson, Henry.
1922. Letter from General Atkinson to Colonel Hamilton. Nebraska Hist., vol. 5, No. 1, pp. 9–11.

Boas, Franz.
1906. Notes on the Ponka grammar. Intern. Cong. Amer., vol. 15, No. 2, pp. 317–337. Quebec.

Boas, Franz, and Swanton, John R.
1911. Siouan (Dakota) . . . with remarks on the Ponca and Winnebago. *In* "Handbook of American Indian Languages." Bur. Amer. Ethnol. Bull. 40, pt. 1, pp. 875–965.

Bourke, John G.
1892. On the border with Crook. London. (New York, 1891.)

718–071—65——12

Brackenridge, H. M.
1904. Journal of a voyage up the River Missouri; performed in eighteen hundred and eleven. *In* "Early western travels, 1748–1846," ed. by Reuben G. Thwaites, vol. 6. Cleveland.

Bradbury, John.
1904. Travels in the interior of America in the years 1809, 1810, and 1811. . . . *In* "Early western travels, 1748–1846," ed. by Reuben G. Thwaites, vol. 5. Cleveland.

Bushnell, David I., Jr.
1922. Villages of the Algonquian, Siouan, and Caddoan tribes west of the Mississippi. Bur. Amer. Ethnol. Bull. 77.
1927. Burials of the Algonquian, Siouan, and Caddoan tribes west of the Mississippi. Bur. Amer. Ethnol. Bull. 83.

Champe, John L.
1946. Ash Hollow Cave; a study of stratigraphic sequence in the central Great plains. Univ. Nebraska Stud., n.s., No. 1.
1949. White Cat Village. Amer. Antiq., vol. 14, No. 4, pp. 285–292.

Connelley, William E.
1918. Notes on the early Indian occupancy of the Great Plains. Kansas State Hist. Soc. Coll., 1915–1918, vol. 14, pp. 438–470.

Cooper, Paul L.
1936. Archeology of certain sites in Cedar County, Nebraska. Chap. in Nebraska Archeol., No. 1, pp. 11–145.
1949. Recent investigations in Fort Randall and Oahe Reservoirs, South Dakota. Amer. Antiq., vol. 14, No. 4, pp. 300–310.

Curtis, Edward S.
1930. The North American Indian. 20 vols. Cambridge.

Densmore, Frances.
1929. Pawnee music. Bur. Amer. Ethnol. Bull. 93.

Dorsey, George A.
1905. The Ponca Sun Dance. Field Columbian Mus., Anthrop. ser., vol. 7, No. 2, pp. 61–88.

Dorsey, James Owen.
1883. The religion of the Omahas and Ponkas. Amer. Antiq. and Orient. Journ., vol. 5, pp. 271–275. Chicago.
1884 a. Omaha sociology. 3d Ann. Rep. Bur. Amer. Ethnol., 1881–82, pp. 205–370.
1884 b. Siouan folk-lore and mythologic notes. Amer. Antiq. and Orient. Journ., vol. 6, pp. 174–176. Chicago.
1884 c. The myths of the raccoon and the crawfish among the Dakotah tribes. Amer. Antiq. and Orient. Journ., vol. 6, pp. 237–240. Chicago.
1885 a. Siouan folk-lore and mythologic notes. Amer. Antiq. and Orient. Journ., vol. 7, pp. 105–108. Chicago.
1885 b. On the comparative phonology of four Siouan languages. Ann. Rep. Smithson. Inst. for 1883, pp. 919–929.
1888 a. Ponka stories, told by Tim Potter, or Big Grizzly Bear, in 1872, at Ponka Agency, Dakota Territory. Journ. Amer. Folk-lore, vol. 1, p. 73.
1888 b. Abstracts of Omaha and Ponka myths. Journ. Amer. Folk-lore, vol. 1, pp. 74–78, 204–208.
1889. Ponka and Omaha songs. Journ. Amer. Folk-lore, vol. 2, pp. 271–276.
1890. The Ȼegiha language. Contr. North Amer. Ethnol., vol. 6.
1891 a. Omaha and Ponka letters. Bur. Amer. Ethnol. Bull. 11.

DORSEY, JAMES OWEN—Continued

1891 b. The social organization of the Siouan tribes. Journ. Amer. Folk-lore, vol. 4, pp. 331–342.

1893. Preface. *In* "Dakota grammar, texts, and ethnography," by Stephen R. Riggs. Contr. North Amer. Ethnol., vol. 9, pp. xi–xxxii.

1894. A study of Siouan cults. 11th Ann. Rep. Bur. Amer. Ethnol., 1889–90, pp. 351–544.

1896. Omaha dwellings, furniture, and implements. 13th Ann. Rep. Bur. Amer. Ethnol., 1891–92, pp. 263–288.

1897. Siouan sociology. 15th Ann. Rep. Bur. Amer. Ethnol., 1893–94, pp. 205–244.

DORSEY, JAMES O., and THOMAS, CYRUS.

1907. Iowa. *In* "Handbook of American Indians north of Mexico." Bur. Amer. Ethnol. Bull. 30, pt. 2, pp. 612–614.

1910. Ponca. *In* "Handbook of American Indians north of Mexico." Bur. Amer. Ethnol. Bull. 30, pt. 2, pp. 278–279.

DUNBAR, JOHN B.

1880 a. The Pawnee Indians: their history and ethnology. Mag. Amer. Hist., vol. 4, No. 4, pp. 241–281.

1880 b. The Pawnee Indians; their habits and customs. Mag. Amer. Hist., vol. 5, No. 5, pp. 321–342.

DUNBAR, JOHN B., ET AL.

1918. Letters concerning the Presbyterian Mission in the Pawnee country, near Bellevue, Nebr., 1831–49. Kansas State Hist. Soc. Coll., 1915–18, vol. 14, pp. 570–784.

EGGAN, FRED.

1937. The Cheyenne and Arapaho kinship system. *In* "Social anthropology of North American tribes," pp. 39–95. Univ. Chicago Press.

FLETCHER, ALICE C.

1893. A study of Omaha Indian music. Peabody Mus., Archaeol. and Ethnol. Pap., vol. 1, No. 5. Cambridge.

1896. The emblematic use of the tree in the Dakotan group. Science, vol. 4, pp. 475–487.

1900. Indian story and song, from North America. Boston.

FLETCHER, ALICE C., and LA FLESCHE, FRANCIS.

1911. The Omaha tribe. 27th Ann. Rep. Bur. Amer. Ethnol., 1905–06, pp. 15–654.

FOREMAN, GRANT.

1946. The last trek of the Indians. Univ. Chicago Press.

FRY, EDWIN A.

1922. The Mormon winter camp on the Niobrara. Nebraska Hist., vol. 5, No. 1, pp. 4–6.

GILMORE, MELVIN R.

1919. Uses of plants by the Indians of the Missouri River region. 33d Ann. Rep. Bur. Amer. Ethnol., 1911–12, pp. 43–154.

GRIFFIN, JAMES B.

1937. The chronological position and ethnological relationships of the Fort Ancient Aspect. Amer. Antiq., vol. 2, No. 4, pp. 273–276.

1946. Cultural change and continuity in Eastern United States archeology. *In* "Man in Northeastern North America," ed. by Frederick Johnson, vol. 3, pp. 37–95 (bibliography, pp. 307–348). R. S. Peabody Foundation for Archaeol. Andover, Mass.

GRINNELL, GEORGE B.

1892. Development of a Pawnee myth. Journ. Amer. Folk-lore, vol. 5, pp. 127–134.

GRINNELL, GEORGE B—Continued
1909. Pawnee hero stories and folk-tales, with notes on the origin, customs and character of the Pawnee people. New York. (1st ed. 1889.)
HAYES, F. A., ET AL.
1935. Soil survey of Knox County, Nebraska. U.S. Dept. Agr., Bur. Chem. and Soils, Soil Surv. Rep. series 1930, No. 25. Washington.
HAYDEN, F. V.
1863. Contributions to the ethnography and philology of the Indian tribes of the Missouri Valley. Amer. Philos. Soc. Trans., vol. 12, art. 3, pp. 231–461.
HERSKOVITS, MELVILLE J.
1938. Acculturation: the study of culture contact. New York.
HOLMER, NILS M.
1945. Sonant-surds in Ponca-Omaha. Intern. Journ. Amer. Ling., vol. 11, No. 2, pp. 76–85.
HOWARD, JAMES H.
1950. The Omaha hand game and Gourd Dance. Plains. Archeol. Conf. News Letter, vol. 3, No. 3, pp. 3–6.
1951. Notes on the Dakota Grass Dance. Southwest. Journ. Anthrop., vol. 7, No. 1, pp. 82–85.
1952. The Sun Dance of the Turtle Mountain Ojibwa. North Dakota Hist., vol. 19, No. 4, pp. 249–264.
1953. An Omaha medicine packet. Plains. Archeol. Conf. News Letter, vol. 5, No. 4, pp. 55–57.
1954 a. Yanktonai Dakota eagle trapping. Southwest. Journ. Anthrop. vol. 10, No. 1, pp. 69–74.
1954 b. The Dakota heyoka cult. Scien. Month., vol. 78, No. 4, pp. 254–258.
1954 c. Plains Indian feathered bonnets. Plains Anthrop., No. 2, pp. 23–26.
1955 a. The tree dweller cults of the Dakota. Journ. Amer. Folk-lore, vol. 68, No. 268, pp. 169–174.
1955 b. Pan-Indian culture of Oklahoma. Scien. Month., vol. 81, No. 5, pp. 215–220.
1956. The persistence of southern cult gorgets among the historic Kansa. Amer. Antiq., vol. 21, No. 3, pp. 301–303.
1957. The mescal bean cult of the central and southern Plains: An ancestor of the peyote cult? Amer. Anthrop., vol. 59, No. 1, pp. 75–87.
1961. Peter Le Claire's buffalo headdress. Amer. Indian Tradition, vol. 8, No. 1, pp. 19–20.
HUMPHREY, SETH K.
1906. The Indian dispossessed. Rev. ed. Boston.
HUSE, WILLIAM.
1896. History of Dixon County, Nebraska. Norfolk, Nebr.
HYDE, GEORGE E.
1934 a. The Pawnee Indians. Pt. 1, 1680–1770. The Old West Series, No. 4, pp. 5–54.
1934 b. The Pawnee Indians. Pt. 2, 1770–1890. The Old West Series, No. 5, pp. 3–50.
IRVING, JOHN T.
1835. Indian sketches, taken during an expedition to the Pawnee tribes. 2 vols. Philadelphia and London.
JAMES, EDWIN.
1905. Account of an expedition from Pittsburgh to the Rocky Mountains, performed in the years 1819, 1820 . . . under the command of Major Stephen H. Long. *In* "Early western travels, 1748–1846," edited by Reuben G. Thwaites, vols. 14, 15, and 17. Cleveland.

JOHNSON, ELDEN.
1955. Carl Bodmer paints the Indian frontier. St. Paul, Minn., Sci. Mus. Indian Leaflets, Nos. 8–10.

JONES, A. D.
1890. Letter to J. M. Wood. MS. Oklahoma State Hist. Soc., Oklahoma City.

KROEBER, A. L.
1939. Cultural and natural areas of native North America. Univ. Calif. Publ. Amer. Archeol. and Ethnol., vol. 38. Berkeley.

KURATH, GERTRUDE.
1950. A new method of choreographic notation. Amer. Anthrop., vol. 52, No. 1, pp. 120–123.
1954. A basic vocabulary for ethnic dance descriptions. Amer. Anthrop., vol. 56, No. 6, pp. 1102–1103.

LA BARRE, WESTON.
1938. The peyote cult. Yale Univ. Publ. Anthrop. No. 19. New Haven.

LA FLESCHE, FRANCIS.
1917. Omaha and Osage traditions of separation. 19th Intern. Cong. Americanists, 1915, Proc., pp. 459–462. Washington.

LE CLAIRE, PETER.
1961. Peter Le Claire, northern Ponca. Amer. Indian Tradition, vol. 8, No. 1, pp. 17–19.

LEHMER, DONALD J.
1954. Archeological investigations in the Oahe Dam area, South Dakota, 1950–51. Bur. Amer. Ethnol. Bull. 158, Riv. Bas. Sur. Pap. No. 7.

LESSER, ALEXANDER.
1933. The Pawnee ghost dance hand game; a study of cultural change. Columbia Univ. Contr. Anthrop., vol. 16.

LEWIS, MERIWETHER.
1904–5. Original journals of the Lewis and Clark expedition 1804–06. 8 vols. Ed. by Reuben G. Thwaites. New York.

LINTON, RALPH.
1943. Nativistic movements. Amer. Anthrop., vol. 45, pp. 230–240.

LOWIE, ROBERT H.
1917. Notes on the social organization and customs of the Mandan, Hidatsa, and Crow Indians. Amer. Mus. Nat. Hist., Anthrop. Pap., vol. 21, pt. 1.

MARTIN, PAUL S., QUIMBY, GEORGE I., and COLLIER, DONALD.
1947. Indians before Columbus; twenty thousand years of North American history revealed by archeology. Chicago.

MAXIMILIAN, PRINZ VON WIED-NEUWIED. *See* WIED-NEUWIED.

MCGEE, W. J.
1897. The Siouan Indians, a preliminary sketch. 15th Ann. Rep. Bur. Amer. Ethnol., 1893–94, pp. 153–204.
1898. Ponka feather symbolism. Amer. Anthrop., vol. 11, pp. 156–159.

MEAD, MARGARET.
1932. The changing culture of an Indian tribe. Columbia Univ. Contr. Anthrop., vol. 15.
1956. New lives for old, cultural transformation—Manus, 1928–1953. New York.

MEKEEL, SCUDDER.
1943. A short history of the Teton-Dakota. North Dakota Hist. Quart., vol. 10, No. 3, pp. 136–205.

MERRILL, MOSES.
1892. Extracts from the diary of Rev. Moses Merrill, a missionary to the Otoe Indians from 1832 to 1840. Nebraska State Hist. Soc., Trans. and Rep., vol. 4, pp. 160–191.

MINER, WILLIAM HARVEY, EDITOR.
1911. The Iowa. Cedar Rapids, Iowa.

MOONEY, JAMES.
1928. The aboriginal population of America north of Mexico. Smithson. Misc. Coll., vol. 80, No. 7.
1896. The Ghost-dance religion. 14th Ann. Rep. Bur. Amer. Ethol.,1892-93, pt. 2

MORGAN, LEWIS HENRY.
1868. Systems of consanguinity and affinity of the human family. Smithson. Contr. Knowl., No. 218.
1959. The Indian journals, 1859–62. (edited, with an introduction, by Leslie A. White.) Univ. Michigan.

MURDOCK, GEORGE P., ET AL.
1945. Outline of cultural materials. Yale Univ., Institute of Human Relations, Anthrop. Stud., vol. 2.

NASATIR, ABRAHAM P.
1952. Before Lewis and Clark; documents illustrating the history of the Missouri; 1785–1804. 2 vols. St. Louis.

NATIONAL ARCHIVES, BUREAU OF INDIAN AFFAIRS.
——— Letters received, 1824–51. St. Louis Superintendency.
——— Letters received, 1824–74. Upper Missouri Agency.
——— Letters received, 1836–57. Council Bluffs Agency.
——— Letters received, 1859–80. Ponca Agency.

NEWCOMB, WILLIAM W., JR.
1955. A note on Cherokee-Delaware Pan-Indianism. Amer. Anthrop., vol. 57, No. 5, pp. 1041–1045.
1956. The culture and acculturation of the Delaware Indians. Univ. Michigan, Mus. Anthrop., Anthrop. Pap., No. 10.

OEHLER, GOTTLIEB F., and SMITH, D. Z.
1914. Description of a journey and visit to the Pawnee Indians who live on the Platte River, a tributary of the Missouri, 70 miles from its mouth. (Reprinted from the "Moravian Church Miscellany" of 1851–52.) New York.

PETRULLO, VINCENZO.
1934. The diabolic root; a study of peyotism . . . . Univ. Pennsylvania.

PIKE, KENNETH L.
1947. Phonemics, a technique for reducing languages to writing. Univ. Michigan Publ. Ling., vol. 3.

PLC, *see* LE CLAIRE, PETER.

PONCA AGENCY RECORDS. Oklahoma State Historical Society, Oklahoma City.

PROVINSE, JOHN H.
1937. The underlying sanctions of Plains Indian culture. *In* "Social anthropology of North American tribes," edited by Fred Eggan, pp. 341–374. Chicago.

REID, RUSSELL, and GANNON, CLELL G., EDITORS.
1929. Journal of the Atkinson-O'Fallon expedition. North Dakota Hist. Quart., vol. 4, No. 1, pp. 5–56.

RIGGS, STEPHEN R.
1893. Dakota grammar, texts, and ethnography. Contr. North Amer. Ethnol., vol. 9.

ROYCE, CHARLES C., COMPILER.
1899. Indian land cessions in the United States. 18th Ann. Rep. Bur. Amer. Ethnol., 1896–97, pp. 521–964.

SCHMIDT, WILHELM.
1927. Die Omaha und die Ponca. *In* "Der Ursprung der Gottesidee," vol. 2, pp. 657–658. 14 vols. Muenster.

SECOY, FRANK R.
1951. The identity of the "Padouca"; an ethnohistorical analysis. Amer. Anthrop., vol. 53, No. 4, pp. 525–542.

SHINE, MICHAEL A.
1914. The Nebraska aborigines as they appeared in the eighteenth century. Nebraska Acad. Sci. Publ., vol. 9, No. 1, pp. 1–23.

SHONLE, RUTH.
1925. Peyote, the giver of visions. Amer. Anthrop., vol. 27, pp. 53–75.

SKINNER, ALANSON.
1915 a. Societies of the Iowa. Amer. Mus. Nat. Hist., Anthrop. Pap., vol. 11, pp. 679–740.
1915 b. Kansa organizations. Amer. Mus. Nat. Hist., Anthrop. Pap., vol. 11, pp. 741–775.
1915 c. Ponca societies and dances. Amer. Mus. Nat. Hist., Anthrop. Pap., vol. 11, pp. 777–801.
1920. Medicine ceremony of the Menomini, Iowa, and Wahpeton Dakota, with notes on the ceremony among the Ponca, Bungi Ojibwa, and Potawatomi Indians. Indian Notes and Mono., vol. 4.

STANDING BEAR, LUTHER.
1928. My people, the Sioux. Cambridge, Mass.

STEPHENSON, ROBERT L.
1954. Taxonomy and chronology in the Central Plains—Middle Missouri River area. Plains Anthrop., No. 1, pp. 15–21.

STRONG, WILLIAM DUNCAN.
1935. An introduction to Nebraska archeology. Smithson. Misc. Coll., vol. 93, No. 10.

SWANTON, JOHN R.
1910. Osage. *In* "Handbook of American Indians north of Mexico." Bur. Amer. Ethnol. Bull. 30, pt. 2, pp. 156–158.

TABEAU, PIERRE ANTOINE.
1939. Tabeau's narrative of Loisel's expedition to the Upper Missouri. ed. by Annie Heloise Abel and trans. by Rose Abel Wright. Norman, Okla.

THOMAS, CYRUS
1910. Quapaw. *In* "Handbook of American Indians north of Mexico." Bur. Amer. Ethnol. Bull. 30, pt. 2, pp. 333–336.

TIBBLES, THOMAS H. *See* Zylyff.

TRUDEAU, J. B.
1914. Trudeau's journal. South Dakota Hist. Coll., vol. 7, pp. 403–474.

U.S. CONGRESS.
1868. Statutes at Large, Treaties, and Proclamations of the United States of America, ed. by George P. Sanger. Vol. 14. Boston.

VOGET, FRED W.
1956. The American Indian in transition: Reformation and accommodation. Amer. Anthrop., vol. 58, No. 2, pp. 249–263.

WALLACE, ANTHONY F. C.
1956. Revitalization movements. Amer. Anthrop., vol. 58, No. 2, pp. 264–281.

WEDEL, WALDO R.
1936. An introduction to Pawnee archeology. Bur. Amer. Ethnol. Bull. 112.
1946. The Kansa Indians. Kansas Acad. Sci., Trans., vol. 49, No. 1.

WELSH, WILLIAM.
1872. Report of a visit to the Sioux and Ponka Indians on the Missouri River. Philadelphia.

WHITE, LESLIE A.
1939. A problem in kinship terminology. Amer. Anthrop., vol. 41, No. 4, pp. 566–573.

WHITMAN, WILLIAM.
1937. The Oto. Columbia Univ. Contr. Anthrop., vol. 28.
1939. Xúbe, a Ponca autobiography. Journ. Amer. Folklore, vol. 52, pp. 180–193.

WIED-NEUWIED, MAXIMILIAN ALEXANDER PHILIPP, PRINZ VON.
1906. Travels into the interior of North America, 1832–34. *In* "Early western travels, 1748–1846," edited by Reuben G. Thwaites, vols. 22–25. Cleveland.

WILL, GEORGE F.
1924. Archaeology of the Missouri valley. Amer. Mus. Nat. Hist., Anthrop. Pap., vol. 22, pt. 6, pp. 285–344.

WILL, GEORGE F., and HYDE, GEORGE E.
1917. Corn among the Indians of the upper Missouri. Little Histories of North American Indians, No. 5. St. Louis.

WOOD, W. RAYMOND.
1955. Historical and archeological evidence for Arikara visits to the Central Plains. Plains Anthrop., No. 4, pp. 27–39.
——— The Redbird Focus. M. A. thesis, Univ. Nebraska, 1956.
1959. Notes on Ponca ethnohistory, 1785–1804. Ethnohist., vol. 6, No. 1.
1960. Nanza, the Ponca fort. Soc. Amer. Archaeol., Archiv. Archaeol., No. 3. Madison.

ZIMMERMAN, CHARLES LEROY.
1941. White Eagle, chief of the Poncas. Harrisburg.

ZYLYFF.
1880. The Ponca chiefs. Boston.

Shoo-de-ga-cha (*Šúde-gàxe* or The Smoke), chief of the Ponca tribe. Painted by George Catlin in 1832. Original painting is in the Smithsonian Institution.

Mong-shon-sha or Bending Willow, wife of Great Chief, Ponca. Painted by George Catlin in 1832. Original painting is in the Smithsonian Institution.

Hee-lah-dee or Pure Fountain, wife of The Smoke. Painted by George Catlin in 1832
Original painting is in the Smithsonian Institution.

Hongs-kay-dee or Great Chief, son of The Smoke. Painted by George Catlin in 1832. Original painting is in the Smithsonian Institution.

"Punka Indians encamped on the banks of the Missouri," painted by Carl Bodmer on May 11, 1833, near the mouth of the James River. From an engraving in Maximilian, 1843.

A battle between the Ponca and the Dakota as drawn by To-tay-go-nai (Standing Buffalo) a young warrior. Copy by A. Z. Shindler, 1858, Washington, D.C.

Group of Ponca men with their agent (seated at left). Standing Bear, the Ponca chief, is standing at right.

a, Big Snake, Ponca warrior.

b, Ponca Indian warrior (possibly another photograph of Antoine, chief of the mixbloods).

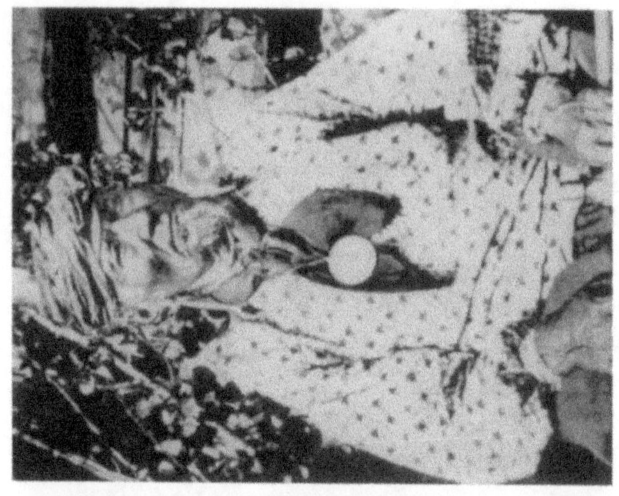

c, Antoine, Chief of the mixbloods.

Four Ponca chiefs. *Left to right:* E-shno^{n}-ni-ka-ga-hi (*Ešnǫ́-nìkagàhe* or He-alone-is-chief); Ta-to^{n}-ga-no^{n}-zhin (*Tatǫ́ga-nǫ́žį* or Standing-buffalo-bull); We'-ga-sa-pi (*Wégasàpi* or Whip); and Wa-shko^{n}'-mo^{n}-thi^{n} (*Waškǫ́-mǫđį*). Photograph by A. Z. Shindler, taken in 1868, Washington, D.C.

Standing-bear (*Montšú-nǫžị*), the Ponca chief who led part of his people back to Nebraska from the Indian Territory. *a*, Morrow photograph, probably taken ca. 1869. *b*, Copied from an original photograph taken ca. 1880.

Ponca delegation to Washington, 1877. *Seated, left to right:* O^{n}'-po^{n}-to^{n}-ga (*Ǫ́pą-tòṅga* or Big-elk); *Tatǫ́ga-nǫžį̀* or Standing-buffalo-bull; Xi-tha'-cka (*Xiđá-ska* or White-eagle); Mo^{n}-chu-no^{n}-zhi^{n} (*Montšú-nǫžį̀* or Standing Bear). *Standing, left to right:* The interpreters, Barnaby and Charles H. LeClaire (father of Peter LeClaire). Photographer unknown.

a. Shu'-de-ga-xe (*Śúde-gàxe* or Smoke-maker), Ponca chief born in 1826. Photograph taken in Washington, D.C., prior to 1877.
b, Mo^n-chu'-hi^n-xte (*Montšú-hịxtè* or Hairy-grizzly-bear), Ponca Indian born 1831–37 in South Dakota. Photograph taken in 1877 in Washington, D.C.

a, Xi-tha'-ca-be (*Xiđá-sabè* or Black-eagle) called Jack Peniska. Born in 1840. Photograph by DeLancey Gill, June 1912, Washington, D.C.

b, Te-zhe'-ba-te (*Težébatè* or Buffalo-chips) also called Nu-do^{n}'-ho^{n}-ga (*Nudą́-hǫgà* or [war] Captain) Photograph possibly by J. K. Hillers, Washington, D.C., 1882.

Two types of burials, Ponca Reservation, Nebraska. Copied from prints furnished by J. Owen Dorsey, 1885–95(?).

a, We'-ga-ca-pi (*Wègasàpi*, Iron Whip or The Whip) of the Dhi-ghi-ga (*Đíxiđa*) gens. Father of Xi-tha'-cka (*Xíđa-skà* or White-eagle). Photograph by A. Z. Shindler, Washington, D.C., 1858. *b*, Mi'-xa-to^{n}-ga (*Míġa-tọ̀ga* or Big-goose), Ponca Indian born in 1848. Photograph by DeLancey Gill, February 1906, Washington, D.C.

Part of the 1906 Southern Ponca delegation. *Seated, left to right:* Horse-chief; Yellow-horse; Little-soldier. *Standing, left to right:* Big-goose; John Bull; White-chief; White-knife. The John Bull shown here is the *Mąžąhatè* of Peter LeClaire's "Ponca History." Photograph by DeLancey Gill, February 1906.

Ponca ceremonials. *a*, Southern Ponca Sun dance (copied from a much-worn print kept by a Northern Ponca as a religious memento). *b*, Northern Ponca Peyote meeting in the 1930's. (Both, courtesy University of Nebraska Laboratory of Anthropology.)

Scenes in the Ponca country. *a*, View looking northwest on the Niobrara River, near Niobrara, Nebr. *b*, View looking south in hilly country approximately 7 miles west of Niobrara, Nebr. It is in this area that Ponca legends say the Ponca once encountered the creature called *Indáḍige*. *c*, Chalk bluffs along the Missouri River near Niobrara, Nebr. These bluffs were the burying grounds of the Ponca. *d*, View looking north from road about 3 miles east of Monowi, Nebr. In the small valley at left the Ponca legends relate that the Ponca encountered the water monster *Wakạ́dagi* for the last time.

Housing and settlement of the Northern Ponca. *a*, View looking west on Main Street, Niobrara, Nebr. *b*, Northern Ponca Community Building, located approximately 2 miles west and 3 miles south of Niobrara, Nebr. The building was formerly used for Indian dances. It is now used for meetings of the Tribal Council. *c*, Northern Ponca home near the Community Building. Homes of this type were built with Government funds and Indian labor. *d*, Typical Northern Ponca cabin, located near the Community Building.

Northern Ponca types. *a*, Joseph Le Roy (JLR), Northern Ponca informant, the son of a chief of the second rank. *b*, The late Alfred Larvie, a Northern Ponca patriarch and Peyote Leader. *c*, The late Otto Knudsen (OK), the last chief of the second rank in the Northern Ponca band. *d*, Silas LeClaire, a Northern Ponca of the South Dakota group, with a powder horn of his own manufacture.

Peter LeClaire (PLC), the Ponca historian. *a*, Wearing a *Hedúška* costume of the "Straight dance" type. The vest is Teton Dakota work. (Photographed in 1951.) *b*, Wearing a buffalo headdress with a costume of the "Straight dance" type. (Photographed at a Dakota Grass dance held at Okreek, S. Dak., in 1949.) *c*, With the Northern Ponca *Hedúška* drum, last used in the 1930's. (Photographed in 1949.) *d*, With the late chiefs Whiteshirt and Birdhead, at one of the last Northern Ponca *Hedúška* dances, held near Niobrara, Nebr., in the late 1930's. (Photograph courtesy University of Nebraska Laboratory of Anthropology.)

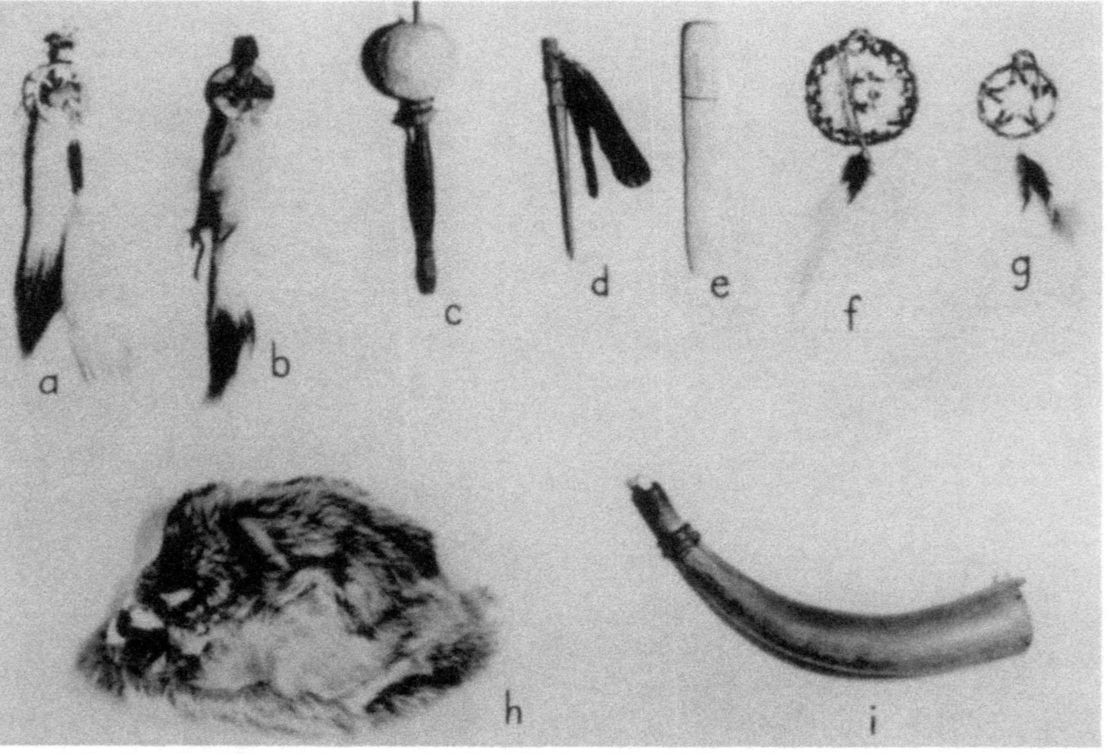

Items of Northern Ponca material culture. *a*, Teton Dakota deer-tail dance ornament of the type attached to bandoliers, with medicine packet tied to center of quillwork wheel. This ornament was formerly worn by Peter LeClaire with his *Hedúška* costume. It is shown here for comparative purposes. *b*, The Northern Ponca version of the same ornament, made by Peter LeClaire. *c*, Northern Ponca Peyote "gourd" or rattle, made by Peter LeClaire. In all respects except size it resembles a *Wá-wą* rattle more than a peyote gourd. *d*, Pipe tamper made by Peter LeClaire. *e*, Corn-shelling device made by Peter LeClaire. *f*, *g*, Bead and wire shirt and hair ornaments used in the *Hedúška* dance, made by Mr. and Mrs. Peter LeClaire. *h*, Raccoon skin "winter cap" made by Mr. and Mrs. Peter LeClaire. *i*, Powder horn made by Silas LeClaire.

Southern Ponca scenes. *a*, Southern Ponca village scene in the early 1900's (Doubleday photograph). *b*, Southern Ponca Soldier dance, 1953. Note the Pan-Indian "feather" costumes.

Southern Ponca types. *a*, Chloe Eagle, Southern Ponca beauty, in powwow costume. Note the "princess crown" type headband, a Pan-Indian innovation. *b*, Southern Ponca beauty in powwow costume. *c*, Obie Yellow-bull (OYB), also known as Little-standing-buffalo, playing the Indian flute. *d*, Edward Primeaux, also known as Pack horse, a Southern Ponca Peyote leader.

INDEX

718-071—65——15

CPSIA information can be obtained
at www.ICGtesting.com
Printed in the USA
LVHW06s1015210418
574378LV00009B/17/P

9 780803 228191